A SATURNALIA OF BUNK

H. L. Mencken

A Saturnalia of Bunk

Selections from
The Free Lance, 1911–1915

Edited by S. T. Joshi

OHIO UNIVERSITY PRESS
ATHENS

Ohio University Press, Athens, Ohio 45701
ohioswallow.com
© 2017 by Ohio University Press
All rights reserved

Printed in the United States of America
Ohio University Press books are printed on acid-free paper ⊗ ™

27 26 25 24 23 22 21 20 19 18 17   5 4 3 2 1

Library of Congress Cataloging-in-Publication Data

Names: Mencken, H. L. (Henry Louis), 1880–1956 author. | Joshi, S. T., 1958– editor.
Title: A saturnalia of bunk : selections from The free lance, 1911 /1915 / H.
  L. Mencken ; edited by S. T. Joshi.
Other titles: Baltimore sun.
Description: Athens : Ohio University Press, 2017. | Selected writings from
  the author's column, The free lance, published in The Baltimore sun,
  1911–1915. | Includes bibliographical references and index.
Identifiers: LCCN 2017018028| ISBN 9780821422700 (hc : alk. paper) | ISBN
  9780821446027 (pdf)
Classification: LCC PS3525.E43 A6 2017 | DDC 818/.5209—dc23
LC record available at https://lccn.loc.gov/2017018028

CONTENTS

INTRODUCTION

LATE IN LIFE, H. L. Mencken (1880–1956) estimated that he had published ten to fifteen million words as a journalist, essayist, reviewer, critic, and general man of letters. With such an immense body of work, it is not surprising that much of it—especially the newspaper work, which by its nature tends toward the local and the ephemeral—remains uncollected. It remains a fact, however, that a great many of the books Mencken compiled in his lifetime—notably his six-volume series of *Prejudices* (1919–27), which established him as America's leading literary and cultural critic of the 1920s—were stitched together from newspaper or magazine articles. It is a bit more puzzling that neither Mencken himself, in his late compilation of a lifetime's writing, *A Mencken Chrestomathy* (1949), nor any subsequent editor has seen fit to preserve one especially notable treasure trove of journalism between the covers of a book: with few exceptions,[1] his 1,228 contributions to his column The Free Lance of 1911–15, comprising a million and a half words, remain embalmed in the pages of the *Baltimore Evening Sun* where they first appeared.

Perhaps the very immensity of this mass of writing has proved intimidating; certainly, most present-day newspaper columnists would suffer apoplexy at the thought of writing a 1,200-word column six days a week for four and a half years. Perhaps, also, scholars have assumed either that this column represented apprentice work that could not stand up to the scintillating journalism Mencken produced in the decades following or that it was exclusively concerned with local affairs and personalities of minimal relevance to contemporary issues. A judicious reading of the best of the Free Lance columns puts the lie to both these assumptions.

By 1911 Mencken could hardly have been considered a cub reporter. Having graduated from high school (the Baltimore Polytechnic Institute) in 1896, he went to work in his father's cigar factory, with the expectation of taking over the business when his father retired; but the work proved most uncongenial, and only days after his father's unexpected death in January 1899 he secured a job at the *Baltimore Herald*, one of the lesser papers in his hometown. His advancement on this humble paper was swift: by September 1901 he had become drama critic; a month later he was editor of the *Sunday Herald;* in 1903 he became city editor of the *Morning Herald;* in 1905 he was appointed managing editor of the *Herald.* Mencken came to dislike the executive or administrative aspects of the newspaper business: writing, whether repertorial or editorial, was his chief passion. When the *Herald* folded in June 1906, he was immediately hired by Charles H. Grasty to be news editor of the *Baltimore Evening News;* but although he did write some unsigned editorials and some installments of a Mere Opinion column, he again felt ill at ease in an administrative capacity and leaped at the chance to write for Baltimore's oldest and most established paper, the *Sun,* when the opportunity presented itself in late July.

For the time being, Mencken was unconcerned about his unceremonious departure from the *Evening News;* for the next four years he put most of his efforts into the *Sun,* writing unsigned editorials, drama reviews, and other work. But in 1910, Grasty (who had sold the *Evening News* to the wealthy magazine and newspaper magnate Frank A. Munsey in 1908), wishing to return to the Baltimore newspaper arena, gained control of the *Sun* after a struggle with Walter, Arunah, and Charles Abell, the feuding descendants of the paper's founder. Mencken expected to be fired for having snubbed Grasty by resigning from the *Evening News,* but Grasty, knowing a valuable property when he saw it, forgave him and kept him on.

Mencken quickly became involved in the *Sun*'s plans to establish an evening paper. As he wrote in his posthumously published memoir, *Thirty-Five Years of Newspaper Work,* Grasty "was notoriously (and correctly) convinced that destiny was on the side of evening papers, and in that doctrine nearly all the other more reflective newspaper men of the time agreed with him."[2] At a time before television or even radio had gained the devotion of the general public, it was assumed that hardworking citizens would wish to absorb the day's news on returning home from the office or factory. Moreover, an evening (or, more properly, late afternoon) paper could actually report on noteworthy events of that day: in later years, Mencken's celebrated reports of the Democratic and Republican national conventions would be telegraphed to the *Evening Sun* offices by early afternoon for immediate publication, providing the closest thing to live coverage then technologically possible in the print medium.

Mencken appeared in the debut issue of the *Baltimore Evening Sun* (18 April 1910) with a column of miscellany on the editorial page—the haven for the great majority of his newspaper writing for the next thirty years. His articles at this time covered a wide range, from local events to literary and dramatic criticism to social and political topics to such whimsies as "Victuals: A Reverie" (19 May 1910). These columns would appear perhaps three or four times a week; Mencken also wrote hundreds of unsigned editorials (traditionally appearing in the first two or three columns of the editorial page, and representing the paper's official policy on issues of the day). It was, however, Harry C. Black, who had recently been elected to the paper's board of directors, who proposed to Grasty that Mencken be given his own daily column. Mencken further suggested "that it would be more effective if it were made more personal, and I were free to ride some of my hobbies."[3] Accordingly, after one column (8 May 1911) titled "The World in Review," The Free Lance was born on May 9.

It should be noted that work for the *Evening Sun* was far from Mencken's only literary activity at the time. He had already published two monographs, *George Bernard Shaw: His Plays* (1905) and *The Philosophy of Friedrich Nietzsche* (1908), and in 1908 had become a monthly book reviewer for the *Smart Set,* a position he would retain until the end of 1923. Writing as many as twenty-five 1,200-word newspaper columns a month, on top of a 3,000-word book review column (necessitating the reading of fifteen to twenty books each month), points to Mencken's prodigious energy as he threw himself headlong into journalism on both a local and a national level.

At this juncture, Mencken as a journalist would have been called a "paragrapher"—that is, his column consisted of discrete paragraphs on a wide range of subjects, separated by a horizontal rule; the rule was present even when Mencken chose to discuss a single subject over several paragraphs or an entire column. (In some anomalous instances, Mencken would be forced to terminate a discussion in midsentence, sometimes even in the middle of a word, and resume it the next day. On some occasions he would promise to resume a discussion but then neglect to do so.) Whether Mencken was influenced by his great nineteenth-century predecessor, Ambrose Bierce—who in his fifty-year newspaper career, first for the *San Francisco News Letter* (1867–72) and later, more famously, for William Randolph Hearst's *San Francisco Examiner* (1887–1906), consistently adhered to this "paragrapher" format—is not clear; but the entire run of the Free Lance retains this structure, and Mencken clearly felt comfortable with it. (His subsequent weekly editorials for the *Evening Sun,* beginning in 1920, finally abandon the "paragrapher" format, although they are customarily, and somewhat mechanically, divided into four numbered sections.)

While a fair proportion of the Free Lance column was devoted to sparring with local political, social, and religious figures—most notably the hapless J. Harry Preston, mayor of Baltimore for the entire period of the column's existence, whom Mencken referred to as a "very vain and sensitive fellow"[4]—it becomes abundantly clear that these debates were merely the springboards for broader discussions of the significant issues of the period. Grasty had once told Mencken that he must not feud with clergymen, for this would undermine the *Evening Sun*'s chosen self-image as a family paper; but Mencken easily got around the restriction by persuading Grasty to allow him, in simple fairness, to respond to attacks by the clergy and others on himself. Mencken facilitated this task through his role as editor of the letters to the editors section, variously called "Editorials from the People" or "The Forum." In this way Mencken gleefully printed searing (but usually inept) attacks on himself in the letters column and rebutted those attacks, almost before they were out of their writers' hands, in The Free Lance.

No one could fairly conclude, however, that The Free Lance was merely a haven of abuse and billingsgate. A systematic reading of the columns allows us to ascertain a nearly complete view of Mencken's political, religious, social, and cultural philosophy as it had evolved up to this point—and that philosophy underwent relatively few alterations in the course of his subsequent career. In the space of this introduction it is possible only to supply the barest outlines of that philosophy, but the columns themselves supply a wealth of detail and nuance.

The central pillars of Mencken's worldview are freedom of thought and action and a sincere devotion to the truth as he saw it. Sundry combinations of these two principles may well account for all the anfractuosities—complex and at times seemingly contradictory—of his views on politics, society, religion, art, and general culture. In today's parlance Mencken would be considered a libertarian, and he explicitly referred to himself as such; but unlike so many present-day libertarians, who frequently restrict the notion of freedom to the sphere of economics, Mencken maintained that freedom of thought and speech were central and essential. In a book review column of 1922 he wrote: "I am, in brief, a libertarian of the most extreme variety, and know of no human right that is one-tenth as valuable as the simple right to utter what seems (at the moment) to be the truth. Take away this right, and none other is worth a hoot; nor, indeed, can any other long exist."[5] The ideal of personal freedom outlined in a Free Lance column of 1913—in which the citizen is "bound to do nothing that will endanger [his neighbors'] lives or imperil their property. He is bound to respect their liberties so long as the exercise of those liberties does not invade his own"—is closely in accord with the principles that John Stuart Mill established in *On Liberty* (1859). Mencken followed Mill in advocating the most minimal government involvement in those aspects of social life (particularly the legislation of morality) that have no direct relation to the protection of the citizen from external foes or internal threats.

Mencken, however, drew a curious corollary to his principle of freedom, especially as it related to the America of his own day: "it follows necessarily that I can be only an indifferent citizen of a democratic state, for democracy is grounded upon the instinct of inferior men to herd themselves in large masses, and its principal manifestation is their bitter opposition to all free thought."[6] That Mencken would so forthrightly expound his hostility to the very principle of democracy—a view so far outside the bounds of acceptable political discourse, then as now, as to be all but unspeakable—is, at a minimum, a testament to his desire to "utter what seems (at the moment) to be the truth."

Mencken's objections to democracy—as with so many other facets of his overall philosophy—derive from his absorption of Nietzsche, although it could well be asserted that he would not have responded so ardently to this feature of Nietzsche's thought if he were not already inclined toward it. It appears that Mencken took quite seriously Nietzsche's ideal of the superman, insofar as it was practicable to do so in the United States of the early twentieth century. In his treatise on Nietzsche he described the concept as follows:

> To put it simply, the superman's thesis will be this: that he has been put into the world without his consent, that he must live in the world, that he owes nothing to the other people there, and that he knows nothing whatever of existence beyond the grave. Therefore, it will be his effort to attain the highest possible measure of satisfaction for the only unmistakable and genuinely healthy instinct within him: the yearning to live—to attain power—to meet and overcome the influences which would weaken or destroy him.[7]

Abstract as this sounds, it gets to the heart of the Menckenian notion that the properly civilized person is under no obligation to restrict his own freedom of action—and, perhaps even more important, his freedom of thought—in the face of the moral dispproval of his "inferiors." There is no sense either in Nietzsche or in Mencken that the superman will be a political or military dictator: it is not that he wishes to fetter other people's thoughts or actions; it is simply that he does not wish his own thoughts or actions to be fettered by others.

Mencken's opposition to democracy has far-reaching ramifications well beyond the sphere of politics and morality. "It is a capital mistake," he wrote in a Free Lance column of 1914, "to assume that the common people are stupid but honest." The common people are, instead, both stupid and dishonest. Democracy was based on envy; it is "a device for giving to the relatively inefficient and unsuccessful (and hence, bitterly envious) majority, by the artificial and dishonest device of the ballot, that preponderance of power and influence which belongs rightfully to the minority [i.e., the supermen] by reason of its superior efficiency, honesty and intelligence." It is thus no surprise that Mencken fought unrelentingly (and, it must be admitted, largely unsuccessfully) to restrain the power of government—in such matters as the direct election of senators by popular vote (instituted by the Seventeenth Amendment in 1913), the initiative and referendum, and even the very existence of a state legislature—because any augmentation of governmental power over the citizenry would inevitably result in limiting the freedom of thought and action of the "minority" by means of onerous laws passed through the influence of an ignorant and morally obtuse majority. Mencken's seemingly audacious proposal to repeal the Fifteenth Amendment, which had granted African Americans the right to vote, rested on the belief that a substantial majority of whites did not deserve the vote either: "the franchise is a thing a citizen must earn by his ability and his industry." There would inevitably come a time for "the frank disfranchisement of those whose incapacity for reason is palpable and undisputed."

Is it, then, a paradox that Mencken persistently advocated woman suffrage throughout his Free Lance column, and would continue to do so until the passage of the Nineteenth Amendment in 1920? Mencken did not see any difficulty in doing so. His remarkable essay on woman suffrage, spanning six columns between 1 and 7 February 1912, systematically destroyed all the then-fashionable arguments against allowing women to vote: that many women don't want the vote; that women are too "refined" to engage in the rough-and-tumble of politics; that women could not "enforce" the laws they pass by brute strength; that working women can rely on already existing laws (passed by men) to protect them.[8] Mencken was pointing out that the paradox, if any, rested on the side of those who professed to support the principle of democracy: prohibiting a large class of citizens from voting merely on the basis of sex was a subversion of the essence of democracy. Let it pass that Mencken later came to oppose woman suffrage: perhaps he, like many supporters, experienced a certain disillusionment when women voters proved themselves no less subject to folly and chicanery than their male counterparts.

Mencken devoted a large proportion of his Free Lance column to battling individuals and organizations who were seeking the moral reform of the city and the nation in such areas as prostitution, alcohol consumption, and cigarette smoking. Here again Mencken's libertarianism and his scorn of popular opinion come to the fore. While recognizing that these things may in fact be vices, and while he himself had no desire to engage in any of them except the moderate consumption of alcohol, he was averse to granting the government a heavy hand in their suppression. Nor was he about to concede the moral high ground to the crusaders: he in fact referred to them as "incurably immoral" for their intellectual dishonesty, their bigotry, and their intolerance. As a signal example he held up Charles J. Bonaparte, a former attorney general of the United States who maintained that anyone who opposed the complete eradication of prostitution from the city of Baltimore must be deriving profits from the trade or seeking to make brothels more accessible to those who wished to patronize them. Such outrageous suggestions of bad faith on the part of one's opponents was, in Mencken's view, typical of the methods of vice crusaders.

Mencken was also well aware that moral legislation was almost invariably unsuccessful. In his Free Lance columns he took delight in showing how ineffective were the various state prohibition statutes in preventing the widespread sale and consumption of alcohol. His argument against the attempt to wipe out prostitution (which on occasion he, as was common during this period, referred to by the euphemism "the social evil"), as expressed in a double-length Free Lance column of 7 November 1912, rested on the practical ground that such an attempt would only scatter brothels throughout the city rather than restricting them to a known red-light district. One of his later columns takes note of the formation of the Baltimore Vice Commission designed to look into the issue of prostitution in the city. He reported on the findings of the commission in three separate articles in late 1915, after his column had come to an end. His conclusions were simple: that it is impossible to obliterate prostitution, because the desire (sexual activity) it seeks to satisfy is a natural and not a pathological one; that segregating prostitutes has a more beneficial effect in the real world than the attempt to eliminate them altogether; and that the real problem with prostitution is not its actual practice but its engendering of venereal diseases—a purely medical problem that can, in principle, be solved.[9]

The issue of prohibition brought down even greater fulminations from Mencken: he came to believe that the imposition of a state, and even a national, prohibition statute was inevitable, but he was no less unrelenting in his opposition for all that. Alcohol was indeed a vice, but is it not the essence of freedom to allow people to engage in a vice, "so long as the enjoyment it produces is not outweighed by the injury it does"? There were already statutes on the books against public drunkenness; was there really a need for the entire elimination of alcohol from the fabric of the nation—an elimination that, in any event, could never be even approximately complete? Here again Mencken relied on his standard distinction between the civilized minority and the boorish majority: prohibition was being fostered only by those who could not use alcohol in moderation, and hence they sought to take it away even from those who could. In this argument—pressed repeatedly both in his Free Lance columns and throughout the long years when the Eighteenth Amendment was in effect—Mencken came close to employing exactly those ad hominem attacks he criticized in others. In the end, of course, he was proven right, but only after the nation had been put through thirteen years of government corruption and unrestrained criminal activity that proved, if any further proof were necessary, that morality could not be legislated.

It was no accident that Mencken took repeated potshots at the clergy, for it was they—especially the leaders of the Baptist and Methodist churches—who took the lead in prohibition and other moral crusades, whether under the aegis of such lobbying organizations as the Anti-Saloon League or on their own hook. Mencken's careful reading of the Bible allowed him to demolish a local preacher's assertion that the prohibition of alcohol was scripturally based; he argued, cleverly, that such a prohibition was not in fact Christian but Muslim. Mencken may not have been a full-fledged atheist, but his anticlericalism—once again derived at least in part from the atheist Nietzsche—was scarcely ever in abeyance. He boldly declared that preachers should get out of the business of politics—not because they should not concern themselves with political (or even moral-political) issues, but because "their training does not give them any appreciable fitness for judging politicians." It was the clergy that repeatedly advocated the retention of archaic laws on the statute books, notably the Sunday laws that, in the Baltimore of Mencken's day, prohibited such harmless activities as baseball, golf, or even a symphony orchestra performance on Sundays. Late in life he came to believe that such an issue as the reform of restrictive divorce laws could not be effected "until the discussion is purged of religious consideration."[10]

When the evangelist Billy Sunday's histrionics garnered public attention in the early 1910s, Mencken saw in him a symbol—not of Christian revival, but of the "decaying corpse of evangelical Protestantism" heading toward its ultimate dissolution in the United States. In this prediction he was sadly off the mark, although it could well be said that his participation in the Scopes trial of 1925 was instrumental in causing fundamentalism to go underground for half a century. Mencken cannot be held responsible for the recrudescence of an aggressive and intolerant Christianity in our day, but he can be credited with prescience in his comment that "the ideal Christian of today [is] . . . one who pursues his brother with clubs and artillery."

Purely literary matters rarely come up in the Free Lance columns: that was the preserve of his *Smart Set* review column, which, in the course of fifteen years, all but established a canon of contemporary American literature, with Theodore Dreiser at the pinnacle and other such worthies as Sinclair Lewis, Willa Cather, Sherwood Anderson, James Branch Cabell, and F. Scott Fitzgerald not far behind.[11] But on occasion Mencken did write on general issues relating to language, literature, and art. Several columns anticipate his vigorous advocacy of an "American language" starkly different from standard (British) English—something he extensively codified decades later in *The American Language* (1936) and its successors. One column reprinted here (11 December 1914) anticipates his famous "Sahara of the Bozart" article (in *Prejudices: Second Series*), condemning the cultural deficiencies of the South. On occasion he wrote brief reviews of some new books, and he also took occasion to skewer the many hopeless poetasters of his day, usually by the simple expedient of quoting the choicest of their lame verses with a minimum of comment.

Where Mencken did speak out was in his repeated warning against censorship of the theater or of literature. Here again the lust of an intolerant majority to take away the pleasures of the civilized minority was the central issue, and it was encapsulated in the figure of the redoubtable Anthony Comstock, who in his half century of lobbying against "obscene" books caused the suppression of thousands of books and magazines and, worse, the self-censorship of many authors and magazine editors who feared prosecution and the destruction of their reputations. As the 1920s advanced, the burgeoning Modernist literature of the period found in Mencken a valuable ally against puritanical attempts to suppress it, and by 1930 Mencken could take justifiable pride in believing that Comstock's notorious legacy had come to naught.

It should not be assumed that The Free Lance is entirely devoted to dour reflections on the weighty issues of the day; indeed, even when discussing substantial topics Mencken is careful to leaven them with pungent wit and satire. He remarked, "My Free Lance job was the pleasantest that I had ever had on a newspaper . . . and I enjoyed it immensely,"[12] and there is no reason to think that his readers were any less entertained. Some of his most engaging columns treat what he called quackery—astrology, Christian Science, the New Thought (a fuzzy mix of mysticism and self-help), patent medicines, antivivisection, antivaccination, and the like. But once again, Mencken's fundamental principles come into play: these quackeries enjoy such widespread popularity because they appeal to the limited understandings of the common people, who—especially in the realm of medicine, where such tremendous strides had been made that the field was now hopelessly beyond the comprehension of the layman—are always quick to seek a simple answer to a complex problem. Quackery, indeed, is the inevitable product of democracy: "the ultimate adjudication of medical controversies, as of all other controversies, lies with the ignorant and unintelligent mob, and . . . this mob is animated by that chronic distrust of learning which always marks the lower orders of men."

Medicine was a particularly sensitive issue with Mencken, who had a touch of hypochondria. He counted among his friends several of the leading figures in the Johns Hopkins Medical School, and he repeatedly defended them against frauds and charlatans—such as those who had organized the National League for Medical Freedom that sought to question their authority and to advance the claims of such dubious professions as homeopathy, osteopathy, and chiropractic. In the case of antivivisection, Mencken had no sadistic desire to carve up defenseless animals but recognized that animal testing was a crucial and indispensable aid in the treatment of human diseases; he also exposed the antivivisectionists in numerous instances of bad faith and bad science. The issue of public health was also a great concern to Mencken: throughout his Free Lance column he would print the standings of what he termed the National Typhoid League—a grisly parody of baseball standings in which the leading cities of the nation were ranked by the number of annual typhoid deaths; Baltimore was, lamentably and shamefully, near the top of the list for years.

Where Mencken parted company with nearly all his *Evening Sun* readers, even those who were sympathetic to his belaboring of clerics, his lampooning of astrologers, his broadsides against public officials, and his nose thumbing of vice crusaders, was in his screeds in the first year of the Great War. Mencken claimed, perhaps a bit disingenuously, that his advocacy of the German side of the war had little or nothing to do with his own German American heritage: "I was born in Baltimore of Baltimore-born parents; I have no relatives, near or remote, in Germany, nor even any friends (save one Englishman!); very few of my personal associates in this town are native Germans," and so on. One suspects that Mencken was protesting too much. Although, as his biographer Fred Hobson has pointed out, Mencken wrote several editorials in 1910–11 critical of Germany,[13] there is more to his fervent defense of Germany and his unrelenting, at times abusive, denunciation of England and the Allies than mere contrarianism or a desire for fair play.

Perhaps central to Mencken's stance in the war was the fact that both English and American propagandists almost immediately blamed the outbreak of war on Germany's absorption of militaristic ideas from the baneful Nietzsche. Mencken, for whom Nietzsche always remained an intellectual mentor, was not about to stand by and see his idol abused. Far from denying such a Nietzschean influence on modern-day Germany, he embraced it: Kaiser Wilhelm was, as his detractors claimed, no democrat, and it was good that he was not; England, in turn, had fallen into decay precisely because it had allowed the democratic principle to run amok and raise such demagogues as Churchill and Lloyd George to power. The bold, courageous Englishmen who had established a worldwide colonial empire had given way to sniveling cowards who drafted other nations to do their fighting for them. And as for Americans, who were theoretically neutral in the early stages of the conflict, their half century of peace since the Civil War had engendered both a military and a moral softness that made them ill-equipped to take a place on the world's stage.

A detailed analysis of the causes of the war—and even a brief analysis of Mencken's views on the causes of the war—is not possible in this space. Let it suffice to say that Mencken's assertions that Germany's rapid augmentation of its military might in the later nineteenth and early twentieth centuries was purely defensive are both largely false and to some degree disingenuous. There is no reason to believe that, even given Germany's increasing economic rivalry with Britain and its threat to match Britain's superiority as a naval power, a confrontation between the two nations, let alone a world war, was inevitable. Mencken's claim that "Germany was doomed to battle for her very life" is mere bluster and after-the-fact exculpation.

Mencken's fanatical support for Germany led him into increasingly untenable positions as the war progressed. He wrote a plangent lament for France, but when he turned his attention to Belgium he shocked readers by declaring flatly that its fate was merely "academic and sentimental"—that, as a weak country, it was destined to be overrun by the strong. When Germany's campaign of submarine warfare began, Mencken was once again an ardent advocate. He argued that commercial or passenger liners that failed to pull up when hailed by a U-boat were themselves to blame if they were subsequently sunk when pursued—an argument that conveniently ignored those numerous instances when vessels had been sunk without any advance warning. Mencken's most notorious column was published the day after the sinking of the British liner *Lusitania* on 7 May 1915; among its 1,200 dead were 128 Americans. But as with other such incidents, the *Lusitania* had, in Mencken's view, brought about its own destruction by being an armed vessel. Americans' outrage over the incident—exacerbated by Germany's unexpectedly belligerent response to President Wilson's demand for an explanation and apology—came close to plunging the United States into war. Such an eventuality was Mencken's (and Germany's) worst fear, for he knew that Germany could not stand up to the united forces of England, France, Russia, and the United States. Americans' isolationism quickly reasserted itself, however, and Wilson won his reelection campaign in 1916 chiefly on promising to keep the United States out of the war.

But that was more than a year in the future; for the time being Mencken had to face the overwhelming obloquy that his Free Lance columns were engendering. In *Thirty-Five Years of Newspaper Work* he states that his cessation of the column on 23 October 1915 was purely a result of lack of time: in the fall of 1914 he and George Jean Nathan had taken over the editorship of the *Smart Set,* and he goes on to state that "when I gave up the Free Lance in October, 1915, it was on my own motion entirely."[14] And yet, Mencken had to face the brutal fact that his war views were opposed not only by the generality of Baltimore citizens but by the *Evening Sun* itself, which was resolutely supportive of the Allied cause. One of his last columns furiously condemns his own paper for "bogus neutrality" and for arousing hostility against German Americans by printing lies about the Germans. Two months after this column appeared, the Free Lance was silenced—though whether by his own decision, or by a joint decision by Mencken and the *Evening Sun's* editorial board, it is now difficult to know.

Matters would get worse for Mencken before they got better. Although he resumed writing separate articles for the *Evening Sun* in 1915–17, he resolutely refused to discuss the war. The United States' entrance into the conflict in April 1917 caused him to withdraw from the paper altogether, since he felt that newly imposed censorship regulations would prevent him from writing freely about the war. (The situation was worse than he knew: a thick file on his wartime activities, such as they were, was kept by the Justice Department, as well as by a notorious private anti-German group, the American Protective League.[15]) Mencken published nothing in either the *Sun* or the *Evening Sun* from 29 March 1917 until 9 February 1920, when his weekly editorials began appearing every Monday. He occasionally sat in on editorial meetings, but no article bearing his name appeared. Of course, he was still writing his book reviews for the *Smart Set,* and some of his most distinguished early volumes—*A Book of Prefaces* (1917), the first volume of *Prejudices* (1919), and *The American Language* (1919)—appeared to good notices. Mencken had grand plans to write a multivolume work on American involvement in the war, but they came to nothing.[16]

By the time his Monday editorials began in 1920, The Free Lance appeared to be ancient history. A number of books produced during this period, including *A Book of Burlesques* (1916), *Damn! A Book of Calumny* (1918), and even the monograph *In Defense of Women* (1918), had been largely assembled from newspaper and magazine work, but for reasons still not entirely clear he chose, with the one exception previously noted, not to use any of the Free Lance material therein. Was Mencken himself overwhelmed with the bulk of his writing? What is not in doubt is his own realization of the lasting benefits of the column. In speaking of the influence of the column on his subsequent work as author and editor (especially in one of his most visible roles, the editing of the *American Mercury*, 1924–33]), Mencken writes:

> My belief is that running the column was very beneficial to me, professionally speaking, for it not only rid me of the last vestiges of executive work, but also served to clarify and organize my ideas. Before it had gone on a year I knew precisely what I was about and where I was heading. In it I worked out much of the material that was later to enter into my books, and to color the editorial policy of the *American Mercury*.[17]

The best of the Free Lance material ranks with the best of Mencken's journalism overall—in its satirical pungency, its rapierlike strokes of logic, its deadpan exposure of fallacy, hypocrisy, and absurdity, and its intellectual cogency as the reflections of a man who had worked out his philosophy of life both in broad parameters and in the smallest details. His trenchant and chilling column (4 January 1913) on witnessing a hanging must rank as one of the most pungent examples of his journalism. It is true that on many occasions Mencken lapses into language that today would be considered highly objectionable (such as his repeated and half-jocular references to African Americans as "niggeros," "darkies," and "blackamoors"); but this is part and parcel of a linguistic exuberance—exemplified by frequent use of German idioms ("katzenjammer," "geheimrat," etc.), esoteric terms ("xanthiate," "saprophytes"), and slang—that Mencken deliberately employed to convey his point as vividly as possible.

The argumentative sparring in which Mencken engaged in his Free Lance column stood him in good stead when he came to tackle the opaque rhetoric of Warren G. Harding, the fundamentalist obfuscation of William Jennings Bryan, and the labored pomposities of the puritans, charlatans, and crusaders with whom he tangled in the 1920s. Even if many of the individuals against whom he battled in the Free Lance columns have now lapsed into merited oblivion, the issues he dealt with remain with us: To what degree should religion influence politics? How can unpopular minorities be protected in time of war?

Can democracy survive if the electorate is, by and large, ignorant and dishonest? Is America, indeed, the land of the free or merely a haven of intolerant conformity? Mencken's answers to these and other questions, whether we agree with them or not, are undeniably those of a man who has thought long and hard about what it means to be a free citizen, and how much would be lost if we ceased to utter what seems, at the moment, to be the truth.

A NOTE ON THIS EDITION

In compiling this relatively slim volume of selections from a million and a half words of Mencken's The Free Lance column, I have perforce made some emendations that result in a somewhat different reading experience from that presented by the original material. First, I have removed the horizontal rules that separate every paragraph from beginning to end of the column's existence; second, I have affixed titles (which I hope I are in keeping with the spirited and satirical tone of the text) to Mencken's discussions of a given subject. I have supplied the date of publication of the excerpt at the conclusion of the selection; I have not felt the need to include page numbers, as all the Free Lance columns appeared on the editorial page of the *Baltimore Evening Sun,* almost invariably on page 6, but occasionally (especially toward the end of the series) on page 8.

Given that Mencken is such an inveterate name-dropper, I have, as in my previous editions of Mencken's work, prepared a glossary of names to present background information on those individuals, many of whom are now obscure, whom Mencken cites. Such a glossary reduces the need for footnotes and allows readers to look up only those individuals with whom they may be unfamiliar. Names that an educated person can be expected to know are not included, except to draw attention to Mencken's writings about them. Other points are clarified in a section of notes.

I am under a considerable debt to Vincent Fitzpatrick, curator of the H. L. Mencken Collection at the Enoch Pratt Free Library in Baltimore, who supplied some texts that were unavailable to me and assisted in the transcription of some items. I secured microfilm copies of most of the Free Lance columns from the McKeldin Library of the University of Maryland, College Park. I am grateful for the general support and friendship provided by Richard J. Schrader, Ray Stevens, Oleg Panczenko, Louis B. Hatchett, Jr., and other devoted Menckenians. And I owe a deep debt of gratitude to my wife, Mary K. Wilson, whose diligent and meticulous proofreading of this book has saved me from many errors.

I

ON BEING
A FREE LANCE

A SATURNALIA OF BUNK

WHY NOT A permanent organization in Baltimore for warring upon stupidity, flapdoodle and buncombe? The fakes and the fanatics, the boneheads and the balderdashians, who swarm here as in few other cities of Christendom, have scores and scores of clubs and unions, and these clubs and unions pour a constant stream of nonsense into the public ear. Pick up a newspaper any day and you will quickly see that nine-tenths of the proposals and propositions before the people are frankly and unequivocally ridiculous. On the one hand, the City Council proposes to build a $2,000,000 tunnel under the harbor at a place where there is not enough business to support a single ferry-boat. On the other hand, the Lord's Day Alliance[1] proposes to make the Baltimore Sunday even more horrible than it is. On the third hand, as it were, the Hon. Mahoni Amicus strikes affecting attitudes in the spotlight, a "martyr" to newspaper "conspiracy." On the fourth hand, various camorras of ignoranti come forward with absurd "proofs" that the Pasteur vaccine will not *cure* hydrophobia. On the fifth hand, some tinpot "improvement" association—what hatcheries of prominent Baltimoreans those parochial parliaments are!—bawls loudly for a new park where none is needed. On the sixth hand, the Health Department sophisticates the mortality returns and claims praise for the deed. On the seventh hand, a half dozen booming bureaux fight one another, announce a multitude of grandiose plans—and never carry one of them out. On the eighth hand, Jake Hook and the Super-Mahon denounce the merit system on the ground that it would force them to employ niggero clerks. On the ninth hand, the common people are anæsthetized by a microscopic lowering of the tax rate and then plundered of their savings by a staggering increase in water rents and special assessments. On the tenth hand, public commissions discuss interminably the paving of streets—and no streets are paved. On the eleventh hand, the improvement of the water supply is constantly and tediously debated—and the water remains putrid and poisonous. And on the twelfth hand (to make an end of this centimanual enumeration), political rabble-rousers burst eternally with schemes for saving money, and yet out of every dollar paid in taxes, either to city or to State, fully 50 cents are wasted, lost, misspent, grafted or stolen.

An endless saturnalia of bunk, of bluff, of stupidity, of insincerity, of false virtue, of nonsense, of pretense, of sophistry, of parology, of bamboozlement, of actorial posturing, of strident wind music, of empty words—even, at times, of downright fraud. If the City Council is not flinging its legs about in some new debauch of clowning, then some faction or other of the boomers is launching a new and extra-preposterous scheme for "saving" the town from imaginary disaster, or some new and useless board is being created by the Legislature, or some new and ridiculous campaign for chemical purity is being started by snooping Puritans, or in some other way, always noisy, usually three-fourths silly, the peace, dignity and well-being of intelligent men are being invaded.

Certainly Baltimore must have a few citizens who do not fall for all or any of this buncombe—who can tell a hawk from a handsaw without a helping diagram—who have no faith in boomery, no faith in militant morality, no faith in political mountebankery—who believe that a fact is eternally a fact, and that all the yowling of a thousand gullets cannot change it—who possess, in brief, the faculty of elementary reasoning, of ordinary logic, and exercise it unemotionally, even while the yells resound and the red fire burns and the smell of punk[2] is in the air. I do not say that there are many such men in Baltimore. In our population, as everyone knows, there is an abnormally large proportion of ciphers—darkies, foreigners, invading yokels, professional loafers and so on. And despite the presence of excellent educational opportunities, the educated man, in the true sense of the term, is still a rarity in the classes above—so much a rarity, indeed, that he exhales a smell of sorcery, and it is always possible for political bawlers to rouse the rabble against him. Again our so-called polite society is shoddy and ignorant: its influence, if it has any influence at all, is frankly on the side of buncombe. And the measure of our "leading" lawyers and "prominent" business men is revealed by the acts and pronunciamentoes of the grotesque organizations which represent them.

But for all this, Baltimore still has its faction of intelligent, unemotional, fully adult men—not a large faction, true enough, but still a faction, and one influential enough, if it would but speak in one voice, to knock out, or at least cripple, most of the wizards whose fallacies now reach the common people as wisdom. A few such men found their way, I suppose by accident, into the recent Red Cross Committee of chartermakers: you will see their hand in the demand that the City Council, that incurable and intolerable evil, that worst and costliest of pests, be destroyed root and branch. And there are others, perhaps a thousand all told—men who are capable of ordinary ratiocination—who don't intrigue for political jobs, who have no desire for the applause of numbskulls, who see the truth with reasonable clarity and can afford to tell it—men, in brief, who approximate, more or less roughly, to the intelligence, or at least to the courage and degree of civilization, of such a man as the late Richard M. Venable.

Why are such men heard from in Baltimore so seldom? Why don't they rise up more often and haul down the ballyho men who try to sell us cure-alls? Why are they silent, knowing the truth, when balderdash in mountainous bales is being unloaded upon the town? Why, in a word, don't they form a *posse comitatus,* launch a counter-reformation, and wage a persistent and useful war upon all that riot of snide politics, of bluff and bluster, of anemonic and anemic boomery, of unintelligent agitation, of grab and guff, of puerility and piffle which now assaults and pesters every Baltimorean, keeps the city in a barbarous wallow and makes it laughable in the sight of all creation? [30 December 1911]

THE CENSORIOUS MENCKEN

From an earnest but ungrammatical essay by the Hon. Thomas G. Boggs in the current issue of the *Baltimoreische Blaetter,* the monthly comic paper of the Honorary Pallbearers:

There are critics and critics. Honest, constructive criticism by able and earnest persons is valuable. The object and service of such tend to betterment, for which every human and communities of humans should and do, as a general thing, strive for. But the critic, or rather he who criticizes in flippant, reckless and even smart Aleck manner, for fun and personal gratification, who offers no remedies for that with which he may justly find fault, is a pusillanimous pest and a damage to his community. We have in Baltimore, connected, unfortunately, with one of our newspapers, such a one. He is given a latitude that is surprising— far beyond the editorial privileges in the same paper. We are told that he writes certain editorials which praise Baltimore and its people, while on the same page, over his own signature, he abuses the city and those who are endeavoring in an unselfish manner, to benefit the community.

Reducing these amazing snarls of verbiage to simple English, one discovers that they set forth two propositions, to wit:

1. That I engage in loathsome critical vivisections wantonly, and with no intelligible plan of improvement in mind.
2. That I am two-faced, or rather two-handed, writing anonymous eulogies of Baltimore with one hand and signed attacks on Baltimore with the other.

Such are the allegations of the Hon. Thomas G. Boggs, editor of the *Baltimoreische Blaetter* and chairman of the standing committee on boggus statistics. My answer thereto may be divided into two asseverations, viz:

1. I deny absolutely that I have ever, at any time since the year 1900, written a single line anonymously, for THE EVENING SUN or any other publication, which has conflicted, in any essential, with any article bearing my signature.
2. I deny absolutely, and with a staggering emission of oaths, that I have ever written a single paragraph about the needs and defects of Baltimore which has not revealed on its face, or by plain implication, a definite and intelligible plan of improvement.

But *what* plan of improvement? A very simple and workable plan. A plan, in brief, involving a rising of the civilized and intelligent people of this town against buncombe and balderdash, fake and fraud, sophistry and salve-spreading—against the Merchants and Manufacturers' Association and its gaseous resolutions, its oblique attacks upon good government, its boggus statistics—against all the other camorras of boomers, with their childish rivalries and back-bitings, their idle *blassmusik* and windjamming, their incessant manufacture of Prominent Baltimoreans—against all the militant moralists who seek to make life in Baltimore as dull and depressing as life in the House of Correction—against the Old-Fashioned Administration, its rabble-rousers and frauds, its chicaneries and indecencies—against that low and revolting form of journalism which apologizes for such things and encourages such things—against all that saturnalia of bluff and bluster, of quackery in business and politics, of disingenuousuess and stupidity, of noise and nonsense, of slobbler-gobble and rumble-bumble, of false starts and false pretenses, of maudlin bawling and tin-horn magic, of rotten respectability and stuffed dignity, which makes every true Baltimorean ashamed, at times, of his city, and honestly fearful, at other times, of its future.

I myself, my dear Tom, am a Baltimorean—a Baltimorean of the third generation, born here, living here in great contentment, and hopeful of finding a quiet resting-place, along about 1975 or 1980, in Loudon Park.[3] I have the greatest faith in Baltimore—and not only in the future of Baltimore, but also in its present. The one thing we suffer from, at the moment, is a plague of bad advisers, of moral, political and economic charlatans. On the one hand we are besought, with loud yells, to make improvements which would not be improvements at all; on the other hand, we are taught that the best way to deal with certain pressing evils is to deny them. Under the first heading fall most of the plans of the so-called boomers; under the second heading, to cite but one example, falls the joint effort of the Health Department and Merchants and Manufacturers' Association to sophisticate the mortality returns.

Such enterprises, I believe, are dangerous. It is dangerous to spread the crazy notion that commercial prosperity is the only measure of a city's progress, and it is dangerous to preach the doctrine that evils are best dealt with by denying them. But despite all this false teaching, despite all this quackery and flapdoodle, this mountebankery and mendacity, this rhetoric and rottenness, Baltimore wobbles along. We Baltimoreans get enough to eat; we live in decent houses; we are pretty well satisfied with our comfortable old town. And if, from baffled boomers, comes anon the allegation that we are stupid, that we are slow to comprehend, that we do not rise promptly to ideas, then we may answer quite safely, in defense of our intelligence, that we still have sense enough to see the essential hollowness and insincerity, the guff and gabble, the buncombe and balderdash of boomery. [24 January 1912]

THE VIRTUE OF HOWLING

From an editorial in the Baltimore *Southern Methodist* entitled "With Our Compliments to the Free Lance" and showing the suave literary style of the Rev. Dr. C. D. Harris:

> We must confess we cannot understand his caustic strictures upon men of this community of the highest integrity and character. Must men who are actively interested in the moral betterment of the city and State be held up to ridicule and scorn?

The objection of a critic who deserves respect—but is he quite fair? I question it. When a man comes before a community with a new pill for the cure of its malaises, and particularly when he proposes to administer it by force of arms, the thing for the community to determine is not whether the man himself is pious and honest, but whether the pill will actually cure. If the probabilities are all against it, then it is the duty of every good citizen to denounce the quack, and that duty increases in direct ratio to the citizen's opportunities. I have no apologies to offer for howling from my own private stump. I am paid to howl; I enjoy howling; it makes me feel virtuous to howl.

The fact that a quack happens to be respectable is no defense of his quackery. The more respectable he is, the more dangerous he is. If the Hon. Charles J. Bonaparte were an obscure shyster, his public advocacy of pharisaical and unenforceable laws would be of no consequence. But it so happens that he is a man of the highest position and dignity, the bearer of a great name, a powerful maker of public opinion, and therefore his errors are of very serious consequence indeed. When he tries to enforce them by the mere weight of his authority, disdaining all honest opposition and grossly libeling its spokesmen, it is an agreeable business to show that vastly weightier authority is ranged against him. And when he tries to prevail by the sheer violence of his whoops, then it is a pious act to whoop even louder.

No word of abuse has ever been printed in this place against any man who sought to persuade people to his honest opinion by fair and honest argument. But there is a tremendous difference between honest persuasion and violent and ill-natured browbeating, and that difference I shall continue to point out from time to time. The objection to the moralists whom the Rev. Dr. Harris defends is not only that they are wrong, but also and more especially that they are intolerant, pharisaical, cruel, ignorant, vindictive, vituperative and disingenuous. In brief, they try to overcome their opponents, not by proving them in error, but by calling them scoundrels. That is a fault so discreditable that it wipes out all the credit of their holy zeal. It is a fault that their pastors should beat out of them with clubs. They should be taught manners before ever they are allowed to teach the rest of us morals.

I give so much space to the Rev. Dr. Harris' accusation because I regard him as an honest man, and hence one among many. What is more, he is a sinner and thus my brother. I myself once caught him in sin, and he frankly admitted it. This lifts him above all suspicion of personal interest. I hold no brief against any moralist save the bogus archangel, the lofty sniffer, the manhater, the pharisee, the bichloride tablet. Let me call on the rev. gent., then, for the name of one gentleman, not obviously of that fair brotherhood, whom I have ever attacked unjustly, and to whom I have ever shown discourtesy. Let him produce one lone *honest* moralist with authentic wounds. [17 October 1913]

BEING ON THE LOSING SIDE

Friendly caution and summons of an anonymous contributor to the Letter Column:

> Sir Lancelot, don't you know you're on the losing side? Can't you discern the signs of the times?

Well, suppose I am? Suppose I can? What of it? Is there any special virtue in being on the winning side? If so, let's hear it. Personally, I have always found it a great deal more exciting to lose than to win, and what is more, a great deal more soothing to the soul. Imagine a man winning with the mob behind him, or, say, the City Council, or the Society for the Suppression of Vice, or the salacious old deacons of the

Anti-Saloon League![4] The immediate fruits of victory, true enough, would be his. He would be applauded, he would be esteemed, perhaps he would even get a good job. But consider the damage to his self-respect, the staggering psychic insult! How he would blush when he shaved in the morning—and looked into his mirror!

But what good is accomplished by combating the irresistible, the inevitable? For example, what good is accomplished by opposing prohibition, which is bound to triumph in Maryland within five years, and perhaps within two years? The answer is as simple as can be: *no* good is accomplished. Utilitarianism sees the enterprise as wasteful and vain, and hence as immoral. But while utilitarianism thus denounces it, hedonism approves it. That is to say, its objective uselessness is outweighed by its subjective pleasantness. Herein lies the beauty of philosophy: it is so full of contradictions that it affords excuse for every imaginable immorality. And herein lies the charm of life: that one man's poison is another man's meat.

Just why it is so all-fired agreeable to object to what the great bulk of "right-thinking" men regard as nice I do not profess to determine with accuracy. My own theory is that the feeling is based upon sound logical and psychological grounds: that the pursuit of the truth is inherently pleasant, and that the pursuit of the truth necessarily involves a conflict with the majority of men, who view it, at best, with suspicion, and at worst, with the most savage hostility. Some one has put the fact into a platitude: What everyone believes is never true. It was voiced by Paul in his famous saying, The truth shall make you free[5]—*i. e.*, shall release you from membership in the stupid and credulous mob.

All belief in the intelligence of the mob—which is to say, all democracy—is based upon the erroneous assumption that logic is instinctive in man, just as lying and theft are instinctive. Nothing could be more ridiculously untrue. The fact is that logic is one of the youngest of the arts, and that relatively few men ever attain to any facility in its practice, even after the most painstaking instruction. Such rare men, I believe, tend to increase just as the men who can read and write tend to increase, but the vast majority still labor under a congenital unfitness or incapacity. These inept ones, whose logical fingers are all thumbs, run the United States today. They believe that Friday is an unlucky day, that Peruna[6] will cure catarrh, that a cat has nine lives, that one American militiaman would be a fair match for 10 Germans or 20 Frenchmen, that all rich men are rogues *ipso facto* and that universal human appetites may be obliterated by a simple legislative fiat. They venerate Theodore Roosevelt as the male Jane Addams, and Jane Addams as the female Roosevelt, and both as profound and revolutionary thinkers.

One of the minor errors we make in considering the logical faculty is that of confusing it with mere education. The two things, of course, are wholly distinct, and in some sense even antagonistic. A man may have a mind richly stored with facts, and yet at the same time he may fall into error in the most elementary reasoning processes. I offer as an example a distinguished member of the Johns Hopkins faculty, whose name and chair I charitably suppress. This gentleman, with the best intentions in the world, once composed a pamphlet that has since been widely circulated by interested persons. It covers but a few pages, but in those few pages the whole science of logic is reduced to madness. The learned professor jumps through syllogisms with the abandon of a hunter leaping a hedge. It would be impossible to imagine a wilder debauch of faulty premises and unwarranted conclusions. And yet the thing was composed seriously, and is accepted seriously by 99 readers out of every 100 today.

When we come to men less trained to purely intellectual processes, by reason, perhaps, of a preoccupation with emotional and hence unreasonable matters, we find even worse examples, if worse be possible, of logical burlesque and buffoonery. At the risk of seeming to push a point too hard, I cite again the astounding chain of reasoning whereby the Hon. Charles J. Bonaparte has established, to his own satisfaction, that all men who oppose the hounding of miserable prostitutes are either frequenters of their studios or friends of their prosperity. This chain of reasoning, it may be said at once, has convinced not only the Hon. Mr. Bonaparte himself, but also many other persons. And yet, at bottom, it is not only at war with the easily demonstrable facts, but also inherently unsound and ridiculous. Here we have a former Attorney-General of the United States—*i. e.,* a recognized leader in a profession based upon logic—backing logic into a corner and beating it to death.

And if there be any further desire to seek clinical material, and no objection is made to visiting the free wards wherein the lowly fight for life, I offer this column gladly. Herein one observes full oft that even an amateur, who ordinarily loves the art he practices, may maul it quite as mercilessly as a professional, who ordinarily hates it. Two or three weeks ago some kind gentleman informed the Letter Column that he had found no less than six separate logical absurdities in my compositions in one week. Obviously a blind man—or a humanitarian. My real score must be well over six a day, with a dozen on Blue Mondays. [6 February 1914]

MENCKEN TAKES A VACATION

Au revoir, dear hearts! *Auf wiedersehen!* In this place, during my absence in the service of the Kaiser, various sophists and wordmongers will purl and cavort. I beseech you to hear and bear their rumble-bumble with patience; I shall return anon, and once more an orthodox and laudable doctrine will be on tap. I need not remind you how many misguided and fatuous persons there are in this town, State, republic, hemisphere and world. You and I are fortunate in that we are not to be reckoned among them. Whatever *we* believe is true, and in most cases, self-evident. We are not deceived by the mere appearance of things. We do not suffer ourselves to be stampeded by the sough and burble of empty words. We never make mistakes. What, never? Well, hardly ever.

Nevertheless, let us not take too much flattering unction to our souls. It is not because of any merit of our own, but simply by the providence of God, that we are not such boobs and suckers as other men are. How thick, after all, is the partition which separates us from the Socialists, the Bryanistas, the uplifters, the peruna-swallowers, the Christian Scientists, the believers in palmistry and international peace, the osteopaths and osseocaputs?[7] Not more than an eighth of an inch. A slight shove in early youth and we would have burst through it, and so come to manhood as forward-lookers and right-thinkers. Think how narrow the escape! And then give thanks for it in all humility of spirit.

Furthermore, let us not underestimate these lowly brothers, for they, too, serve their benign uses in the world, and have human needs and feelings. Even a Socialist, for all his stupidity, may yet be a very respectable specimen of a man. He may labor diligently at some necessary, though perhaps ignoble, trade, art or profession—for example, vestcutting, journalism or beer-bottling. His wife may love him, and even venerate him. His children may look up to him as to a pillar of wisdom. He may be esteemed in his submerged circle for qualities which do credit to his heart however they may expose and denounce his head. He may go, in the end, to Heaven, and shine the shoes of Karl Marx for all eternity. Such a man is not to be sniffed at. He may be foolish, but he is surely not quite degraded.

So with all other uplifters and press agents of the millennium. You and I know, true enough, that they are bughouse, but let us not fall into the error of assuming that they are therefore wholly devoid of merit. Within his narrow sphere, within the circumscribed and unyielding circle of his capital ivory, the uplifter may even be faintly creditable to the human race, just as an industrious peasant may be creditable, or even an Englishman. I know, in fact, a number of such uplifters. They approach a capacity for human reason very closely; they are at least anthropoid; mammals without a doubt, they bring forth their young alive, and their ideas in passable English. I hope I am not one to sneer at these worthy creatures. A few seidels of authentic Pilsner would convert the best of them into excellent second-rate men.

Even Sunday-school superintendents, I dare say, are occasionally full of virtue, though the impression to the contrary seems to be widespread and ineradicable. Personally I do not share in the common suspicion of them. I am willing to admit, of course, that their vulnerability to temptation is greater than that of bartenders, and that more of them thus go wrong, but perhaps this is only because they are exposed to greater temptations—which is also the case, I suppose, with working girls. The bartender, let it be remembered, is protected by the cash register, a device which interposes such obstacles to his cupidity that it must often save him when he would otherwise sneak a yellowback.[8] The Sunday-school superintendent enjoys the protection of no such checks and balances. Widow ladies with insurance money to invest continue to place it in his hands; dealers in Mexican mine stock never overlook him; many women fall in love with him. Is it any wonder that he so often ends as a fugitive from justice, a price upon his head?

I did not start out, however, to defend Sunday-school superintendents, but to protest gently against a too contemptuous view of the boneheads of the world. Secure behind the ramparts of our superior sagacity, let us look down upon them, gents, with kindly feeling and genuine brotherliness. They do their darndest with their meager machinery and angels could do no more. It is surely nothing against them that their skulls are somewhat tight, and so give little play to the peristaltic action of their pituitary bodies. You and I, for all our amazing acumen, would be in the same boat if some footpad were to sneak up behind us when we were in our cups, and dent our trapeziuses with a blunt weapon. In brief, our infallibility resides chiefly in a purely physical accident, or, at any rate, in a physical immunity, and so we should be no more uppish about it than we are about our bulk or our loveliness. The Lord giveth and the Lord taketh away. Some are born virtuous and some are born cunning. [4 January 1915]

MENCKEN ATTACKED

The Hon. John Stonewall J. Healy's pious ranting in today's Forum is pathetically typical of the new "Americanism"—that fantastic compound of cheap bullying and cheaper moralizing. It is a first principle of this tin-pot "Americanism" that any man who dissents from the prevailing platitudes is a hireling of the devil; it is a second principle that he should be silenced and destroyed forthwith. Down with free speech; up with the uplift! Because I presume to believe, along with such men as Prof. Drs. John W. Burgess, William M. Sloane, Herbert C. Sanborn and Henry Wood, that Germany is right in this war and England wrong, I am a foe to the true, the good and the beautiful. Because I presume to argue, along with the Hon. William J. Stone, chairman of the Committee on Foreign Affairs of the United States Senate, that the *Lusitania* was a belligerent ship and that her passengers knowingly risked their lives in boarding her, I commit an offense against the United States. And because the Editor of THE EVENING SUN, despite his open partiality for the Allies, is still fair enough and courageous enough to let me present my contrary views in this place, he is a low scoundrel, selling his honor for a few miserable dollars.

What puerile buncombe! What a vain making of faces! What a deadly exposure of the true dignity and manliness of the new "Americanism," by Judge Lynch out of Chautauqua! And how beautifully the Hon. Mr. Healy, with his virtuous bluster and empty charges, serves as an exponent and example of it! Consider his logic: THE EVENING SUN, eager for profit, outrages and alienates the overwhelming majority of its readers in order to tickle a small minority! What a syllogism is here, Messieurs! What an Aristotle performs upon the tragic bassoon! And consider again his plain allegation that I have "gloated over the suffering" of the *Lusitania* victims (When? Where?) and his allegation that I have denounced Dr. Wilson "in language so foul and indecent that at times it was unfit for publication in a decent family journal" (Examples, I prithee!), and his allegation that I am employed "for the special purpose" of signing my name to "the inspired and prepared stuff sent out by the German propagandists" (Am I, then, incapable of writing my stuff myself?), and his allegation that "the German papers published in this country are subsidized by the German Government" (Why subsidize them? How long would they last if they opposed Germany?). What ludicrous yawping, indeed! What a feeble and childish rattling!

I do not offer the Hon. Mr. Healy the affront of assuming that he actually believes these allegations to be true. On the contrary, I assume that he knows very well that they are false. That he makes them at all is sufficient evidence of the lamentable state of mind into which he has fallen, and with him a vast number of other such high-falutin' and hysterical moralists. England has long rung with these frenzied charges and hollow threats; they are now heard *fortissimo* in the United States. Let the Hon. Mr. Healy cast his eye toward the Germans, observing them studiously through his pious tears. He will find that they are not moralizing, but fighting; that they make steady progress against the enormous hordes of their foes; that they draw tighter and tighter the rope around John Bull's neck; that they face the future resolutely, bravely, confidently, paying no heed to the moral slobber-gobble of their enemies, whether open or disguised. Let him ask himself which race is better fitted to prevail in the world—the Germans with their homeric strength and daring, or the English with their white livers and their womanish screams for help.

As for the hon. gentleman's impatience with my own heterodoxy, I regret that I can offer him no assurances of reform. Strange as it may seem to him, I am a good American (only partly, by the way, of German blood) and eager to serve my country. Unfitted by fastidious prejudices for that petty job-seeking which has been the hon. gentleman's avenue of service, I devote myself to combating what appear to me to be elements of decay in the national philosophy and the national character. I believe that the American people would be a stronger and more respectable race if they could get rid of the intellectual dishonesty and slimy hypocrisy that they have inherited from England, and take on something of the German's respect for the eternal and immovable facts. To the promotion of this transformation I shall devote the time intervening between the present moment and my inevitable arrival at Loudon Park. And if not in this place, then in some other place. [12 May 1915]

II

THE CENTRAL QUESTIONS
OF EXISTENCE

LESSONS OF A LIFETIME

I OFFER THE following conclusions after 42 years of unremitting observation and reflection, aided by consultations with hundreds of other
observers, dead and alive:

1. There is no such thing as honest politics, in the strict sense. All
persons who aspire to public office, without a single exception, are
mountebanks. Even those who start out honestly, with a sincere desire
to sacrifice their private comfort to the public good, become mountebanks the moment they face an assemblage of voters, just as every man
becomes a mountebank the moment he faces a woman. Under a republic, with the vote of a farmhand counting exactly as much as the vote of
a Huxley, intellectual honesty in politics is inhibited by the very nature
of things.

2. It is a capital mistake to assume that the common people are
stupid but honest. The exact contrary is more nearly true. The common
people never sacrifice their own good to the general good. They are
always in favor of the man who promises to get something for them
without cost to them—*i. e.*, to steal something for them. This capacity
for predatory enterprise they venerate above all other human qualities.

Even when it is turned against them, they have a sneaking respect for it. They may laugh at a college professor or an archbishop, but they never laugh at a Charles F. Murphy. One cannot laugh at a man one envies— at the man one would like to be.

3. Virtue is often a mere symptom of meanness, or of poverty, which is the same thing. The mildest vice is an overhead charge, a dead expense. A man of intense and unyielding virtue is often merely a man of overpowering meanness. This explains why it is that such virtue is usually found in combination with lack of generosity, boorishness, suspiciousness—why it is, in brief, that a virtuoso of virtue is seldom a gentleman. It costs something, even to be merely polite. One cannot show any genuine toleration for the other fellow—the essence of being a gentleman—without at the same time practicing, or at least freely condoning, his vices, *i. e.,* his unutilitarian acts. The true test of a man is not the way he gets his money, but the way he spends it. Men are drawn into firm friendship and understanding, not so much by common occupations, as by common vices. Professional musicians usually dislike one another, but amateur musicians are strongly attracted to one another. Thus it appears that good will between man and man is largely based upon common vices—*e. g.,* music, politics, alcoholism, gambling, or the pursuit of women (either openly, as Don Juans, or in disguise, as vice crusaders).

4. Women and actors have this advantage in common: that any sign of intelligence in them, however slight, causes surprise, and is therefore estimated above its true worth. In the case of actors this surprise is justified, but justified or not, it works to the same end. No one gets excited over a man who has read Kant, but a woman who has done so, or who merely gets the reputation of having done so, becomes a sort of celebrity *ipso facto.* In the same way an actor who is able to put together a dozen intelligible paragraphs about Shakespeare is hailed as a Shakespearean scholar and invited to address universities. I say "intelligible," mind you, and not "intelligent." No actor has ever written anything actually intelligent about Shakespeare, or even about acting. Of all the professions open to males, acting is the only one whose practitioners have never contributed anything of value to its theory.

5. A man who has never faced the hazards of war is in exactly the same position as a woman who has never faced the hazards of maternity.

That is to say, he has missed the supreme experience of his sex, and is hence an incomplete being. There is something in all of us which makes us crave these natural hazards—some impulse toward danger and courage—and when they are not experienced we are prone to invent imaginary substitutes. Thus it is that the men of a nation long at peace become old maidish: they torture themselves with artificial austerities and hobgoblins—for example, prohibition and the Rum Demon. The remedy for such vapors is war, just as the remedy for hypochondria is a knock in the head.

6. Whatever may be the demerits of Dr. Sigmund Freud's scheme of psychoanalysis, there is at least sound support for his theory that the thing we hate most is the thing most dangerous to us—that a man's prejudices afford an index to his weaknesses. The most cruel and vindictive judge is the one who is most a criminal at heart. The loudest whooper for prohibition is the man who is most tempted every time he passes a saloon. But perhaps the best proof of Freud's theory is to be found in those strange fanatics who specialize in denouncing nude pictures and statuary. The argument of these gentlemen is that such pictures and statues incite the beholder to lewd thougthts. This is a faulty generalization from their personal experience. Their error lies in the assumption that all men, or even any considerable number of men, are as dirty-minded as they are themselves. Wasn't it Arnold Bennett who said that a novelist must always get his psychology from himself? The same thing is true of a moralist.

7. The prosperity of such bogus healing schemes as osteopathy and Christian Science is largely based upon the fact that they offer simple and intelligible theores as to the causation of disease. In this department scientific medicine has made but little progress. It can tell us clearly *what* nephritis is, but it cannot tell us *why* it is. Even when it ventures to answer—as in the case of typhoid fever—it really begs the question. The *bacillus typhosus,* in itself, cannot cause typhoid: there must be a preliminary state of receptivity in the body. What that state of receptivity is and how it is produced are questions that scientific medicine has yet failed to answer in simple terms. The answers given by osteopathy and Christian Science, of course, are not true, but they are at least simple, and to the popular mind they thus become plausible. Even an anti-vivisectionist is intelligent enough to understand the theory that typhoid

is caused by the pressure of hard bone upon soft nervous tissue. But only a few persons can understand the warring hypotheses of immunity, and even these are left in doubt and darkness.

8. I have spoken above (in paragraph 5) of the impulse to danger and courage that is inherent in all of us. Its psychological roots are to be found in the *wille zur macht,* the will to power—a thing differing considerably from Schopenhauer's will to live, despite many elements in common. The impulse to do something daring is simply an impulse to give an exhibition of efficiency—in particular, of the sort of efficiency that few other men possess. And added to this psychical impulse (and no doubt underlying it) is the purely physical impulse to function: in brief, the life force. That the life force, working thus through the medium of the impulse to daring enterprise, may produce its own destruction—*i. e.,* may produce death—is not an objection of any importance. We all know that nature is an ass. She is constantly failing, through what may be called excess of zeal, to accomplish her own purposes. She is extraordinarily inept, clumsy and wasteful. Even when her purposes seem to be clear (which is not often) her means of accomplishing them are commonly fatuous to the point of unintelligibility. Nature's plans are magnificent, but her workmanship is almost always bad. An optician who made a microscope as defective as the human eye would be taken out into the alley and shot.

9. The hardest job in the world is that of a clergyman. If he preaches a scheme of life that is actually livable, he is condemned as a compromiser with evil, and if he preaches a scheme that is ideal, and hence unlivable, he is condemned for not living it himself. No other man is watched so closely, or judged so harshly. And not only are the judgments upon him harsh, but they are also wholly unfair. He is expected to have sympathy for every human weakness, even the worst, and yet to show no human weakness himself, even the least. Imagine a grown man, perhaps with sciatica, Mexican mine stock and a mother-in-law, who is forbidden to utter so much as a single damn! Imagine a man whose material rewards in his profession are exactly in *inverse* proportion to his sincerity, his industry and his enthusiasm! Again, recall this staggering fact: the clergyman is the only professional man who cannot, in decency, abandon his profession. And yet, being founded wholly upon faith, without any support whatever in

exact knowledge, it is precisely the profession which exposes its practitioner to the most insidious doubts. A lawyer who begins to doubt
the law may switch to business or politics, and still hold up his head.
But a clergyman who is unfrocked, even at his own request, remains a
suspicious character to the end of his days.

These, at least, are my honest views. If I err I shall be very glad to
apologize. [25 March 1914, 30 March 1914, 10 April 1914]

BEST OF ALL POSSIBLE WORLDS?

The Hon. Charles J. Ogle, secretary of the Maryland Tax Reform Association, in THE EVENING SUN of yesterday:

> It is all very well, so long as we ourselves have beer and
> skittles, to say that the vast majority of us get exactly what we
> deserve, and that all is as it should be in this best of all possible
> worlds. But in our hearts we know that it's a lie while our lips
> are saying it. * * * Resign from the World's Boomers' Association,
> Brother Mencken! * * *

For shame, Charles! Oblique and unmanly advice! When have
I ever preached any such rubbishy doctrine? The best of all possible
worlds, forsooth! How can this ever be the best of all possible worlds so
long as I have hay fever, and grow bulky to the verge of immobility, and
have to work eight hours every day for a meagre living, and owe $7 on
my Sunday clothes?

Best of all possible worlds? Bosh! One of the worst worlds I can
imagine. The fact that I never blush is proof enough that I did not
make it, and do not defend it. Huxley once ventured the modest guess
that he could improve upon the weather. I go much further. I think that
I could improve upon sciatica, upon the human liver, upon the tonsils,
upon mud, upon jiggers, upon snakes, upon babies, upon chilblains. If I
were manager of the world there would be no whiskers, no bunions, no
twins. No fat women, incrusted with diamonds, would loll provokingly
in automobiles. Vice crusading would develop swiftly into convulsions,
coma and dissolution. The Hon. Mr. Anderson would choke upon his
own sinister eloquence.

No, Charles, I am no apologist for this world, no press agent for nature. I know very well that the human eye, so loudly praised as nature's

masterpiece, is really the most fragile and undependable of optical instruments, that any man who made a microscope so badly would be heaved out of the union. I wonder that so clumsy a banjo as the glottis should ever make music at all. I deny that katzenjammer[1] is either a logical or a moral necessity. I believe that many men die too soon, and that a great many more men do not die soon enough.

But after all, what would you? Say what you will, the massive fact remains that the world is as it is. You and I didn't make it, we are not consulted about its management, we do not even know why it exists, we can do precious little to change it, even in minor details. Was it Romanes or Lankester who said that we human beings sometimes prevail modestly against nature, that we sometimes gain a puny and trivial victory of outposts, but that every time we do so we lose as much as we have won? Taking man as he stands, is he better off than his anthropoid fathers? Is he healthier, happier, more fit? In many ways he undoubtedly is. In many other ways he undoubtedly isn't. And in so far as he is, it is probably due as much to nature's victories over advancing civilization as to civilization's victories over nature.

In brief, the world, as it stands, at least works. By hook or crook it wabbles along. Revile it as you will, my dear Ogle, you must always admit, in the end, that you and I have survived in it, and that, to that extent, it is humane, benevolent, intelligent, praiseworthy, and a success. Our survival, true enough, has had a million times more luck in it than merit—but who are we to complain against luck? Why try to discount it, deplore it, account for it? Why worry so much about the other fellow? Is he worrying about us? I doubt it. His one great passion is to increase his own luck, his own beer, his own skittles—and nine times out of ten he tries to do it by decreasing ours.

Therefore, let us admit freely the injustice and savagery of the world, and at the same time put the matter out of mind. Nothing that we can do can set aside, for more than an inconsequential moment or two, the great natural law that the strong shall prey upon the weak. In the most lovely Utopia that you and I could plan, there would still be men who were less fitted to survive than the best man, or even than the average man. And nothing that laws or philanthropy could accomplish would make these men more fit. [21 August 1912]

THE ESSENCE OF EDUCATION

The Rev. Charles Fiske, D. D., in the course of an article on "The Debt of the Educated Man":

> Some years since Senator Lodge expressed the opinion that the chief defect of our modern educated life was its tendency to arouse unduly the critical spirit. * * * There are plenty of intellectual mugwumps[2] in the world, and they are always barren of lasting achievement. They sit complacently on judgment stools, passing cynical criticisms on evils which they make no effort to correct.

To which, perhaps, the most apt of answers was made by Immanuel Kant fully 150 years ago, to wit:

> *So viel ist gewiss: wer einmal Kritik gekostet hat, den ekelt auf immer alles dogmatische Gewäsche.*

Which may be put into English as follows:

> So much is sure: Whoever has once tasted Criticism, is disgusted forever after with all dogmatic twaddle.

That is to say, once education and experience have aroused the critical spirit in a man, he straightway loses all belief in brummagem schemes for making the world a one-horse paradise overnight. The chief impression left on a healthy mind by a sound education, indeed, is an impression of what may be called the infinite complexity of the social reaction. An ignorant man believes in short cuts, ready answers, sovereign specifics. He believes, for example, that Peruna will cure Bright's disease, that such terms as "good" and "bad" have definite and unchangeable meanings, that a simple act of the Legislature is sufficient to stamp out such things as prostitution, avarice, cleverness, drunkenness and the law of natural selection. The educated man is simply a man who knows better. The fact that he knows better is the one practicable test of his education. It may not be a sufficient and infallible test, but nevertheless it is the only test that actually works.

There is no need, I take it, of supporting this proposition with a host of examples, for a large number of them will immediately occur to every reflective man. All proposals for the reduction of enormously complex phenomena to simple equations come from the dreamers of the race, *i. e.*, from those persons whose pressing sense of what ought to be is uncontaminated by any appreciable sense of what is. Viewed romantically, such persons are prophets. Their thinking is not grounded upon reason, but upon intuition—and it is always pleasant to argue that intuition is superior to reason. But viewed realistically, the thing they offer is not prophecy at all, but merely ignorance. It is the business of the persons who possess superior knowledge—that is to say, of those who are better educated—to combat this ignorance with criticism, and to pull off its successive husks, one by one, until finally the inner kernel of truth is revealed. Sometimes that kernel is microscopic, but it is very seldom, of course, that it has no existence at all, for even error is unimaginable save as it is an exaggerated and distorted statement of truth.

The operation of this process is seen most plainly, perhaps, in the field of medicine, for it is probable that men have done more thinking in that field, first and last, than in any other, not even excepting religion. Everyone of us is ill at times, and everyone of us wants to get well. The result of this universal yearning has always been an effort to dispose of ancient difficulties, to find short cuts, to reduce the complex and baffling to a beautiful simplicity. Such has been the origin of all the quack healing cults since the day of Hammurabi. For example, Christian Science. Mrs. Eddy was able to devise her puerile magic, and to believe in it after she had devised it, not because she was educated, for she wasn't, but precisely because she was incredibly ignorant. Difficulties and objections that would have halted an educated person at the very start did not bother her in the slightest. She was ignorant of the most elementary facts of anatomy and physiology, and so she went blundering on. The result was a healing scheme of unparalleled simplicity—but also one of unparalleled imbecility.

But didn't it convince many persons who *were* educated? It did not. It convinced only those who *thought* they were educated, who *passed* as educated. It convinced, in the first place, a crowd of women with no more genuine education, whatever their pretensions, than so many chorus girls or Slavonic immigrants. And it convinced, in the second place, a crowd of male boobies so powerful in intellect that they were willing to take the simple word of a vapid old woman, on an extremely recondite and technical question, against the sober and unanimous judgment of men who had devoted their whole lives to studying it. Many of these persons, male and female, were highly estimable. Most of them belonged to Sunday-schools. All of them, so far as I know to the contrary, paid their taxes, beat their children daily and sent money to the heathen. But in the whole lot there was not one who showed the slightest development of that critical faculty which is the chief fruit, sign and essence of true education. They were refined, peaceable and honest—but they were infinitely credulous and ignorant.

The same phenomenon is frequently witnessed in the domain of morals. Speaking generally, the most ignorant man is always the most immovably moral man. That is to say, the most ignorant man is always the most sure that *his* right is *the* right, and that all other rights are bogus, and that no change in moral values will ever be possible in future, and that the world would be perfect if all dissenters were clapped into jail. Such is the fine, blatant, bumptious morality of vice crusaders, prohibitionists, Sunday snouters and all other such gladiators of Puritanism. The thought that their easy solution of all the problems of the world may be wrong—that civilization may be a vastly more complex affair than they assume it to be—this thought never crosses their minds. They are so sure that they are right that they are ecstatically eager to shed the blood of every man who raises any question about it.

Is it the duty of educated men, who should and do know better, to join in this preposterious bellowing? Or is it their duty to stand forever against it, to expose its weaknesses, one by one, to oppose it with all their might? I leave the answer to every man who esteems the true above the merely sonorous, to every man who feels any responsibility of gratitude for his opportunities to acquire knowledge, to every man who believes that deceit, cant, fustian, hypocrisy and stupidity are evil and shameful things, however virtuous their wrappings. [14 June 1913]

WAR IS GOOD

War is enormously destructive, not only to life and goods, but also to platitudes and platitutidinarians, the *pediculidæ*[3] of civilization. Once the band begins to play and men are on the march there is no audience left for the Bryans and the Billy Sundays, the Carnegies and the Lydia Pinkhams. It is not good but bad fortune that keeps the United States out of the present mix-up. More than any other people we need the burden of resolute and manly effort, the cleansing shock of adversity. A foreign war—and, in particular, a foreign war in which we got the worst of it—would purge the national blood of the impurities which now pollute it. The Civil War had that effect, and for all its horrors, it was of profit to the race. It cut short an era of moralizing, posturing and tub-thumping and ushered in an era of action. It rid us of the abolitionist forever, and of the prohibitionist, the revivalist and the prude at least temporarily. It cleared the way for the unimpeded and unmoral enterprise of the 70's and 80's, during which decades the new nation found itself and came to genuine greatness.

The warlike qualities of daring and pugnacity are inherent in all healthy peoples and individuals, and a race must be far gone in decadence before they fall into ill repute. There is something deep down in the soul of every man worthy of the name which makes him crave power and consequence for himself and his own, that he and they may stand clearly above the common run of men. This craving is at the bottom of all that we know of human achievement and all that is loftiest and noblest in human aspiration. It moves the saint in his sheet of flame no less than the general on the battle field; it is as much responsible for the higher forms of sacrifice as for all forms of conquest. Human progress would be impossible without this inborn and irresistible impulse, this eternal will to power.

But civilization, as we all know, attempts a vain but none the less pertinacious war upon it. That security which is one of the chief fruits of civilization gives artificial advantages to the man who has it only faintly— to the poor-spirited, harbor-seeking sort of man—to the compromiser, the "right-thinker," the joiner, the mob member, the hider behind skirts. And at the same time civilization tries to put an artificial restraint upon the man in whom the will to power is unusually strong, and who makes no effort of his own to throttle it—that is, upon the man of daring enterprise and intelligent self-seeking, the violator of precedents, the assertive and bellicose man, the "bad" citizen. In both directions the pressure is toward conformity, peaceableness, self-effacement. But in neither direction is it strong enough to achieve more than a mere appearance of prevailing. The yearning for self-functioning is still powerful in every healthy individual, and the measure of that self-functioning, in civilized societies, no less than in the sea ooze, is power.

War is a good thing because it is honest, because it admits the central fact of human nature. Its great merit is that it affords a natural, normal and undisguised outlet for that complex of passions and energies which civilization seeks so fatuously to hold in check. Let us not forget the fatuity of the effort. Let us not forget that man, under peace, is just as much urged and bedeviled by his will to power as man in war. The only difference is that war makes him admit the fact and take pride in it, whereas peace seduces him into lying denials of it. And out of that difference grow all the evils that a long peace nourishes—too much moralizing, petty and meticulous fault-finding, a childish belief in soothsayers, a sentimental reverence for poverty and inefficiency, a cult of self-sacrifice, a universal fear, suspiciousness, over-niceness, prudishness and hypochondria. In brief, a nation too long at peace becomes a sort of gigantic old maid. It grows weak in body and aberrant in mind. The energies that should be turned against its foes and rivals are turned against itself. It seeks escape for its will to power by flogging its own hide.

No need to dredge up examples out of history. We have a capital one under our very noses. The American people, too secure in their isolation and grown too fat in their security, show all the signs of deteriorating national health. The very qualities which won a great empire from the wilderness are the qualities which they now seek to deny and punish. Once a race of ruthless and light-hearted men, putting the overt act above any metaphysical significance of it, they now become introspective and conscience-stricken, and devote their chief endeavors to penalizing one another for artificial crimes, and to brooding maudlinly over dangers and "wrongs" that their healthier fathers never gave a thought to. In every evidence of superabundant energy, in every manifestation of sound wind and quick blood, they see only the spectre of disaster. They become afraid of everything, including even themselves. They are afraid of women, they are afraid of alcohol, they are afraid of money. And their fear, playing upon their sick will to power, arouses them to that abominable orgy of spying and hypocrisy, that disgusting mutual pursuit and persecution, which is fast becoming the chief mark of American civilization in the eyes of other peoples.

A war would do us good. It would make us healthier in body, cleaner in mind. It would put an end to our puerile brooding over petty "wrongs" and ills, our old-womanish devotion to neighborhood gossip and scandal-monging, our imbecile following of snide messiahs. No race can long hold a respectable place in the world which shrinks from the hazards amd sacrifices of honorable, stand-up combat, and hangs instead upon the empty words of fact-denying platitudinarians. At this moment the peoples of Europe are preparing to fight out the great fight that must inevitably select and determine, in man no less than among the protozoa, the fittest to survive. And at this moment our ranking officer of state, taking his place between the performing dogs and the Swiss bell-ringers, is wooing the ears of marveling hinds with his grotesque repeal and re-enactment of the law of natural selection.[4] [4 August 1914]

THE CASE AGAINST DEMOCRACY

The Hon. S. Broughton Tail, the Walbrook thinker, continues to fill the Letter Column with his solemn proofs that the German Kaiser is not a democrat. When this great labor is over let us hope that the Hon. Mr. Tail will present his reasons for holding that the Hon. Tom McNulty is not a Jewish rabbi, and that the Hon. Jack Johnson is not an albino, and that Sir Almroth Wright is not a militant suffragist, and that I myself am not a bishop in the A. M. E. Church. A man of such gifts for convincing argumentation owes the human race a high duty: he must exercise them constantly if he would go to Heaven when he dies. Let us all rejoice that one so suave and sapient is in our fevered midst.

Seriously, it is as vain to argue that the Kaiser is not a democrat as it would be to argue that dogs have fleas. If it means anything at all, democracy means government by men in the mass, without any regard whatever for the personal fitness of the individuals composing the mass for that difficult and highly technical business. It is grounded firmly and immovably upon the doctrine that, in the voting booth at least, all men are equal—that the opinion of a corner loafer or a farm hand is just as good as the opinion of a Lincoln, a Bismarck or a Huxley. The Kaiser is wholly opposed to that doctrine. He regards it as windy nonsense, as utter puerility and damphoolishness. And what is more, the overwhelming majority of intelligent men, not only in Germany but everywhere else, agree with him.

I know a great many Americans of position and influence, but save for professional politicians and a few sentimentalists I do not know three who even make a pretense of believing in anything approaching genuine democracy. Not many of them, true enough, argue against it publicly. They look upon the question as a closed one in the United States, at least for the present, just as the question of a state church is a closed one, and the question of free education. But though they thus dodge the empty and thankless job of bucking the enraptured rabble, they by no means confess thereby that they are in accord with it. On the contrary, they are opposed to it, and they will remain opposed to it until the last galoot's ashore.

The very theory of democracy, in fact, is unintelligible to men accustomed to reflection, just as the theory of Christian Science is unintelligible. And the cause thereof is as plain as day: it is because democracy is not founded upon an idea at all, but merely upon an emotion. That emotion is the lowly one of envy, perhaps the most degraded in the whole human repertoire. Democracy is a device for giving to the relatively inefficient and unsuccessful (and hence, bitterly envious) majority, by the artificial and dishonest device of the ballot, that preponderance of power and influence which belongs rightfully to the minority by reason of its superior efficiency, honesty and intelligence. In brief, democracy is an attempt to wreak punishment upon successful men for the crime of being successful, and its charm lies in its promise of loot. The one thing that may be said in favor of it is that it seldom works.

Here in the United States, for example, we have had to dilute and modify genuine democracy over and over again in order to save the nation from utter destruction and ruin. The enfranchisement of the negro was a device of genuine democracy: it set up the frank doctrine that the opinion of a Georgia field hand, but three generations removed from cannibalism, was as good as the opinion of Gen. Robert E. Lee—that his desires and ideals were just as respectable, that his notions of civilized government were just as sound. Lincoln and other sane men stood against that doctrine, but it was forced upon the country by a typically democratic process, *i. e.,* emotionally, unintelligently, in a villainous spirit of revenge.

But it had no sooner been adopted than everyone saw that it would not work. The States south of the Potomac begin to suffer from it even more than they had suffered from the Civil War and some of the Northern States also found it an unmitigated curse. The result was an organized attack upon it, resulting in the gradual pulling of its teeth. To abandon it bodily, of course, was beyond the American imagination, but hypocrisy, as is usual in democratic nations, did the work that honesty was unequal to. Today there is not a Southern State in which the Fifteenth Amendment is actually in force. Self-preservation demanded that this supreme masterpiece of democracy be reduced to a mere shell of words.

What is more, very few professed democrats advocate its restoration. Not a word in favor of that folly ever comes from the Hon. William Jennings Bryan, or from the Hon. Theodore Roosevelt, or from the Hon. Bob La Follette, or from the Hon. Woodrow Wilson, or from any other great apostle of the plain people. What is still more, the few lingering impossibilists who yet weep and argue for it are open opponents of democracy in other directions. I cite the Hon. C. J. Bonaparte as an example. This eminent statesman looses a tear ever and anon for the stolen "rights" of the virtuous niggero—but let us not forget that he was against local option,[5] and that he devotes himself ardently to opposing self-government at Back River.[6] The persons who make Back River an inhabited place are almost unanimously in a favor of an open Sunday, but Mr. Bonaparte and his friends frankly endeavor to block their attainment of it by arousing the passions and prejudices of remote yokels who have never been nearer to Back River than Watson street and the Monumental Theatre. [21 October 1914]

MORALITY AND IMMORALITY

The Hon. James A. Dunham, in the long-suffering Letter Column:

> THE SUN has ideals and standards, while [the Hon.] Mr. Mencken apparently has neither.

The traditional verdict of stupidity upon the unfamiliar. Because, forsooth, the ideals and standards to which I adhere are not the sweet and soothing ones to which the Hon. Mr. Dunham himself adheres, he comes to the solomonic judgment that I have no ideals and standards at all! But do not laugh. The absurdity into which this virtuous and well-meaning, if somewhat naif and unreflective, gentleman falls is one which occasionally engulfs the best of men. The most difficult of all mental processes, indeed, is that of grasping the other fellow's point of view, particularly with sympathy. And when we enter the domain of morals that difficulty becomes a practical impossibility. It is a first article of faith with all of us that those whose morals differ from our own have no morals at all. We habitually denominate them, indeed, by the simple word "immoral."

Nine times out of ten, of course, this use of the word is idiotic, for very few persons, in point of fact, are wholly immoral. Even those persons whose immorality is assumed by an almost unanimous public opinion are often devotees of a rigid and austere moral code. For example, the unfortunate women whose pursuit and persecution are so significantly attractive to a certain type of "moral" man. These women, true enough, habitually violate one of the Ten Commandments, and are thus immoral by our prevalent standards, but it would vastly surprise some of their pursuers to know how sternly moral they are in other respects—for example, how honorable they are in their dealings with one another, how violently they disapprove the man who seeks to bring other women to their plight, and how unyieldingly they frown upon that snivelling hypocrisy which sometimes offers them a way out. Ask one of these women what she thinks of any conspicuous moralist of our vicinage, and it is a safe bet that she will tell you he is cruel and mendacious—*i. e.,* that he is immoral.

So much for the morality of a class generally admitted to be sub-moral. What is constantly forgotten is that there are also classes which properly deserve to be called super-moral. That is to say, there are classes which accept all, or at least nearly all, of the restrictions imposed by the current popular morality, and then add restrictions that the popular morality does not demand. The gentlemen of the monastic orders offer a familiar example: some of them reach a degree of morality quite impossible, and even unimaginable, to the average man, or even to the average professional moralist. And one finds something of the same sort, though in less degree, among prohibitionists, vegetarians, Sabbatarians, Moslem dervishes, and the breed of kill-joys and uplifters in general.

No need to say that all of these super-moral persons have been, and are today, regarded as atrociously immoral by other persons of sound mind. The doctrine that asceticism is immoral once attained to such wide acceptance that it contributed very largely to an epoch-making schism in the Christian church, and it is still held today, I believe, by fully eight

Protestants out of ten. (Even among those who approve of asceticism some of its earlier manifestations are now regarded as immoral; for example, self-mutilation, flagellation and immersion in filth, all of which had countenance, popularly if not officially, in the first centuries of our era.) And one need not walk 20 steps to find a man who believes the prohibitionists to be tyrannical and dishonest, and hence immoral, or another man to denounce the Blue Laws, or animal-worship, or the Moslem holy war.

Thus it appears that morality, considered broadly, is a gem of many facets, and that the man who clings to one of them gets a sadly distorted view of the men clinging to the others. On some rules of morality, true enough, most civilized men agree, for example: on the rule against punching out the eyes of sleeping babies with tack pullers. But on the vast majority of rules opinion is anything but unanimous, even among persons who regard themselves as conventionally moral. I know hundreds of men who would rather starve than steal, and yet most of them habitually violate the Sabbath without the slightest sense of sin, and some of them swear like archdeacons, or gamble for money, or go to burlesque shows, or perform some other act that would give the Hon. Jack Cornell the fantods. Worse, all of them regard Jack as an immoral and abhorrent fellow, basing their opinion upon the very snoutery that is the foundation of his moral eminence among professional moralists!

Viewing the Hon. Mr. Dunham's allegation from such lofty peaks, I can well afford to pronounce upon it a superior Pooh-pooh! and so let it go. My own personal morality seems to me to be vastly more austere and elevating than that with which the hon. gent. contrasts it—to wit, the morality of the *Sunpaper*. I could fill this whole column with a list of things that the *Sunpaper* has done in the past, and that I myself wouldn't dare to do. For example, I would never print a line in praise or defense of such a charlatan as the Hon. William Jennings Bryan, knowing his character as I know it, and as the *Sunpaper* knows it, and as every intelligent American knows it. Again, I would never make a noisy pretense of neutrality in a great and bloody war, and then attack one of the contestants unfairly under cover of it, as the *Sunpaper* did in August last, and as Monsignor Russell properly denounced it for doing. Yet again—

But no more examples! I am not going to gloat over the poor old *Sunpaper* because my moral code happens to be too harsh and exacting for it. Nor am I going to revile the Hon. Mr. Dunham because that code is beyond his comprehension. He is, I take it, a virtuous man, and he probably does his darndest within his limitations. If the higher sort of honesty is over his head, he is at least in numerous company. To the average, everyday, unreflecting, platitude-eating man, the truth ever bears a sinister and forbidding aspect. He regards it as immoral, and with reason. If it prevailed in the world, then nine-tenths of the things that he believes in, and that give his life a meaning, and that soothe him and comfort him, and fill him with a pleased, boozy feeling of rectitude and security, would be blown up. [5 November 1914]

MENCKEN AND MATERIALISM

Some anonymous friend in the long-suffering Letter Column:

> [The Hon. Mr.] Mencken's * * * eyes are earthbound. Ethics of
> the mud. A gross materialist, that fellow, with only earth fires to
> lighten him.

Empty nonsense, true enough, but nevertheless it bobs up in the Letter Column regularly. One of the hardest of all things for a professed idealist to believe is that the man who dissents from his particular idealism may be an idealist also. This difficulty is at the bottom of most of the political and theological wars that rack the world. The first charge that one disputant makes against another is always that he is a materialist, that he has no idealism. And the counter-charge is always exactly the same. The whole dispute between Catholic and Protestant, Democrat and Monarchist, Christian and Jew, may be reduced to just such terms. The Englishman scorns the German as a worshiper of force; the German scorns the Englishman as a worshiper of ease; the Frenchman sniffs at both as gross and materialistic; both denounce the Frenchman as a voluptuary and an atheist. And so on and so on.

Every man is thus convinced, not only of the brutish materialism of the other fellow, but also and more especially of his own lofty idealism. I myself, for example, though constantly accused of neglecting the things of the spirit (and, from the standpoint of my critics, with excellent cause), am nevertheless an almost fanatical idealist in my own sight. As I look back over my life I see a long record of more or less steady devotion to worthy ideals, often at a heavy sacrifice of material benefits. The picture is intensely agreeable to me; in it I take on a sort of mellow, romantic aspect; I am positively touched. And yet my life, to many other men, must needs appear grossly materialistic, for its net results, to date, are that I am fat, that I have stopped going to Sunday-school, and that my conscience seldom bothers me.

Even when two men pursue one and the same ideal, they often fall into irreconcilable differences over the manner of its attainment. Consider, for example, the commonplace ideal, visioned by practically all of us, of a carefree and happy human race. I should like to see it realized, and Dr. Kelly would like to see it realized. But observe how vastly we differ in our plans for its realization. My plan is to let people do whatever they please, so long as they do not invade the right and freedom of other persons to do the same: that is, I see liberty of desire, of taste, of action as the capital essential to happiness. But Dr. Kelly, with the very same end in view, advocates a diametrically contrary route to its attainment. That is to say, he proposes to make people happy by force, by terrorism, by compulsion. His plan, in brief, is to decide what sort of life is a happy one, and then compel them to live it. This seems to me to be utter nonsense, almost a contradiction in terms. And yet Dr. Kelly and his friends undoubtedly believe in it, and (setting aside the natural pleasure that all of us get out of pursuing and punishing our fellow-men) undoubtedly work for it in good faith, and with a keen and even overpowering sense of virtue.

The correspondent I have quoted bases his accusation that my "eyes are earthbound" chiefly on the fact that I defend and advocate the German cause in this war. This seems to him an effective proof that I am no idealist, but a "gross materialist." In all friendliness, could anything be more absurd? Even supposing me to be a "gross materialist" as a general thing, certainly the fact must stick out plainly that I am far from being one in this particular case. What have I to gain, materially, by arguing for the Germans? Is there any reward hung up for that advocacy, save the wholly impalpable one (but far from unreal one!) of the idealist? Surely, it would be far more comfortable to drift with the tide. And surely the material rewards of such drifting could not be less.

But perhaps the learned writer means to say that I am not an idealist because the Germans themselves are not—that is, that the attorney shares the culpability of his client. Another absurdity. No people in history have made heavier sacrifices for their ideals than the Germans; no people in history have had ideals that were higher. The German is not content with material prosperity; he also wants to see his country great and venerable. And as a means to that end he counts in Beethoven's Fifth Symphony quite as much as he counts in the War Machine, and such men as Siemanns[7] and Ehrlich quite as much as such men as Hindenburg and Bismarck. The German civilization that he sees ahead is a civilization vastly transcending anything that the world knows today, and he is not only eager to work for it but also ready to fight for it. Does the attainment of his ideal demand the risk of his life? Then he risks it gladly and gallantly, and his womenfolk urge him on. (What a golden page of history belongs to German women in this war!)

I believe fully in this German idealism, and what is more, I believe that it will prevail. The truth is behind it, and the truth has a mailed fist. The snuffling and the sobbing dies; the moralists and the mob-masters depart. What stands is the immutable law of human progress: That the more fit shall conquer and obliterate the less fit. This present war is merely the first skirmish. The real battle will be fought out later on. On the one side will be a vigorous, an intelligent and a courageous people, and an ideal that sets great deeds immeasurably above empty words. On the one[8] side will be a group of peoples crippled by fear, suspicion and irresolution, and an ideal that makes weakness a virtue and truth-telling an unforgivable sin. I have no doubt of the outcome. [23 December 1914]

III

THE FOLLIES OF AMERICAN
GOVERNMENT AND SOCIETY

ABOLISHING THE STATE LEGISLATURE

WHAT AMERICAN STATE will be the first to abolish its Legislature? At least 20 States have already gone halfway—by introducing, in some form or other, the checks of the initiative and referendum—but not one has yet gone, as the poet hath it, the whole hog. That very thing, however, is bound to be done some day, and perhaps it will be done in the near future. The American people, after more than a century of bitter experience, are beginning to see the light. They now realize that the Legislature in the State, like the City Council in the city, is inevitably the headquarters of all governmental incompetence, stupidity and corruption. An honest Legislature is as rare as a modest actor. Here in Maryland we have not had four in 80 years. And an intelligent Legislature is rarer still.

Not, of course, that every lawmaker is necessarily a rascal. Our system of choosing Legislators and Councilmen gives enormous advantage to those aspirants who happen to be rascals, and the next most noticeable advantages to those who happen to be jackasses, but all the same not a few honest and intelligent men are returned at every election. It must be apparent, however, that such men are nearly always in the minority and that, in consequence, their influence for good is much less powerful than it ought to be. The normal Legislators, like the normal Councilman, remains a fellow of low intelligence and barroom morals. It is only fear that keeps him on the track—fear of his decenter colleagues, of the newspapers, of public indignation, of the penitentiary. Whenever the chance offers to turn a trick, safely and to his profit, he is sure to turn that trick.

There is scarcely need, at this late day, to attempt to show why this is so—why it must always be so. We all know how Legislators and Councilmen are commonly chosen—how it happens that they represent, not the people of their districts, but the professional politicians of their districts—how their training makes it practically impossible for them to regard public service save as a game of grab—how, once they are in office, they quickly yield to the double influence of the bribers who offer them money and the bosses who threaten them with extinction.

The trouble with the average Legislator is not that he is essentially dishonest, but that he is essentially stupid. Representing a small group of electors, he is himself small—a neighborhood notable—a paddler in a little puddle. This rule, of course, is not invariable; like all other generalizations it falls down before exceptional facts. Men of broad intelligence, of large vision, are sometimes candidates for the Legislature, and now and then they are actually elected. But it must be plain that three times out of four the man who aspires to any such lowly and ill-rewarded office is a dwarf. He can understand, perhaps, the needs of his own little mudpuddle, and he may even make a sincere effort to serve those needs, but when it comes to the needs of other mudpuddles he is not interested, and when it comes to the needs of the State as a whole, or of any large section of it, he is unable to grasp them and utterly disinclined to make the attempt.

This explains the sordid drama that is played out at Annapolis at every session of the Legislature. Country legislators, reaching the State capital with their pockets full of local bills, put through those bills—and then lay back and watch the show. Soon there is something going on in each of 10 rings. The city of Baltimore is in conflict with its professional politicians or with half a dozen piratical corporations. A dozen other corporations, menaced by bellringers, roar and sweat blood. The country solon[1] cannot understand half of these combats—but in every one his vote will count. So he is approached, tempted, won over. The bait used may be nothing more poisonous than the flattery of some "big" politician. Again it may be cash in hand. But whatever it is—whether the lawmaker himself is paid for his vote directly or his vote is delivered for ready money by some professional manipulator who acquires control of it by promises or threats—the fact remains that a vote has been influenced by corrupt means.

Not every countryman is open to such approaches—nor every city man. But there are always enough fools and rascals in the crowd to make the game worth while. Six votes may be enough to deliver the goods—and it is always possible to buy the six votes.

The same thing happens in City Councils. The average Councilman in the average American city is, if anything, a more stupid and venal man than the average Legislator. He is, speaking generally, either a ward boss himself or the disgusting slave of a ward boss—and the aim of a ward boss, it must be plain, is not to work for the city's good, but to work for his own good. In most cases he pursues politics as a trade. It is his only means of livelihood. Therefore, it is not astonishing that he should fall with alacrity upon every opportunity to turn his influence into cash. To ask him to neglect or spurn such opportunities would be, indeed, to question his sanity.

The remedy for all this, of course, is plain. Get rid of your small and purchasable men and you will get rid of bribery. But how are you going to get rid of them? By abolishing Legislatures, City Councils and all other such asylums of the ignorant and corrupt. But laws must be made! Some one must run the city and State! Well, why not hire a few first-rate men to do that work—*and then watch those men?*

That plan, in various forms, has been actually tried by various American cities—and always with great success. In some cities, such as Baltimore, for example, the City Council has been deprived of the absolute power which once made it a cesspool of corruption, and a small and efficient Board of Estimates now does most of its old work. In other cities—nearly 150 of them—the Council has been abolished altogether, and a board of three or four men has taken its place. Membership upon such boards is attractive to first-rate men—men who would not think of entering a City Council. And the people, watching three or four men, can see what each of them is doing. It is difficult to keep tabs upon 30 or 40 councilmen, or 100 Legislators, too often it is impossible to distinguish between an honest vote and a bought vote. But it is easy to keep tabs upon three or four commissioners. [22 May 1911]

USELESS LAWS

The estimable Wegg, of Belair, continues to flood the Harford county hinterland with his tears. Not until the Back River resorts are turned into Chautauquas and the plain people who patronize them are pumped full of pink lemonade will he have done with his wailing and get the sleep he needs. Wegg has never been to Back River—he is, I take it, rather proud of the fact—but that, of course, doesn't disqualify him as a critic. All day Sunday he broods over the crimes of those happy beer drinkers, flying-horse jockeys, fried-fish eaters, wife-beaters and child-stealers, and by the time night comes he is entirely fluid. But by Monday morning he is always well enough to dispatch, by special courier, an indignant letter to THE EVENING SUN.

One of those letters got into print yesterday, and—to adopt without shame an orthodox lie—it has just been called to my attention. In it Wegg makes the admission that it is not "sin, as such," that inflames him, but "the open, bare-faced violation, not to say defiance, of statute law." In other words, the act itself is not so bad, but the fact that it is forbidden by statute makes it heinous. With all due respect to a distinguished moralist I must permit myself the word "bosh!" Certainly the cause of the virtuosi of virtue is in extremis when they must bolster it up with any such idle absurdity.

As a matter of fact, no law carries within itself any mysterious inviolability. The thing which makes a law worthy of respect and which gives it, in practice, the respect of decent men, is its essential reasonableness, its direct and certain appeal to the good sense of the community, its practical social usefulness. One such good law is that which prohibits murder. Now and then the best citizen, for private reasons, may lament that it is on the books and even question its wisdom, but on the whole it is approved by the vast majority of folk without reservation, and they believe that its repeal would work them harm. The man who violates it commits a definite offense against the community: he strikes at that security which is at the bottom of civilization.

But it must be apparent that the statute books of most communities are overloaded with laws which have no such reasonableness behind them—laws which represent, not the community's sane effort to protect itself, but the bumptious yearning of one part of the community to boss some other part. Of such sort were the sumptuary laws of old England, by which Parliament prescribed, in great detail, just what clothing the common people should wear, and just what victuals they should eat. Of that sort, too, were those Puritan laws of Massachusetts which forbade a man to feed his hogs or kiss his wife on Thanksgiving Day. And of the same sort is that law of Maryland which forbids free citizens to go fishing on Sunday or to look at moving-pictures, or to play baseball, or to buy cigars, or to drink beer (or even soda water), or to do any of 100 other things which, in themselves, are no more indecent or disorderly or anti-social than the act of swatting a fly.

Such laws invade the rights of every citizen whose tastes run to the things they forbid, and so he is perfectly justified in violating them not only occasionally but persistently and as a matter of lofty principle. Wegg himself, I daresay, has bought soda water in his time on Sunday—and yet he must have known that it was unlawful. No doubt he has also bought Sunday newspapers on Sunday, and ice and milk, and perhaps candy for the children—and yet the sale of all these things was and is specifically forbidden. In the same way and in the exercise of the same freedom the folk who go to Back River buy beer and fried fish on Sunday. The act, true enough, is unlawful, but the answer is that the law forbidding it is even more unlawful, in the higher and better sense of that term.

Wegg tries to confuse the issue by comparing Sunday drinkers to prisoners in the penitentiary, arguing that the former, like the latter, cannot be trusted to govern themselves or even to decide what they want. Here we have an echo of that absurd presumption which causes a prohibitionist to bawl for local option when the majority is for prohibition and to denounce it—as at Back River—when the majority is against prohibition. In brief, the doctrine is laid down that drinkers are inherently immoral—that they form a class distinctly inferior to teetotalers. It may be so, but you will have a hard time convincing most fair men that it is, for their experience of life teaches them that no such difference exists.

A few more words and I leave Wegg to his smug idols. He argues, in one place, that I have been unjust to the present crusaders—that they demand, not a state of universal coma on Sunday, but merely the observance of the liquor and gambling laws. He even hints that they are not opposed to Sunday baseball, Sunday tennis and so on. If that is true, I should like to hear a specific statement of the fact. Meanwhile, I deny it and in support of my denial point to history. The same crusaders who now denounce Back River have denounced every other invasion of the blue laws. They are opposed to Sunday baseball as well as to Sunday drinking, to Sunday concerts as well as to Sunday gambling. There is upon the statute books of Maryland at present a law which forbids any man, upon penalty of a heavy fine, to give a public performance of Beethoven's Fifth Symphony in Baltimore on Sunday. If any crusader in good standing will sign a petition for the repeal of that atrocious law, I shall be glad to offer him my abject apologies and to buy him a box of five-cent cigars.

But how do such laws get upon the books? If the majority of intelligent men are opposed to them, how are they forced through our Legislatures, and how is every effort to repeal them blocked? Wegg does not actually frame these questions, but his letter asks them. The answer is to be sought in the superior frenzy of the moralists, in their vast talent for making a noise, in their extraordinary skill as wire-pullers and brow-beaters. That skill enabled them to get the Anti-Canteen law through Congress—aided and abetted by the natural cowardice and stupidity of politicians.[2] Four-fifths of all the officers of the army were in favor of the canteen. Two-thirds of the members of Congress, I am told, were also in favor of it. And yet the crusaders knocked it out, and the army suffers thereby today, and will continue to suffer until the fates give us, by chance, a Congress unalarmed by bawling. [4 August 1911]

STEALING LIBERTY

Discoursing lately, with great rage and eloquence, upon the moral mania which now afflicts this fair land, and particularly this fair city, I ventured the view that a plain fallacy was at the bottom of it, but did not go to the length of revealing that fallacy. In response to many polite requests from the clergy and laity, I now do so. It is the fallacy of assuming, as an axiom of morals, that a man's duty to his neighbors is superior to his duty to himself, that whenever his own desires come into conflict with theirs, he is bound to yield to theirs.

As a matter of fact no such grotesque and homicidal excess of social responsibility is laid upon the individual by any really civilized society. He has, true enough, a duty to his neighbors, but it is a duty rigidly limited and defined. He is bound to do nothing that will endanger their lives or imperil their property. He is bound to respect their liberties so long as the exercise of those liberties does not invade his own. But he is *not* bound to yield himself docilely to their mere whims and prejudices. He is *not* bound to obey their mandates in his private life. He is *not* bound to put their theory of what he *ought* to do above his own theory of what he *wants* to do.

Many moralists forget, or, if they remember it, try to conceal it, that this republic was founded as a protest against the very militant morality they now advocate. The colonists who came here did not object to respecting the *rights* of the majority they left at home; what they did object to was the need of respecting the mere *opinions* of the majority. Those opinions, it happened, were chiefly of a theological nature, and so it was religious freedom that attracted the rebels to the New World. But opinions of a purely moral nature may be just as gratuitous and just as tyrannical, and the battle against them, by the same token, may be just as worthy the enterprise and sacrifice of a civilized white man.

It is moral tyranny that now afflicts These States, and the worst of the matter is that thousands of Americans seem disposed to submit to it without protest. If theological tyranny were revived tomorrow, they would loose a bellow loud enough to shake the earth, but in the face of moral tyranny they remain silent and sit still. Thus it is that militant moralists, moved by that will to power which is universal in man, have proceeded from excess to excess, until now an almost endless roll of wholly harmless acts is under the ban of the law.

It is unlawful in Baltimore for a citizen to hear Beethoven's Fifth Symphony on the Sabbath. It is unlawful for him to buy a cigar. It is unlawful for him to have his hair cut. It is unlawful for him, on a summer Sunday, to recreate himself by playing baseball. In various large areas of his city he is forbidden to buy a bottle of wine, even on a week-day. Many plays that he may want to see, indubitable works of art, are barred from the theatres he patronizes. He is forbidden to possess certain great and valuable books, or to send them to his friends by mail. The law decides what games of chance he shall play and what games of chance he shall not play, and the division is purely arbitrary and nonsensical.

What is more, this invasion of his common rights is still going on. Here in Baltimore there are half a dozen organizations devoted exclusively to the concoction and prohibition of new and wholly artificial crimes. And in Washington the Congress of the United States is preparing to pass a law making it a crime for a man to have a bottle of beer in his possession—not to sell it or give it away, remember, but merely to *have* it.

What is the theory at the bottom of all this oppressive and intolerable legislation? Simply the theory that no man shall do, even in his own house, anything which the majority of his fellow-citizens do not care to do in *their* houses. His act need not be vicious in itself; it need not be dangerous; it need not be disturbing nor even physically visible to his neighbors. All it need be is abhorrent to the opinion of those neighbors, or, to be more exact, to the opinion of 51 per cent. of them. This is the theory at the bottom of moral snouting and moral legislation, and this was also the theory at the bottom of the hanging of Jews and Quakers, the Massacre of St. Bartholomew and the Inquisition in Spain.

No sane man, I take it, objects to laws necessary to the public security, even when they limit his own liberties. I have never heard anyone defend burglary, or arson, or rape. I doubt that any such defense has ever been made in Christendom. But is it necessary to the public security that boys who work hard all week be forbidden to take reasonable recreation on Sunday? Is it necessary to the public security that a sane man, fully competent to take care of himself, be forbidden to drink a bottle of beer? Is it necessary to the public security that a good citizen be forbidden to hear Beethoven's Fifth Symphony one day out of every seven, or that he be forbidden to read the books he wants to read, or to see the plays be wants to see?

I think not. On the contrary, it seems to me that such prohibitions are wholly intolerable and indecent. It seems to me that any person who essays to enforce them upon free citizens is a far more dangerous criminal than that poor wretch who essays to pick their pockets. The pickpocket steals only a watch, and a man without a watch is still a man.

But the militant moralist tries to steal liberty and self-respect, and the man who has lost both is a man who has lost everything that separates a civilized freeman from a convict in a chain-gang. [11 January 1913]

THE PUNISHMENT OF CRIMINALS

Marshal Farnan's[3] sensible suggestion that pickpockets be punished by amputating their fingers is not likely to get any attention from the Legislature of Maryland. It sums up the experience and reflection of an intelligent man, and therefore it is offensive, *ipso facto*, to lawmakers. Besides, even if the lawmakers were able to see its merit, the bawling of sentimentalists would make it impossible for them to put it into a law. A politician may safely laugh at reason, but he must beware of sentiment. The common people, whom he represents and visualizes, do all their thinking emotionally. A sob impresses them vastly, but they distrust and detest a syllogism.

However, as I have said, Marshal Farnan's suggestion has sense in it, and some day, after mob rule has been overthrown and a natural aristocracy has seized the reins, it may be dug up and put into effect. The rise of democracy during the last 400 years has brought about a correlative augmentation of judicial sentimentality, and the result is that all the ingenious and varied punishments of a more clear-sighted age have disappeared. Today we have but two ways of punishing crime. One is that of killing the criminal—a punishment reserved for a few extra-heinous crimes and (with an accidental exception now and then) for poor men. The other way is that of compelling the criminal to live, for a definite time, in some given place. This last is the punishment commonly called imprisonment. It is a real punishment only to those criminals who hold to the old delusion that the joys of freedom outweigh its responsibilities, or to those who find the house in which they are confined less comfortable than the house they have left.

The so-called punishment of fining the criminal is really no punishment at all. On the contrary, it is a means of evading punishment—a scheme whereby the occasional criminal who can afford it is permitted to escape the just penalty of his crime by paying a bribe. The Chinese culprit bribes the judge personally; the American culprit bribes the judge as wiskinski[4] for the community. The effect is exactly the same in the two cases; it makes no difference to the culprit what role the judge professes to play. All he knows is that, having money, he may go free, whereas if he were without money he would have to go to jail.

What we need, of course, is a revival of the fluent and scientific punishments of the feudal ages—punishments which bred ingenuity and honesty in judges, and worked exact justice. A medieval judge had to keep his wits about him. His highest duty was that of making the punishment fit the crime. If, having one day punished a perjurer by cutting a schnitzel from the fellow's tongue, he next day essayed to visit the same punishment upon a pickpocket, a kidnapper or a strolling actor, the superiors to whom he reported would probably set him down an osseocaput and take away his commission. He had to be alert—or quit.

But today a judge labors under no such incentive to intelligence. He is esteemed, not as he displays ingenuity, but as he suppresses ingenuity. He works entirely by rote. If the murderer before him is a pauper and friendless, he must pronounce sentence of death. If the murderer is rich and well-lawyered, he must grant the classical series of stays and appeals. If the drunkard has no money—seven days in jail. If the drunkard has a wad—a slice of that wad for the communal tin-bank. And in dealing with all intermediate crimes, he can impose only imprisonment, with the occasional alternative of accepting a bribe from an extra-opulent rogue. His sole discretion lies in determining the length of the imprisonment, and even here rigid laws limit his range of choice, and other laws condition and modify his choice after it is made.

How much better and saner the old system! How much better and saner the plan of Marshal Farnan! Cut off a pickpocket's fingers and you at once make it impossible for him ever to pick pockets again. Here is the ideal combination of punishment and prevention. The crime is penalized and the criminal is cured. Imprisonment, it must be obvious, never cures a pickpocket. All it does is to forbid him, for a limited time, to practice his profession. As soon as he is liberated he goes back to that profession, and to it he clings until the last horn blows.

If, now, picking pockets is a profession that we are justified in suppressing, just as we have suppressed piracy, then it certainly follows that we should adopt the means best adapted to suppressing it. The physical disablement of the pickpocket is that means. It is not only the best means, but also the only means. Moral suasion will not do the trick.

Imprisonment will not do it. Espionage will not do it. But mutilation *will* do it—and therefore Marshal Farnan, as a police officer of long experience and as a man of common sense, is in favor of mutilation.

But only, of course, theoretically. He knows very well, as all of us know, that the Legislature of Maryland will never adopt his plan. Sentiment stands against it—and sentiment is always an ass. We do not hesitate to send pickpockets to jail and there kill them in the shops, or to send them to the penitentiary and there convert them into consumptives, but at the simple, efficient, cleanly, humane and aseptic device of chopping off their watchhooks our virtuosi of virtue stand aghast. [28 December 1911]

A HANGING

Attending at the City Jail yesterday morning, as the guest of the Hon. Bernard J. Lee, to witness the official exitus of a gentleman of color, I was surprised to find no suffragettes at the ringside. In view of their late advocacy of the wholesale hanging of sinners and their plain promise to begin the business as soon as they are in power, which will undoubtedly be very soon, I was full of hope that some of them would be on the scene to observe and master the somewhat ticklish technique of strangulation. But, as I have said, I could find none in the select company of scientists present, and the Hon. Mr. Lee assured me that none were concealed behind the draperies of the lethal chamber.

A pity, to be sure. It was a first-class union hanging and would have given the sweet girls valuable tips for future use. For I assume, of course, that they will participate personally, and even joyfully, in that copious slaughter of the licentious of which they now but dream. When women go to the polls and vote for the practical extermination of the male sex, and then go to the Legislature and put that enterprise into laws, and then sit upon juries and condemn the guilty to the noose, it will be their plain duty, not to say their lofty privilege, to carry the thing through to its affecting finish upon the scaffold. They will do it, I daresay, because they will want to do it, and they will have to do it because few men will be left, after a while, to do it for them. A matter of simple mathematics: on the one hand they tell us that 90 per cent. of all men are scoundrels, and on the other hand they argue that all scoundrels should be exposed to the utmost rigors of the law.

But they missed their chance yesterday, and so I hasten to supply them with particulars of the art, in fear that they may get some friend of mine as their first victim, and disgrace him by bungling him. I pass over, as irrelevant, the affecting preliminaries—the awakening of the condemned by his death-watch; his riotous meal of bacon, fried eggs, French fried potatoes, stewed tomatoes, celery, pound cake and drip coffee; the last visit of his spiritual adviser; the singing of the parting hymn; the composition of dying messages; the goodbys to deputy wardens, newspaper reporters and fellow-prisoners—and proceed at once to the execution proper.

It begins with the fateful footfall of the Sheriff in the corridor. "Come, Johnson, your time is up!" The prisoner rises, the cell door is swung open and the first part of the march is begun. It is to the warden's office, a deputy sheriff leading and guards walking on each side of the condemned. There a crowd of men has gathered—perhaps 30 in all—and as the little procession enters they take off their hats and crane their necks. The prisoner wears a new suit of black clothes and a low, low collar. He stands up in the middle of the room, unsupported and silent, and the deputy sheriffs begin to strap his arms.

First, his wrists are brought together and a long strap is wound around and around them and buckled tight. Then his elbows are drawn back and strapped together behind his back. Then a gruesome black gown, with a monkish sort of black hood, is shaken from its wrappings and put on over his head, with the hood hanging down. The gown has been used before. The straps have been used before. The deputy sheriffs have been there before. It is a very swift and businesslike proceeding.

Now comes the march to the scaffold. Ahead go several deputies, and then follows the condemned with his spiritual adviser. The rest follow in disorder. Through the jail, down the jail yard, and so to the actual place of execution. The condemned, his lips moving, his eyes staring, looks up and sees the great beam, the clumsy trap, the dangling noose. A long flight of steep steps, perhaps 18 or 20. He must walk up them with his arms tied and his long gown flopping about his feet. If he stumbles, his spiritual adviser lends him a hand and a deputy pushes him from behind. The crowd groups itself around the base of the scaffold. Nobody says anything.

Once on the platform the condemned is led to the trap and there makes ready for his farewell to the world. Two heavy boards are laid across the trap, and on these the busy deputies stand, so that in case the trap falls prematurely they will not go through. One of them, kneeling, straps the feet and knees of the condemned together. Another reaches up for the noose, draws it down and deftly slips it over the culprit's head. The rough rope scratches him: at its touch he winces. It is drawn tightly around his neck, with the huge knot under his left ear. The black hood is pulled over his head. The deputy sheriffs step back and draw their protective boards out of the way. The crowd holds its collective breath.

Then the chief deputy waves a handkerchief, there is the squeak of a wire, and bang! the trip falls with a loud rattle. The Sheriff, concealed in his booth behind the scaffold, has pulled the lever. Down shoots the condemned man, a shapeless, black bag—to stop with a jerk that shakes the whole scaffold. The sound of that jerk I shall not attempt to describe: it is much like a single low C, *pizzicato,* by 100 bass fiddles. The spectators, white and clammy, blow out their breaths; sometimes one or two of them faint. Down below, under the trap, a doctor mounts a chair and begins work with his stethoscope.

But this is not always easy. The condemned man may kick. Yes; he may kick with both feet, and swing round like a top, and draw up his knees, and heave his shoulders, and struggle with his straps. A pretty sight! And his nose may bleed and he may otherwise—a sight to see! A warning to evildoers! The majesty of the law! Society at a holy duty! Something to remember!

But soon he stops kicking and then they let him down until his toes barely touch the ground. The doctors cluster around him and listen at his chest. By and by one of them sings out "No heart beat!" and the time is taken down. "How long?" asks some one. "Twelve minutes," says one of the doctors. "Not so bad," agree the deputy sheriffs. And then a couple of darkies bring up a coffin and the late Mr. Johnson is lowered into it. The rope is slipped from his neck, and the spectators begin to cut it up. Souvenirs! The gown is carefully taken off him, and wrapped up. Some other fellow will need it next week.

Alas, that the suffragettes were not present yesterday. It was a first-rate union hanging, swift, businesslike and instructive. It was full of interest to the connoisseur. [4 January 1913]

ON NOT PAYING TAXES

From one wriggling upon the sharp spears of doubt and misgiving:

Is it ever decent for a good citizen to dodge the payment of taxes?

Yes; ever. That is to say, always. And it is not only decent, but also highly sagacious and moral. Theoretically, of course, every citizen is bound to pay his due share of the expenses of the State, and that due share is justly calculated by determining the value of his property. But if we proceed from the theory to the facts, we find that the taxes levied upon an individual are sometimes vastly in excess of his due share of the expenses of the State, and that, in consequence, he is brutally robbed if he pays without effort at evasion.

Consider, for example, the case of any taxpayer in Baltimore. If the taxes of the State of Maryland were evenly distributed, he would pay his proportionate share of 58 per cent. of the whole sum raised—that being the fair share of Baltimore city. But as a matter of fact, Baltimore city, by the arbitrary and indefensible fiat of the peasants at Annapolis, is forced to pay 78 per cent. of the State taxes, or nearly 35 per cent. too much, and in consequence each individual taxpayer in Baltimore is robbed of 35 cents every time he pays $1 in State taxes.

What is he to do about it? Submit like a fool, or make resistance? Make resistance, of course. But how? By deducting 35 cents in the dollar from his tax bill? Alas, that would be useless. The sheriff would seize his property and sell it for the unpaid balance. The device of concealing his property remains—not all of it, but 35 per cent. of it. And that is a device practiced by hundreds of Baltimoreans, and with justice, decency and honor. It is the duty of every honest man, to his creditors, his heirs and himself, to conserve his resources. If he wantonly wastes money in paying unjust taxes, his conduct is just as much to be reprehended as if he lavished money upon chorus girls or games of chance.

And beside the obvious overcharge as in this case, there is also, as a rule, a more subtle overcharge. It is represented by the difference between the actual running expenses of the Government and the sum extorted from the taxpayers. For example, the budget of Baltimore for 1912 provides for an expenditure of $23,580,038.95, and of this great sum more than $15,000,000 will have to be raised by direct taxes. But a considerable portion of the money thus raised, it is plain, will be wasted.

The lighting department, to begin with, will spend thousands of dollars in an effort to make all Baltimore as hideous as the front of a moving-picture parlor—an indecency opposed instinctively by every truly civilized man. Again, the City Council will gobble $65,000—money for which the taxpayer will get not a cent of return. Yet again, hundreds of thousands of dollars will go into the hands of the work-shirking ward heelers employed in the various departments and on various public works. Yet again, other thousands will be wasted upon political contracts and upon silly schemes for augmenting the glory of this or that politician.

Is it fair to ask the self-respecting property owner to pay for all this debauchery? Of course it isn't. He is responsible for his just share of the legitimate expenses of the city government, but he is certainly not bound to pay more. When, in violation of his common rights, he is forced to make that extra payment—when, in brief, he is robbed by legal process for the benefit of loafers and parasites—then he is certainly justified in opposing ingenuity to extortion and in thus saving his money. In other words, it is perfectly moral for him, being unable to procure a fair reduction of the tax rate, to procure, by whatever means may be at hand, a reduction of his assessment.

Thus the ethics of it. In practice, the honorable taxpayer is confronted by the difficulty of determining just how much of the money annually raised by taxation is actually needed for the conduct of the government, and how much is merely coveted by political bravos and thimble-riggers.[5] In the case of Maryland State taxes, as we have seen, he is justified in chalking off 35 per cent at the start. But how much of the remainder is really needed? Here opinions must differ widely. One man whom I consulted this morning ventured the view that half is well spent and half is wasted. Another put the well-spent portion at 60 per cent. A third put it at 40 per cent. A fourth insisted that it could not be greater than 30 per cent.

In the case of city taxes the same difficulty arises. There are persons who believe that of every dollar entering the City Hall, 75 cents is wasted, while others hold that a full half of it is well spent. My own opinion, based upon 40 years of close study, is that the proportion of avoidable waste is commonly over-estimated. In some of the city departments, I believe, not 20 per cent. of the money spent is actually thrown away, and in none is the proportion greater than 60 per cent.

Perhaps 33⅓ per cent. would be a fair average. That is to say, it is fair to assume that, of every dollar collected in taxes, 66⅔ cents is spent with reasonable honesty and intelligence.

Thus the taxpayer is justified in "swearing off" 33⅓ per cent. of his assessment, or, to be more accurate, in concealing 33⅓ per cent. of his property. So much for city taxes. When it comes to State taxes he is justified in chalking off 35 per cent. at the start, and 33⅓ per cent. afterward—or 68⅔ per cent. in all. But inasmuch as the assessments for city and State taxes are levied together and are identical, he must strike an average between the two reductions. What the average should be I do not profess to determine. My private opinion—a mere opinion, of course—is that 50 per cent. would be about right.

The essential thing is that the taxpayer is under no moral obligation to submit to extortion. If, in the effort to protect himself and his children, he is forced to lie, then that lie is of the purest white. A self-respecting man, of course, prefers to tell the truth, but he is not justified in carrying that inclination to suicidal extremes. If, for example, a lie will save him from the murderous attack of a lunatic, it is not only his right but also his bounden duty to lie like a politician, and by the same token it is his duty to save himself and his property, by artful mendacity, whenever the so-called Government—a band of private individuals seeking their private profit—attempts to rob him. [4 April 1912]

Note from a moralist with a superstitious reverence for his own sophistry:

> In advocating tax dodging you forget the Social Contract. Is it decent for a citizen to evade his fair obligations to other citizens? Suppose everyone did as you recommend? What would become of the State?

An interesting objection—if only because it proves that the corpse of the late Dr. Immanuel Kant is still dancing. But though it may thus dance, it is nevertheless indubitably dead—and with it the crazy doctrine of a universal moral law. There is, of course, no such thing. Nothing is ever moral for all men—at all events, not with equal horsepower—and by the same token nothing is ever immoral. It may be wrong for a rich man, with so much money that he doesn't know what to do with it, to dodge his taxes, but it is certainly not wrong in the case of a man whose family must suffer if he pays them. An individual's first and paramount duty is to himself and his second duty is to his children. Then, in order, come his duties to his wife, his parents, his friends. his brothers and sisters, his creditors, his nieces and nephews, his uncles and aunts, his cousins, his second cousins, his third cousins and so on. Finally come his duties to his enemies, his wife's relatives and the community in general.

If the Social Contract were really a free contract, made in cold blood by autonomous principals, then it would lay upon every man a plain duty to pay his taxes in full. But it is really nothing of the sort. On the contrary, it is a contract forced upon him without his leave, and one which he couldn't evade if he would, and what is more, its terms are grossly unfair and extortionate. The State, in brief, is a professional swindler. Its incessant effort is to make every taxpayer pay $2 or $3 or even $10, for something worth but $1. Theoretically, it collects only enough money each year to pay the actual expenses of government—not a cent more. But actually it collects enough in addition to pay a handsome profit to thousands of men—men who are theoretically servants of the State, but in sober truth are private individuals engaged in the universal human business of getting as much money as possible for as little work as possible.

Certainly, it is no crime for a taxpayer to refuse to submit to this brigandage, and to oppose it with whatever means are at hand. The members of the so-called Government, it is obvious, enter the contest with all of the advantages on their side. Not only have they the police power of the State behind them, to enforce their extortionate demands, but they are also supported by the indifference and superstition of the vast majority of taxpayers, some or whom are too lazy or too ignorant to protect themselves, and others of whom think it would be wrong to try. Therefore, it is perfectly moral, in warring upon such unfair assaults, for the intelligent taxpayer to use devices which, in themselves, may be frowned upon by his private code. In brief, it is moral for him to meet brute force with guile, with chicanery, with downright mendacity—to lie like an anti-vivisectionist whenever the truth would expose him to indefensible and ruinous robbery.

But hark! the corpse of old Immanuel rises to ask a question, to wit: What would happen if *every* taxpayer swore off most of his taxes? How could the State exist? A silly question—like most of those asked (and answered) by that cadaver—for it must be obvious that the majority of taxpayers are so poisoned by moral ptomaines that they will never get the courage to save themselves. The average man is, and always will be, a born sucker. What with his stupidity on the one hand and his morality on the other, he is paralyzed from birth, and so he goes through life a chronic victim. The temptation to rob him is irresistible. Even his wife, his pastor and the policeman on the beat can't keep their hands off him. He almost begs the world to take his money.

But, supposing the question to be intelligible, it may be answered quickly. And here is the answer: If every taxpayer refused to pay more than, say, 50 per cent. of his taxes, *the efficiency of government would not only suffer no diminution, but would probably be vastly augmented.* Economy, which is now a mere abstraction, would then become a reality, a necessity. And in the business of cutting down expenses, thus suddenly made the chief concern of the State, nonessentials would go first. If, by any unyielding stupidity of the heads of the State, they *didn't* go first—if essentials were thrown overboard to protect supernumeraries and grafters—then the people would rise against the Government and take things into their own hands, and for the first time in the history of the Republic the State would be run as honestly and as economically as the average coal yard, or newspaper, or building association.

The curse of our present scheme of government lies in the fact that it puts no limitation upon taxation. The men who run the State are able to rob us as they will. Naturally enough—since their one aim is to get all they can for themselves and their friends—they lay on all the traffic will bear. The present tax rate on realty in Baltimore, counting in direct and indirect taxes, is fully $3 on the $100—a rate wholly indecent and proposterous. In the absence of legislation reducing it to $1—which rate, if constantly maintained, would be ample to pay all the legitimate expenses of the government—it is the supreme duty of every self-respecting taxpayer to reduce his own bill himself, and in that endeavor he is justified in employing any means, however "immoral," that may achieve the desired end. Every time he pays a cent more he hands over his good money to meet the costs of pediculine debauchery. [16 April 1912]

POLITICAL CHICANERY

That clergyman who writes me down in today's Letter Column is an extremely plausible fellow, and so he seems to make out a very good case against me, but all the same that case of his is based upon a wholly gratuitous and erroneous assumption: to wit, the assumption that I hold the war against political chicanery and buffoonery to be certain of success; or, at any rate, that I hold it to be more likely to succeed than the war against poverty. In point of fact, I cherish no such theory, nor have I ever cherished it, nor have I ever said that I cherished it. On the contrary, my private view is that political chicanery is as nearly immortal as thirst or mendacity. It will last as long as civilization lasts, and maybe two or three days longer. The difference, in tenacity of life, between it and poverty is a difference no greater than that between tweedledum and tweedledee.

But why, then, waste time heaving chunks of onyx and porphyry at politicians? Why bawl so lustily against the irremediable? Why roll such nauseous pills for the incurable? The answer is simple and shameless: because it is good sport. Political mountebanks are *ferae naturae*.[6] They lurk in every bramble bush and people every copse. What is more, they are sound in wind and limb, and so make graceful and amazing jumps from clod to clod. Therefore, it is pleasing, on a fine morning, to whistle for the dogs and go in pursuit of them. Their leaps are agreeable to the eye. Their yelps are music to the ear. They show fight. A gallop after them stirs the blood and sharpens the appetite. I know of nothing in the world more stimulating, save perhaps Florestan cocktails and laparotomy.[7]

Beside, the chase has its high uses, its social value. Unless politicians were regularly hunted they would multiply enormously and grow too bold. As it is they invade our corncribs and raid our henroosts. Unchallenged and unpursued they would chew up the washing on the line. Therefore, it is not only extremely diverting, but also very virtuous to go after them with hounds and slings. The man who brings one down is soothed by the thought that he has done a good day's work. He has rid the world of one pest more—and he has had a high old time at the business. If, in addition, he happens to be a hired professional, if he is paid for his work by people too fat or too lazy to take the high fences themselves, then his satisfaction is all the greater. Imagine, dear friends, the delights of an enterprise which is both virtuous and entertaining—and lucrative to boot!

Is all of this cheap cynicism? Bilious pessimism? Not at all. It is merely elemental determinism. The politician is inevitable and inexplicable, and so is the man who hunts him. You can't tell me why one exists and you can't tell me why the other exists. They are both immemorial figures in a world made up wholly of incomprehensible reactions. That I myself happen to be a newspaper reporter and not a politician is an accident utterly beyond my control, and even beyond my understanding. All I know is that newspaper reporting comes naturally to my hand, while politics excites my aversion. To take orders from the super-Mahon or any other such political manipulator would cover me with shame. *But don't forget that the super-Mahon would die of it if he had to take orders from the proprietors of The Evening Sun!* So goes the world.

But determinism, like free will, is only a half truth. Most of the things I do are forced on me: I couldn't avoid doing them if I tried. But over the *way* in which I do them I seem to have some control. (Notice that I say *seem:* here I merely accept the report of my consciousness, which may be a liar.) In brief, I may do my work with good will or with bad will, willingly or protestingly. It is easier and more satisfying to do it willingly. If my job is to heave bricks, why not choose hard bricks and heave them with a glad heart? Why not get as much pleasure as possible out of an incomprehensible necessity? Why struggle against fate? Why not yield to it, ratify it and give three cheers for it?

But this conception of necessity, let me here point out, is by no means a conception of divine inspiration, of transcendental duty. If I myself were to cut my throat tonight the trade I pursue would probably be carried on just the same tomorrow. And its progress through all future time would be unchanged. The individual is nothing in such great affairs. He is part of the process, he may even be necessary to the process, but the final issue of that process does not depend upon his volition. The politician is just as inevitable as the anti-politician; disease is just as natural as health. What such combats of yes and no may mean I don't know, but I do know that they exist, and I do know that their course is just as incomprehensible and just as much beyond human influence as their beginning. [24 August 1912]

THE DIRECT ELECTION OF SENATORS

The ratification of the constitutional amendment providing for the direct election of Senators strikes one more blow at the prerogatives and profits of the State Legislatures. In the palmy days, now unhappily no more, a Senatorial fight was worth from $50,000 to $500,000 to a Legislature. Here in Maryland, a cheap State, the price ran low, but out in the West it seldom dropped below six figures, and on more than one occasion it climbed close to $1,000,000. But now that ancient and honorable graft is scotched. The Senatorial candidate of the future will have to deal directly with the voters.

This is only one symptom, alas, of a wasting disease that is fast reducing the Legislatures to a state of pitiful senility. One by one their old perquisites and usufructs are being taken from them. Nearly every State, for example, now has a Public Utilities Commission, with complete power over the public service corporations, and so the old-time bellringers cease to ring. It is now practically impossible, here in Maryland, for the Legislature to shake down the Gas Company—a thing done regularly in the old days, to the joy of all concerned. The United Railways is not worth 10 cents a session: even the City Council can't get to it any more. And the railroads, once so juicy and tempting, now bear the aspect, to the baffled legislator, of dry and decrepit prunes.

The Lord giveth and the Lord taketh away! The sun do move! Time was when a ward heeler sent to the Legislature from Baltimore city was sure to return with enough money to open a saloon. But no more. If any money is made at Annapolis hereafter it will have to be by blackmailing the orphan asylums and one-horse hospitals which reach out so eagerly for the public funds. The old grafts have sunk into the sere and yellow leaf. The old-time lobbyists are selling life insurance or working on the street cars. The old-time statesmen flee from a legislative nomination as from the sneaking, Levantine pestilence. The Garden of Allah, seen by cold daylight, is now observed to be an alkaline and forbidding plain.

A virtuous reform, to be sure. A laudable revolution. But, after all, are its fruits all sweet? Is there no stray lemon among the apples? Alack, I fear there is—and not only one, but at least two. Will the Seventeenth Amendment actually purge the Senate of plutocrats? Will the voters prove more resistent to hard cash than the Legislatures? To come to Maryland again, is there any reason for believing that the average voter is less eager for the mazuma, or less willing to see virtue in its benevolent distributer, than the average legislator? And supposing the answers to all these questions to be such as to caress the pious, what assurance have we that the resultant deadhead Senators will be richer in actual talent than the paid admissions of yesteryear?

No assurance whatever! On the contrary, we have a pretty sure promise that the plain people, once they begin choosing Senators according to the best of their knowledge and belief, will quickly flood the Senate with the worst bunch of mountebanks and rabble-rousers ever assembled under one tent. The process, in fact, has already begun. The Western States, pioneers of the direct primary, have rooted out all their plutocrats and sent boy orators as substitutes. The upper house is now rapidly filling up with Progressives of the extreme left—local optionists, pursuers of white slaves, initiators and referendors, baiters of the judiciary, preachers of perunas, Chautauqua tear-squeezers, clowns and contortionists of all imaginable sorts. For the first time in history, a professional vice crusader is a member of the United States Senate!

And the effect upon the Legislature will probably be as lamentable as the effect upon the Senate. Once the old grafts are all knocked out, the men who sought election in the palmy days will keep out, and so the way will open for the reformers and utopians. Instead of auction sales and bellringers we shall have tournaments of idiotic lawmaking, with each quack battling valiantly for his own panacea, and public order handed over to the devil. All the sorrows of the world will be tackled seriatim. New and more preposterous messiahs will arise daily. The business of government, in the end, will become a sort of wild debauch, with each professor flinging his legs in the air and bringing down his heels upon the hard, flinty caput of some other professor.

Such is the present prospect, unless all signs fail and the prognostications of the prophets go for naught. Does it please you, messieurs? To go back to the Senate, would you rather be governed by the men of which Hoar and Aldrich were types, or by the men of which Bourne and Kenyon are types? You have to hire some one, remember, to govern you: you can't do it yourslf. Which do you prefer: to be governed by your superiors or to be governed by your inferiors? [10 April 1913]

REPEALING THE FIFTEENTH AMENDMENT

Under the somewhat vapid title of "The Rehabilitation of the Republican Party," the Hon. J. M. Vale contributed to yesterday's EVENING SUN a straightforward and impressive argument for the repeal of the

Fifteenth Amendment to the Constitution of the United States. The time has passed, he believes, for defending that amendment on sentimental and patriotic grounds. We have seen it at work for nearly 50 years, and we know it for what it is. It has been, from the very start, a source of bitter hatreds and disorders, an obstacle to the sound progress of the negro, a nourisher of crooked and degraded politicians, a potent agent of national disgrace and degeneration. It would be difficult, indeed, to imagine a piece of organic law less intelligently adapted to its ostensible purpose, or more productive of uncivilized and intolerable abuses. It is perfect proof that there were plenty of political Munyons before Roosevelt, just as there were heroes before Agamemnon.

But is the time quite ripe for repealing this grotesque error of the step-fathers, this masterpiece of bosh? For one, I doubt it. The objection to the Fifteenth Amendment is not that the men it enfranchises have black skins, but that the great majority of them are ignorant, stupid, corrupt and half-savage. In other words, the objection to it is that it is grounded upon the doctrine that every specimen of the *Homo sapiens* is actually, or at least potentially, sapient—that the lowest negro differs only in degree, and not at all in kind, from Galileo and Huxley. This doctrine, in the opinion of most reflective men, is unsound and monstrous. But why, after all, should we abandon it before we have fairly tried it? Why should we begin to lop off the legs of democracy before we have actually tested it on the track? Why disfranchise the negro man before we have trusted the vote to the white woman?

Certainly, there is infinite absurdity in a political theory which holds it to be unjust to disfranchise the negro on the ground that he is not white, and yet holds it to be just to disfranchise the white woman on the ground that she is not a man. The one law denounces and repeals a purely physical test; the other sets up and ratifies a purely physical test. Why not destroy all such tests, whatever their precise character, and so abandon finally the notion that voting is a physical function? Why not start all over again, and from the standpoint that the franchise is a thing the citizen must earn by his ability and his industry, and not a mere tertiary sexual character?

This is what we must come to soon or late, if civilization is to be rescued from the mob. But the time, I believe, is not yet. Before we may begin to edit and denaturize democracy, we must first give democracy a fair trial, and it has not yet had that fair trial. So far as I know, there is not a single State of the Union in which universal suffrage actually prevails, nor even one in which universal manhood suffrage prevails. In every one of them some class or other of citizens is forbidden the polls for some reason not founded upon individual wrong-doing or deficiency, and in all save a few of them the whole female sex is deprived by law of a right which lies at the bottom of all other rights of a freeman. Until this last injustice is rectified, until democracy is actually put into effect in the United States, it will be absurd to talk of turning our backs upon it. That which has never been the law cannot be repealed.

But in the long run, of course, after we have given the vote to everybody, there will have to be a thorough overhauling of the whole scheme, and the natural leadership of the alert and intelligent minority will have to be restored to it. All human progress, not only in the practical arts, but also in government, religion and virtue, originates in this minority and is promoted by it. The great masses of the people are against all change, and in particular, they are against all those varieties of change which involve risk and sacrifice—*i. e.,* the most radical and valuable. Their proper function is to execute the ideas of their betters. It is highly dangerous to let them manufacture ideas themselves.

But the validity and value of a human being's ideas are not determined by pigmentation, nor even by sex. There are good negroes and bad negroes, wise women and foolish women; and even if it be established that the majority of negroes are bad, or that the majority of women are foolish, the absurdity of the current tests remains. The badness of a bad negro is not a function of his color, for a white man may be just as bad. And so with the foolishness of a foolish woman: it is more than matched by the foolishness of many a man whose right to vote goes unchallenged—for example, the Hon. Dashing Harry.[8] Away, then, with all such physical standards and criteria. Let us say, simply, that the intelligent and self-respecting shall have a voice in the government of the State, and that the unintelligent and degraded shall not—and then let us say no more. A black Lincoln would be just as much a Lincoln as Abe himself, and a Pasteur in skirts would still be worth hearing and heeding. But the average white ward heeler is no more like Lincoln than the average black ward heeler. Both lack utterly all the special qualities which made old Abraham what he was. [5 June 1913]

THE INITIATIVE AND REFERENDUM

The Hon. Charles J. Ogle in defense of the initiative and referendum, tipple and chaser of the uplifters:

> Switzerland, sometimes called the ideal republic, has had the initiative and referendum for half a century.

Well, what of it? Does the Hon. Mr. Ogle seriously maintain that whatever is workable in Switzerland is also workable everywhere else? Certainly, I hope not—if only as one jealous of his reputation for ordinary horse sense. The President of Switzerland is elected by the Nationalrath (Senate) and Standerath (House of Representatives) in joint session. His term is but one year, and he is ineligible to serve again until the expiration of another year. Does the Hon. Mr. Ogle advocate the adoption of this system in the United States? It is a logical development of the initiative and referendum. It naturally follows from the doctrine that all public officials are undoubtedly numskulls and probably thieves, and that the only way to keep them from running away with the national treasury is to keep them in constant peril of their jobs.

This argument, by example, is one that the initiators and referendors use incessantly, but there is very little actual force in it. I haven't the slightest doubt that the initiative and referendum may work satisfactorily in Switzerland, which is more a neighborhood than a nation. It may even work in Oregon, though on this point the overwhelming preponderance of fair testimony is against it. But would it work in Maryland? We have here an incredibly ignorant and corrupt electorate. In Baltimore city fully 60 per cent. of the voters are meek followers of professional politicians, most of whom are for sale. In the counties, unless I am grossly misinformed, fully 75 per cent. of the voters will take money for their votes. We are burdened down by foreigners who haven't the slightest idea what they are voting about, and by negroes who sell out invariably, almost as a matter of conscience.

The Legislatures springing from this electorate are bad enough, goodness knows. But I think every fair man must agree that they are appreciably better than the electorate. They represent a degree of intelligence that is plainly a trifle higher, putting it at its worst. They can, as a rule, at least *understand* the problems they presume to deal with, whatever the defects of their solutions. Would it improve matters to hand over the law-making power to a body of men who are obviously more ignorant, and certainly not less corrupt? Would it do us any good, for example, to get rid of the Eastern Shore delegates and throw ourselves into the arms of the Eastern Shore blackamoors?

I seriously doubt it. The adoption of the direct election of Senators has shown us how little is gained by such exchanges. It still takes a lot of money to go to the United States Senate from Maryland—a great deal more than most men of the first ability are able to muster. It takes more, in fact, than ever it took in the old days, when Legislatures did the choosing, and took tips for their pains. And the quality of our Senators is not being improved. An honest candidate is just as sorely handicapped today as he was 30 years ago. His unwillingness to use money corruptly is just as heavy a disadvantage to him. And the money he must pay out honestly, even under the most favorable circumstances, is sufficient to break him.

The Hon. Mr. Ogle's belief in the virtue and intelligence of the common people is so little supported by the plain facts that it must be denied the quality of a logical conviction altogether, and considered merely as a benign superstition. Let him go back, for proofs against it, to the *Politics* of the late Mr. Aristotle, an author seldom consulted in these romantic days, but one still full of sense. Let him read Aristotle's discussion of natural castes, and make a note o't. And as auxiliary reading, let him turn to Senator Elihu Root's little book on "Experiments in Government," just published by the Princeton University Press. [24 July 1913]

OPENNESS IN ELECTIONS

The Rev. Dr. Oscar Woodward Zeigler's proposal, in THE EVENING SUN of Wednesday, that the corrupt practices act be so amended that all organizations taking part in political campaigns be required to make returns of their expenditures is one that must commend itself to all fair men. If a candidate himself is forced to report every campaign contribution he receives and every expense he incurs, certainly it is only just to exact the same open dealing by those who oppose him, whether they be individuals or societies. As things stand, it is perfectly possible for such an organization as the Anti-Saloon League, for example, to spend large sums of money in the effort to defeat a candidate who refuses to submit to its orders, and neither the source of this money nor the exact manner of its expenditure need be accounted for. Not only is this possible, but it has actually been done, and not once, but many times.

It is to the interest of good government, of course, that the discussion of a candidate's fitness for office, during a political campaign, be perfectly free and that every citizen be allowed to take part in it, but free discussion is one thing, and systematic wire-pulling is quite another thing. The Anti-Saloon League, as we know it in Maryland, is frankly a political machine, practicing exactly the same methods that other political machines use. It has its professional sluggers, lay and clerical, who are paid for their electioneering, and it has its bosses and backers who hide behind them. It is highly important that the identity of these bosses and backers be clearly established, and that the extent of their contributions to the campaign fund be made public, to the end that the voters may take due account of their general reputation for wisdom and honesty, and of their probable motives for going into politics. The majority of them, no doubt, are men of the highest character, but there are others whose lack of sense is so marked that their simple unmasking would be sufficient to set off the effect of their secret replenishing of the bar'l.

Soon or late, the law will have to deal with such organizations, which are increasing in number and power all over the United States. Many of them—in fact, most of them—are mere devices for providing easy jobs for their paid whoopers and game-beaters. It is thus to the advantage of such professionals to provide a lot of public excitement, regardless of the effect on the public welfare, for it is excitement that attracts spectators and subscribers. Hence the senseless raids of the Lord's Day Alliance, the lawless mountebankeries of the Society for the Suppression of Vice, the patent-medicine show methods of the Anti-Saloon League and the pornographic enterprises of the so-called Maryland Society of Social Hygiene, an organization run by vice crusaders (*i. e.,* huntsmen, showmen) masquerading as scientists. Half the energy of all such dubious societies is frankly devoted to shaking down the pious, the other half being devoted to getting the pious in good humor by giving them spicy shows.

Personally, I believe that it would be highly injudicious to adopt legislation forbidding the formation of such private sporting clubs. They do a lot of harm, true enough—first, by filling the statute books with donkeyish and unenforceable laws; secondly, by giving poltroons and boot-lickers an advantage over honest men in politics, and thirdly, by facilitating blackmail. But any attempt to meet and overcome these plain evils by a frontal attack would necessarily involve a limitation of the right of free speech, and free speech, under a republic, is a thing of such capital value that everything else must be sacrificed to its preservation.

But though the prohibition of such societies would thus be dangerous, there still remains the device of requiring them to submit their inner works to public inspection. As things stand, their chief power for evil lies in the fact that they afford an excellent cloak for two classes of anti-social persons—first, men of means who enjoy persecuting their fellow-men but are not courageous enough to do it in the open, and secondly, professional snouters and sneaks. Both classes, I think, would be reached by a law requiring all such societies to be registered and licensed, and forcing them to make public, at least once a year, a full list of their contributors, a statement of their receipts and expenditures, and the names and addresses of their hirelings. [13 February 1914]

THE LEO FRANK CASE

Incidentally, it is interesting to note certain remote effects of the late vice crusade in Atlanta—a crusade which, according to one of its gladiators, was "more fun than a fleet of airships." This crusade, which was managed by the usual book peddlers, male old maids and *sforzando* preachers, kept the police so busy that they had no time for other work, and so Atlanta began to enjoy what the local newspapers called "a wave of crime." The public indignation arose thereat, and there were loud demands for blood. The police responded by grabbing the handiest man and trying to railroad him to the gallows. He was the Hon. Leo M. Frank.

The Frank case is now invading the newspapers of the entire country, to the great glory and benefit, one may be sure, of Atlanta. Bit by bit it is becoming apparent that the accused was denied all his common rights, that evidence in his favor was suppressed, that his trial was a hideous farce. Thus the causes thereof, as described by the Atlanta correspondent of the *American:*

> The Police Department was in bad repute because of the
> failure to solve several important cases. The Atlanta newspapers

called on the Police Department, in bold type, to avenge the murder of the girl, to catch the criminal had convict him. *The Police Department had to do something.*

One of the important things to remember in the Frank case is the part that sensational preachers, no less than sensational newspapers, played in it. These noble men of God, having tasted blood in the vice crusade, were ripe for an even larger demonstration of their powers. They found it in the Frank case. The accused was a member of a strange and contumacious race, with small respect for the new perunas. It was horrible that such a person should live in moral Atlanta, practicing his levantine crimes. So the pulpit joined heartily in the uproar against him, and with loud whoops he was started for the gallows. The uplift was vindicated. Atlanta was purged of sin.

Let it be said to the credit of the clergy of Atlanta that there are decent men among them, and that they now appeal for sanity and justice. Such men, of course, are to be found everywhere. But in times of public hysteria, of reform by orgy, of "moral" saturnalia and blood-letting, their voices are drowned out by the harsh, staccato yelps of the peruna-mongers and mountebanks. It is only after the debauch has spent itself and comparative quiet is restored that they can make themselves heard. [18 March 1914]

DEMOCRACY IN THE SOUTH

The eminent Charleston *News and Courier,* the *Sunpaper* of South Carolina, gives over an editorial article no less than 27¾ inches in length to a criticism of my doctrine that civilization in the South has been seriously crippled by the rise of the so-called "poor white trash" to power in politics. The *News and Courier,* it should be said, does not specifically deny the truth of that doctrine. On the contrary, it admits that "there is no disputing the fact that under our [present] civilization it is increasingly difficult to secure the services of the best men for public office." But following the usual democratic habit, it pretends to believe that this evil effect is but temporary—that the common people, once they have made all the mistakes possible, will begin to acquire elementary sense and discretion, and even, it would appear, a measure of honesty—that, in Macaulay's words, "the scattered elements of truth will cease to contend and begin to coalesce," and "at length a system of justice and order" will be "educed out of the chaos."[9]

So much for the democratic theory and the democratic hope. Both are frequently set forth by the *Sunpaper,* and both illuminate the essays and harangues of such great Americans as Dr. Woodrow Wilson, the Hon. William Jennings Bryan, the Hon. Theodore Roosevelt and the Hon. Josephus Daniels, the distinguished Tar Heel thinker. But how much truth and probability are in them? Alas, not much. And what is worse, their hollowness is well revealed by some of the very arguments that the *News and Courier* brings forward in support of them. These arguments go back to the period of reconstruction. They show how the South was saved from anarchy and pillage then, and they show the only way that the South is to be saved from mob-rule and its crazy frenzies now.

What the South suffered from in reconstruction days was democracy pure and simple. All the adult males of the sub-Potomac region, without regard to their color, their intelligence or their degree of decency, had been thrown together as absolute political equals, and the natural result was that the more ignorant and vicious of them, being in an overwhelming majority, had boldly grabbed the government and proceeded to a career of what practically amounted to organized piracy. Life and property were wholly unsafe; law and justice were jokes; civilization existed only as a name. Well, what did the intelligent minority do in this emergency? Did it allow the embattled freemen to continue in their "mistakes," and so learn the art of government by experience? Did it assume that "a system of justice and order" would be "educed out of the chaos"? Not at all. What it actually did was to pit its intelligence and resourcefulness against the brute might of the mob, and so got back, half by cunning and half by intimidation, its old power in the State. And, having once regained that power, it straightway employed it in an effort to make forever impossible a repetition of the reign of terror just ended. That is to say, it took the ignorant and degraded negro's vote away from him, Constitution or no Constitution, and ever since then it has kept him from getting it back.

But in this business the ignorant and degraded white man was overlooked, and ever since then the South has been paying for that error. Steadily increasing in relative number under the new industrialism, and no longer stimulated to decency by his elemental race pride, for the menace of the negro is now past and forgotten, he is showing more and more the sinister characteristics of his class. That is to say, he is showing emotionalism, hatred, envy, stupidity and dishonesty, and out of that complex of bad qualities is coming the political insanity which now disgraces the South, with Bleaseism for its chief symptom in South Carolina, and prohibition as its masterpiece almost everywhere else.

Why should the decent people of the South submit? Why should they live under a "civilization" mirroring this ignorant and degraded white peasant's unfitness for freedom? Why should they assume that *his* right to enact his stupidity and ill-nature into law is more sacred than his no more stupid black brother's? If democracy is actually a divine ordinance, if it is true that the right to vote is inherent and inalienable, then how do the people of the South justify their disfranchisement of the negro? And if democracy is no such thing, if the right to vote is really not a right at all, but merely a privilege, then how do they justify the extension of that privilege to men so thick-witted that they believe in every new mountebank who comes along, and so evil in their hatreds and envies that they are hot for every fresh scheme to invade and destroy the property, the peace and the security of their betters?

It is easy enough to say that such men will learn by experience, that the contemplation of the effects of their errors will teach them prudence—but our experience in the United States shows clearly that this is not so. The common people do not grow more prudent; they grow more imbecile; our laws today, taking them by and large, are vastly worse than our laws of 50 years ago. Again, it is easy enough to say that democracy, whatever its evils, is necessary, that it alone offers any reasonable measure of justice and freedom—but once again the facts are to the contrary. No despotism of modern times, not even the abhorrent German, has ever produced government so thoroughly antagonistic to peace and order, and so disheartening to honest, industrious and law-abiding men, as that which the Hon. Cole L. Blease and his wool-hatted followers saddled upon South Carolina. If this was democracy, then surely every intelligent man will yell for absolutism. And yet it was on view in a State that had been free for a century and a half—a State not lacking, in the past, in prudent and patriotic leaders and teachers—a State in which, if anywhere, the worst errors of democracy had been suffered and recognized, and in which the desire to avoid repeating them should have been extraordinarily strong.

Considering all these things, I am unable to follow the argument of the estimable *News and Courier*. On the one hand, it admits that the facts I offer in evidence are substantially sound, and on the other hand, all that it brings against my conclusions is a mass of hopes, prophecies and unsupported assumptions. If it seriously believes, with Macaulay, that "in a few years men learn to reason," then it must surely attach some cryptic and magnificent meaning to the word "years," as certain Christian apologists have done with the "days" of the first chapter of Genesis. The majority of the voters of the United States, after more than a century of experience, have not yet learned how to reason. They still do their thinking emotionally, ecstatically, orgiastically—not with their cerebrums at all, but with their midriffs and their livers. One blast of wind music counts more with them than all the logic since Aristotle. [11 December 1914]

HOORAY FOR THE I. W. W.!

The estimable *Public Ownership*, the local socialist weekly, in the course of a long and eloquent effort to prove that I am a hireling of the Money Power:

> Men of the Mencken type and the class he serves view a producing wage earner as so much mud.

With the highest respect, Pish! "Men of the Mencken type" do nothing of the sort. But neither do they fall into the contrary error, so beloved of the Socialists, of viewing "a producing wage earner" as so much gold, frankincense and pâté de foi gras. This is the fundamental fallacy of Socialism: the assumption that the man who wants something and can't get it is, in some recondite fashion, more creditable to his species and more pleasing to a just God than the man who wanted something and has got it. In brief, they idealize and sentimentalize failure, and finally make of it a sort of fetish. Any man who gets on in the world is a scoundrel in their sight; any man who tries to get on and fails is an angel.

Nothing could be more absurd. The truth is that the aims of the typical Socialist and the aims of the most avaricious capitalist unhung are identical, and that their degrees of virtue are thus also identical.

The capitalist hogs all he can get, using force if necessary; the Socialist dreams of taking his booty from him in precisely the same manner. Both proceed from wholly selfish motives, and both seek to have the power of the State on their side. If there is any difference between them, it is in favor of the capitalist, for he usually mingles a considerable intelligence with his enterprise, and intelligence, even when it sheds few benefits, is something admirable in itself. The Socialist, as a brief glance at any one of his antagonistic programs is sufficient to show, is not burdened with intelligence. His stock in trade consists almost exclusively of hatred, laziness, bombast, pusillanimity and envy—especially envy. He denounces his brother because his brother is more successful than he is.

The only Socialist who is worth a hoot is that one who is willing to fight for what he wants—for example, the gladiator of the I. W. W.[10] The average, the typical Socialist is capable of no such courage and resolution. Like all other groveling and complaining men, he worships Law. Law will get for him what he can't get himself. He bases all his hopes upon a Law that will confiscate the property of other men and give it to him. When these men show signs of resisting, he proposes another Law forbidding resistance. Law is his hope, his sheet-anchor, his sugar-teat, as it is of all other weak and hateful men. Bellowing against the police and the militia, he yet expects them to protect him in his looting of civilization. In brief, this typical Socialist is an irresolute and disingenuous fellow, a silly mush-master, a sorry specimen of a man.

As I say, he attains to respectability only when he gives over his empty dreams and his pothouse economics and becomes an I. W. W— that is to say, when he shows a willingness to risk his hide for his ideal. There is something inherently masculine and decent in any man who will take that risk. His cause may be a bad one, but if he gives it his genuine devotion, not grudgingly and timorously, but defiantly and gladly, it at once takes on a certain measure of dignity. The I. W. W.'s, true enough, do not face a hazard that is very great. The chance that they will have their heads knocked off is infinitely less than the chance that they will merely go to jail. But all the same, the former chance really exists, and I cheerfully join the more violent I. W. W.'s in hoping that it will rise steadily until it becomes an absolute certainty.

I hope I am not one to contemplate with pleasure the misfortune and disappointments of any man, but why should I hold that those misfortunes confer a special virtue upon him? Why, if they consist of inherent incapacities, should I hold that he is more worthy of respect that one who, in our common speech, is "a better man"? I may be sorry for him, and even try to help him, but I cannot waste my whole time weeping over him, nor have I any sound reason for venerating him. No man gets all that he wants in this world. Disappointment is the inevitable portion of every one of us. But when it comes to a choice between the man who does his darndest and then accepts what fate grants him and shuts up, and the man who is forever bellowing that his brother has got more than he, and forever seeking to prove thereby that his brother is a rogue—when it comes to that choice, I am wholly in favor of the man who does his darndest and then shuts up. [24 December 1914]

THE DEMISE OF FREE SPEECH

The canning of the Hon. Scott Nearing, B. S., B. O., Ph. D., instructor in economics in the University of Pennsylvania, has caused a painful impression among the *intelligenzia* and one notes a number of protests against it in the newspapers, but there seems to be little likelihood that the great masses of the plain people will show any interest in the learned doctor's martyrdom, or that the gentlemen who boss the university will be constrained to give him back his job. The only persons who appear to be genuinely concerned about his case are those who stand, as it were, in his shoes—that is, those confronted by the danger of sharing his fate if they do not mind their p's and q's. The rest of the American people are not worried about him. It is impossible to get them excited over a question of academic freedom.

On the contrary, they grow more and more disposed to deny the necessity and value of that freedom, and of the right to free speech which lies under it. Free speech in this country is gradually coming to mean, not freedom to say what one honestly believes, but merely freedom to say what the mass of so-called right-thinkers believe. As Owen Wister has lately put it, the democrat believes in the right of everyone to agree with him. One finds evidence of it on all sides—for example, in the astounding attack upon Dr. Münsterberg, of Harvard, and again in the Sanger prosecution, and yet again in the efforts made to suppress such journals as the *Menace*.[11] One finds it, too, in the curious doctrine, now so prevalent and with such high support behind it, that it is treason for a native American to support the German cause in this war.

There is, of course, a certain accuracy of instinct in this doctrine, as there is in most doctrines of unreflective men, but there is grave danger in substituting instinctive remedies for intelligent remedies. Perhaps the *Menace* case will make my meaning clear. The demand made by certain Catholics that the *Menace* be denied the mails can have only two imaginable grounds, first, the ground that the *Menace* tells the truth about the Catholic Church and that a universal knowledge of this truth will destroy the church; or, secondly, that it lies about the church, but that large numbers of Americans are so ignorant that they believe its lies. The first contention, it goes without saying, is never actually raised by Catholics. This throws us upon the second. But what does this second contention really mean stripped of all side issues?

It means, I take it, that there is a body of Americans so stupid and so credulous that its members can be deceived by representations that every man of ordinary intelligence laughs at, and that it is of such size that its political might is sufficient to menace even so large and well-organized an institution as the Catholic Church. In other words, it means that free speeeh is dangerous in the United States, not because the truth is dangerous, but because falsehood is dangerous, and because a large number of Americans are incapable of distinguishing between the one and the other. It means, even further, that these naif and numerous Americans, with both the truth and falsehood before them, are very apt to choose the latter.

What we have here, it is obvious, is a doctrine that would appear to be far more at home under an autocracy than under a republic, for what it amounts to is a substantial denial of the fundamental theory of democracy, *i. e.*, that the common people are shrewd and wise. But though it thus offers a destructive criticism of democracy, I doubt that any reflective man will venture to dispute its essential truth. Everyone knows, indeed, that the populace is not actually shrewd and wise, but stupid and ignorant, and everyone also knows that, given a free choice between a sound idea and an unsound one, it almost always chooses the latter. What is thus known, however, is by no means what is said openly. On the contrary, the very limitation upon free speech that I have been discussing makes it an unhealthy thing for any man to say such things, and so the issue is constantly beclouded by platitudes and evasions—*e. g.*, by the hollow effort to draw a dintinction between freedom and what is vaguely called "license."

But soon or late, of course, the issue will have to be met more honestly and courageously, and some remedy will have to be found for the present tyranny of ignorance and emotionalism. That remedy, I believe, will be found in the frank disfranchisement of those whose incapacity for reason is palpable and undisputed. Once such persons have been deprived of the massive political power they now exert—a power sufficient, on occacsion, to overcome the whole force of the national intelligence—the question as to what they think or don't think will cease to have any place in practical politics. No one troubles to find out what the minors of the country, or the insane persons, or the prisoners in the penitentiaries think of the Catholic Church, or of Germany or of Dr. Scott Nearing. The time must come when the same indifference will greet the reflections of those present voters whose salient character is their utter inability to reflect at all.

The upsetting of the so-called Grandfather's Clause by the Supreme Court,[12] though it appears, on the surface, to mark a reaction, is really an enormous step forward. Unable hereafter to disfranchise the incompetents by transparent and degrading trickery, we shall have to deal with the problem they present more frankly and openly. In other words, the Supreme Court has forced a head-on fight—and head-on fighting is what this country needs beyond all things. The effort to mix the water of democracy and the oil of civilized government has led us into an endless maze of absurdities and equivocations, and hypocrisy is even more the national vice today than it was in the days when the American people carried the Declaration of Independence on one shoulder and slavery on the other. It will do us good to look the eternal facts of life in the eye. At the start, they will give tremors to many a right-thinker's knee, but in the long run we shall find them a good deal less uncomfortable than the buncombe that we have been cherishing so long. The truth is bitter, but it never kills. [30 June 1915]

IV

THE BOZART

THE AMERICAN LANGUAGE

WHY DOESN'T SOME idle philologist write a treatise upon spoken American, for the information and entertainment of future generations? In all countries there is a tendency for the written and spoken languages to diverge, not only in vocabulary, but also in grammar. The schools, of course, all teach the written language, but that language is seldom spoken by the common people, nor even, for that matter, by the majority of persons of the upper castes. Whatever they are taught in school, children actually speak the language they hear at home. Not until a child gets beyond the sixth grade—a feat accomplished by not more than one child in 10—does the influence of the written language begin to show in its speech.

A year or so ago I called attention to certain peculiar rules governing the conjugation of American verbs. For example, here are the changes that the verb "to see" undergoes in the first person singular, indicative mood, first in written English and then in spoken American:

	English.	*American.*
Present	I see	I see
Present perfect	I have seen	I have saw
Past	I saw	I seen
Past perfect	I had seen	I had saw
Future	I will see	I will see
Future perfect	I will have seen	?

It was my hope, at the time, that other investigators, far better equipped for the task of reducing American grammar to rules, would undertake it, but, so far, that hope has been in vain. Why doesn't some Johns Hopkins man leap into the breach? Certainly an exhaustive thesis upon the tongue spoken by fully 50,000,000 Americans would be worthy the reward of a doctorate.

The philologists, whenever they condescend to discuss our spoken tongue at all, commonly reveal their gross ignorance of it. For example, they announce the discovery, every now and then, that the vocabulary of the average American is limited to 500, 1,000 or 2,000 words. What could be more absurd? As a matter of fact, the average American's stock of nouns alone probably exceeds 2,500, and he constantly uses at least 500 adjectives and 250 verbs. Most children of 6 years know more than 500 nouns. It you don't believe it, make an experiment on your own infant, pointing to object after object and asking the child their names. It may pronounce many of those nouns incorrectly, but it knows their meanings and differentiates between them.

Even foreigners use much larger vocabularies than the pundits are disposed to allow them. I lately read the statement that the average Italian immigrant, after two years in this country, still staggered along with a vocabulary of but 200 words. It may be so, but I doubt it. No matter how stupid the foreigner may be, if he actually essays to make himself understood in English, he is bound to acquire nouns and adjectives rapidly—perhaps at the rate of 10 a day. In two years he should have at least 1,500.

But to get back to the difference between our book language and our common spoken language. That difference is not merely one of grammatical structure and inflection, but also one of pronunciation and meaning. Practically all words of recent foreign derivation, such as cafe, reservoir, boudoir, bouillon and lingerie, are pronounced differently by those who speak the precise book language and those who speak the common patois. And many words of identical pronunciation vary in meaning in the two tongues. There is, for example, the word clever. In the English taught in the schools it means accomplished, shrewd, adroit, efficient, while in the American spoken on the streets it means agreeable, polite, considerate, affable.

Why not investigate the whole subject? Why not study American as Scotch, Bayerisch, Neapolitan and other dialects have been studied? Why not plat its grammar and penetrate to the baffling secrets of its syntax? [19 June 1911]

ON CENSORSHIP

A board of censors for the local moving-picture parlors seems to be one of the certainties of day after tomorrow. Just how a board of three men will manage to inspect all of the films shown in the city each week, or even half of them, is so far unexplained. But a little detail of that sort need not halt a moral jehad. The aim of such crusades, as everyone knows, is not to accomplish results, but merely to strike postures and emit affecting music.

Meanwhile there are many Baltimoreans (including, I believe, Mayor Preston) who hold that the present demand for a censorship is but ill supported by the facts. How many positively indecent and de-moralising pictures are shown here during the average week? If any at all, where are they shown? Why, in brief, don't the crusaders come forward with names and dates—and turn their evidence over to the grand jury? Whether or not we have a law specifically forbidding improper representations in theatres, it must be obvious that *any* gross violation of public decency, whatever its character or scene, is an indictable offense. If such offenses are being committed, why are not the offenders brought to book?

As a matter of fact, most of the present complaints are probably coming from persons of exaggerated and preposterous sensitiveness—from persons whose noses are so miraculously acute that they smell indecency in almost everything. Not long ago, for example, I heard a man complain against a certain moving-picture film on the ground that it represented a case of marital infelicity, ending in fisticuffs and flight, and that children should be kept from all knowledge of such things. Could anything be more ridiculous? How many children of 10 years are yet unaware that married folk sometimes fall out, that wives sometimes take new husbands and husbands new wives. Every second American family and every American neighborhood has its domestic tragedy and scandal, its divorced couple. What good would be accomplished by withholding all knowledge of such dreary commonplaces of life from the young?

If there are any parents who feel that their children would be better off without such knowledge, let them forbid their children to go to moving-picture shows altogether. But let them then prove their sincerity by extending that prohibition to the public schools, the Sunday-schools, the playgrounds, the streets and all other places where the young of the human species congregate. The only way, in brief, to bring up a child in such utter and chemically pure ignorance as these connoisseurs of impropriety dream of is to cut off its ears, put out its eyes, deprive it of all books, bore a hole in its head and empty its brains. [24 June 1911]

Those Baltimore clubwomen who now propose to agitate for the appointment of a theatrical censor in Baltimore have virtue on their side, but when that has been said for them all that is honestly sayable has been said. The demand, as everyone knows, is not new. It is raised every year or so by militant moralists—usually by militant moralists who openly confess that they themselves never go to the theatre. It is but a single symptom of that unquenchable thirst for chemical purity which racks this town. On the one hand, imaginary evils are combated furiously and with a suffocating effusion of platitudes. On the other hand, real evils are neglected.

The fact is, of course, that the appointment of a theatrical censor, whatever good it might accomplish, would undoubtedly accomplish a great deal more harm. It would put an arbitrary and despotic power into the hands of one man or of a small body of men; it would keep public attention constantly concentrated upon indecencies; it would work a hardship upon the authors, managers and performers of many truly meritorious plays; it would tend to corrupt a serious art with the prejudices and stupidities of parochial virtue.

If the censors showed toleration—if, for example, they approved such a play as Ibsen's "Ghosts"—they would lay themselves open to bitter assaults by moralists. And if, on the contrary, they permitted moralists to lead them by the nose, they would do irreparable damage to the local theatres and make Baltimore a laughing-stock from end to end of the country. It would be next to impossible to steer a middle course. The frenzy of moralists would be a constant stumbling-block, a constant obfuscation, a constant irritation.

What is more, the very existence of such censors would be super-erogatory and ridiculous. We have today an ample remedy against all plays and other spectacles which actually offend the decencies. It is to be found in Article 25, Section 101, of the Baltimore City Code, as follows:

> Every person who shall, within the city of Baltimore, act, exhibit, show or perform in, or cause to be acted, exhibited, shown or performed, or be in any manner concerned in the acting, exhibition, showing or performance of any indecent or blasphemous play, farce, opera, public exhibition, show or entertainment or performance whatsoever, or of any indecent or blasphemous part of any play, farce, opera, public exhibition, show, entertainment or performance whatsoever, shall forfeit and pay for every such offense the sum of twenty dollars.

Why should the purists ask for more than this ordinance? Doesn't it, in point of fact, open the way for the prompt prosecution and pun-ishment of every person, whether actor or manager, engaged in the per-formance of an offensive play? Why don't the foes of the theatre, if they are really outraged by occasional salinity, institute prosecutions under it? Why didn't they take out a warrant for Mr. Ford when "The Follies of 1910"[1] was played at his theatre? Why didn't they send a copper for the late Lehmayer when "The Girl from Rector's"[2] was at the Academy of Music? Here was, and is, an easy road to purity—a road charted since 1879—and yet no moralist has ever ventured to fare along it.

The reason therefor is not far to seek. The trouble with this ordi-nance, in the eyes of crusaders, is that it gives the accused manager a fair chance to defend himself. It is not sufficient merely to charge him with indecency: the thing must be proved. He may, if he desires, demand a jury trial; he may call witnesses in his behalf; he may employ counsel to cross-examine and flabbergast his accusers; in brief, he may have a white man's chance to meet and controvert a most serious accusation against his professional honor and his manhood. Do moralists think it fair to give him that chance? They do not. The essential characteristic of a moralist—the thing which sets him off sharply from all other men—is his firm belief that his own unsupported fiat should be sufficient to disgrace and ruin a fellow-man.

Failing the opportunity to exercise such a despotic power personally, the fanatical purist wants it given to some person of his own nomination, to some censor under his thumb. The demand for a censor, in other words, is also a demand for an alert and uncompromising censor—for one who will attack, not only all undoubted indecencies, but also all merely *questionable* things. And there is where the whole plan runs aground. In theory, a censorship is no more than a safeguard against gross indecency. In practise, it is invariably a conspiracy against free speech in the theatre. The English censor, theoretically unfettered, is really the slave of fanatics. He made the whole English nation ridiculous back in the nineties by prohibiting "Ghosts." He made it thrice ridiculous, a few years ago, by prohibiting "The Mikado."[3]

These considerations—stated, perhaps, with some heat, for the art of the theatre has my highest respect—should be borne in mind by the ladies who now propose to resuscitate and renovate a pernicious and mischievous scheme. That their motives are good I haven't the slightest doubt. Some of them, perhaps, have been outraged in the past by vulgar plays. But let them bear well in mind that, if their ire is real, an easy way of getting redress is always open to them—that they have a clear right, as citizens, to enter complaints against offending managers, and to summon the whole of the State's Attorney's force to the prosecution of those managers. And let them not forget, again, that when it comes to indecency, there is often room for an honest difference of opinion, and that the persons who happen to differ from them are not thereby convicted of immorality. [10 January 1912]

THEODORE DREISER

Theodore Dreiser's new novel, "The Financier," seems to be getting the same shy, uncertain reception from the newspaper reviewers that greeted his "Sister Carrie" and "Jennie Gerhardt," both of which now have safe rank among the few genuinely first-rate novels of our day and generation. Even those daring spirits who admit frankly that the book is better than any best-seller ever hatched from an Indiana egg—even these fair ones insist that the author has a deficient feeling for form, that he neglects amazingly every shining chance to fatten up a scene, and that his English has far more iron and flint in it than goose-grease.

What is more, these dubious and hem-hawing critics are so near to making out a respectable case that it is hardly worth while to quarrel with them. It is perfectly true, as they allege, that Dreiser is an inept and ponderous craftsman, that he has no instinct for *crescendo* and *sforzando*, that he is deaf to the lascivious music of the Paterian phrase, that he puts too much of his trust in heavy hammering and too little, or none at all, in the finer rapier thrusts. And yet—and yet—when all is said and done, when all objections have been brought forward and admitted, what superb effects he gets, how gorgeous his colors when he has finally laid them on, how nearly perfect the illusion of reality in the end!

The truth of the matter is that we must learn to take Dreiser as he is, faults and all, if we are to get at the real merit of his work. The fact that he doesn't write at a gallop may be a bit disconcerting to the steady novel reader, but it is not, after all, sufficient in itself to condemn him, for it is precisely that galloping, flambuoyant style of writing which is responsible for most of the artificiality and peurility of our current fiction. In real life events do not commonly fall into well-modeled acts and scenes, nor is the discourse of men and women a succession of stings and flashes. On the contrary, the stream of life moves sluggishly and torturously, like some puny river feeling its way across an illimitable and inhospitable plain. Most of us live and die, not only without drama, but even without direction. What Dreiser tries to do is to produce, by the written word, this effect of blundering and pointless striving, of meaninglessness, of eternal ineffectuality, and with the high achievements of that method we must also take its necessary defects and limitations.

Frank Cowperwood, the central figure of "The Financier," is a Philadelphian who comes to manhood at the time of the Civil War and plays an important part, but not dominating part in the great game of grab of the 10 years following. He is meant, I suppose, to be a sort of archetype of the first generation of American money-barons, and despite a good many variations in detail he is probably typical enough. The main thing to remember about him is that he is anything but a mere chaser of the dollar, that avarice as a thing in itself is not in him. For the actual dollar, indeed, he has only the toleration of an artist for his brushes and colors. What he is really after in life is power, and the way power always visualizes itself in his mind is as a means to beauty.

He is, in brief, a sort of refined and super-sensitive voluptuary. He likes all things that sooth the eye—a fine picture, a rare rug, a good horse, a pretty woman, particularly a pretty woman. And the delight that he takes in such things is always vastly more intellectual than sensual. A perfect eyebrow seems to him to be a phenomenon worth sitting down before and thinking about, soberly and profoundly. The world, in his sight, is conceivable only as a repository of beauty. In other aspects he seldom thinks of it, and can scarcely even imagine it.

Naturally enough, this over-development of the æsthetic sense carries with it an under-development of the ethical sense. The man, indeed, is a sort of moral vacuum, with no more feeling for right and wrong, as immutable principles of conduct, than a schoolboy or a hyena. When he sees a chance to make a lot of money by allying himself with political buccaneers, he takes it without the slightest questions of its essential virtue. And when, later on, the buccaneers themselves lay open for a bit of pillage, he pillages them with a light heart. Away from actual business the same crude hedonism is the mainspring of his acts. When he discovers that old Edward Malia Butler, his political and financial ally, has a radiant and venturesome daughter, he debauches her under old Butler's very nose, and carries on the affair with the skill and impudence of a Tom Jones.

In this affair, indeed, he has little sense of wrongdoing, either to Butler, to young Aileen, or even to the wife of his youth. The only idea that presents itself to him with any force is the idea that Aileen is very pleasing, and to it he yields without analysis. Even when fortune turns against him, and he is the conquered instead of the conqueror, not much feeling that an act of conquest involves a moral wrong is apparent in him. Old Butler, discovering his affair with Aileen, knocks over his financial house of cards and has him railroaded to prison, but he shows little rancor against Butler, and less against Butler's helpers in the business, but only an unemotional sort of disgust that fate should be so unkind to him, and keep him from beauty so long.

Nor does a year in prison change him. He comes out just as he went in, convinced that life is merely a tedious game and that beauty is its one valuable prize. He has been defeated once, true enough, but next time he is determined to win—and win he does. Black Friday[4] gives him his chance, and his chance precipitates a million. On his feet again, he calmly prepares to leave Philadelphia for Chicago, where the scenes are being set for the wildest deeds of money and chicanery ever seen in the world. And as the curtain falls he is on his way—with Aileen under his arm.

A great rogue, of course, but still a rogue who rises above all mere hoggishness and takes on something of the heroic, and even of the tragic. The achievement of Dreiser lies in this very fact: that he has made the man wholly comprehensible, and, as they say in the theatre, sympathetic. As the tale of his exploits in finance, politics and amour is slowly spun, a serene sort of dignity begins to appear in his sophistries and tergiversations. He is no common crook, but an immoral Prometheus, bound fast to a rock which seems to him to have no substance. And so seen he evokes that sympathy which inevitably goes with understanding. Dreiser's laborious piling up of detail, his onerous progress uphill and down dale, his solemn matter-of-factness and disdain for trickery—all this has the effect, in the end, of showing you Cowperwood's point of view, and once you have it, Cowperwood himself becomes as real as Falk or Barry Lyndon.[5]

Dreiser, I am convinced, is the most considerable novelist, by long odds, now at work in America, and in saying this I do not forget Edith Wharton, nor even the sere and fluttering Howells. His philosophy of life, I am well aware, is wholly un-American, for Americans are all optimists, and he is the most abject of pessimists, but once you have granted him that philosophy of his and made allowance for his peculiarities of method, you will find it difficult to escape the admission that he is a truly great artist, with the firm grip upon realities which distinguished Zola and Dostoevsky, and something of the rude poetry which illuminates the romances of Joseph Conrad.

Nothing finer than "Sister Carrie" has been done in our time, saving only "Huckleberry Finn," our one great contribution to the literature of the world. "The Financier," compared to this earlier book, leaves an impression decidedly less vivid, but that is chiefly because the central figure is a man instead of a woman. A hero, true enough, may outshine any heroine, but between the soiled lady and the villain the choice is always for the former. Beside, the book, for all its 780 pages, is incomplete, for it leaves Cowperwood at the very beginning of his real adventures. Those adventures will make the second volume, and Chicago will be their scene.[6] Of the stature and appeal of that second volume I have no doubt whatever. Dreiser has got a secure grip upon his materials. He knows Chicago as few other men know it, and what is more, he knows Cowperwood inside and out. [15 November 1912]

ANTHONY COMSTOCK: HIS LIFE AND WORK

The news that Anthony Comstock, that venerable and insatiable smuthound, has decided to suppress the *Suffragette,* the official organ of the militants, comes just in time to help the sale of his "authorized biography."[7] This curious work, from the pen of the Hon. Charles Gallaudet Trumbull, an ardent disciple, is now on the book stalls, and all connoisseurs of moral endeavor will find it juicy and edifying reading. It was written under the eye of Anthony himself, and its ecstatic greasing of him may be fairly accepted as in accord with his own notions of his merit. From end to end there runs the proud humility of one on confidential terms with the Creator. Every time Anthony throws some one into jail, it is by the direct behest of the Almighty. And every time he escapes punishment himself, it is by Divine interference. An archangel in sidewhiskers! A *geheimrat* of Heaven!

The hon. gent. was born, it appears, at New Canaan, Conn., on March 7, 1844, and began his moral career at the age of 18 by shooting a mad dog in the nearby village of Winnipauk. After an honorable service in the Civil War, in the course of which he rose to the rank of private, he became a drygoods salesman in New York. It was in 1868 that he made his first actual raid. The initial victim was one Charles Conroy, a publisher of obscene books—that is, Comstock *says* they were obscene. Conroy went to jail, and after him went several other publishers. The whisper went round in moral circles—and also, one fancies, in circles not moral at all—that a new live wire from Connecticut was in town. The science of Comstockery dawned.

But during this first phase, good Anthony had two handicaps upon him, the first being lack of means and the second being lack of suitably virulent legislation. The first was quickly remedied by certain ancients of moral fervor—among them, Morris K. Jesup, William E. Dodge and Henry R. Jones.[8] These old fellows, all of them hot to jail as many sinners an possible, formed a sort of underwriting syndicate to back the new virtuoso, and out of that syndicate grew the New York Society for the Suppression of Vice, the papa of our own pious camorra of the same name. With plenty of money behind them, Comstock now proceeded to the purification of the human race upon a wholesale scale, and soon he was grabbing sinners with both hands and keeping two or three courts busy with his cases

But the laws were still inadequate to his needs, a good many of his victims got off, and some of them even defied him. Accordingly, he addressed himself to the arduous task of obtaining laws of a greater virtue and ferocity, and after a long, long fight he succeeded. On March 3, 1873, encouraged by his big stick, Congress passed the postal law which now adorns the books—a statute prohibiting the mailing of obscene literature, but conveniently neglecting to define obscenity. This statute has been Comstock's standby ever since. Under it he can institute the prosecution of any publisher who attracts his baleful eye, including even a publisher of Bibles, and under it he has diligently and enthusiastically done so. Very often, of course, he has failed in the end, for juries sometimes succumb to the suggestions of the devil. But fully five times out of ten he has succeeded, and today the fear of him is in every publisher's heart. Mention his name in publishing circles, and every hearer thereof goes pale. He is a permanent and paralyzing bugaboo.

The Hon. Mr. Trumbull gives an interesting summary of his hero's work during 40 years. Unfortunately enough, the figures of the hon. gent. do not always agree with themselves. On page 157, for example, he says that Anthony has brought 2,718 culprits to trial since 1873, and that 98½ per cent. of them have been convicted, but on page 239 he gives the total number of arrests as 3,646 and the number of convictions as 2,682, which works out to but 73 per cent. Be that as it may, the figures are still very impressive. "If all the persons he has arrested were to be transported," says the Hon. Mr. Trumbull, "61 passenger coaches would be needed, each with a seating capacity of 60 persons—60 cars filled, and the other nearly full." Marvelous, indeed! And along with these arrests, he has destroyed 60 tons of books, 28,425 pounds of stereotype plates, 16,900 photographic negatives and 3,984,063 photographs. Alas, for poor Anthony: Paris is still turning out those photographs by the million! Every incoming ship brings a consignment of them; every returning Sunday-school superintendent has a few of them in his inside pocket!

Let me advise you to buy and read this "authorized biography" of the emperor of moralists. Put beside him, our own best scourgers of sin shrivel to mere pin-points. The Hon. Samuel E. Pentz is a wart in the mighty shadow of Ossa; even the Hon. Charles J. Bonaparte begins to shrink and look sick. Say what you will against him, belabor and revile him as you choose, you must still admit a certain hearty masculinity in him. He is no puling cry-baby, surrounded by sympathizing old maids of both sexes. He is not a cheap grafter, a moralist for revenue only. He does not shake down the Sunday schools. He does not try to touch the hearts and pocketbooks of suckers with tales of conspiracies against him. On the contrary, he is a hearty old buck with many likeable qualities, and if he hadn't taken to malignant morality in his youth he would have made a genial and popular saloonkeeper. Even his victims have a sneaking respect for him. [25 October 1913]

V

MEN, WOMEN, AND THE VOTE

ON WOMAN SUFFRAGE

TEN THOUSAND DOLLARS reward to any rhetorician or logician who will come forward with a single argument, not obviously fallacious or facetious, against the extension of the suffrage to women. The nearest approach to such an argument—the only one with the slightest plausibility in it—is the pestiferous version of the *argumentum ad hominem* which rests upon the admitted absurdity and grotesquerie of some of the suffragettes. But, as Oscar Wilde long ago pointed out, the truth of a doctrine has nothing whatever to do with the respectability, or even with the sincerity of its advocates. Francis Bacon was a corruptionist and a hypocrite—in short, a politician—and yet his platitudes remain as true as any proposition of Euclid. Nietzsche was a lunatic, and yet his gospel, in the main, is a clarion bellow for sanity in thinking. Johannes Mueller drank beer incessantly and read novels on Sunday, and yet his contributions to biology remain the glories of that science. Newton recanted on his knees, and yet the things that he recanted were undying truths, and he knew it.

Therefore, it is silly to argue against the extension of the suffrage on the ground that some of the suffragettes do not darn their husbands' socks, or on the ground that others drug their hearers with alcohol, or on the ground that others are mere social climbers, with far more interest in the society column than in the great problems of political economy and jurisprudence. Admitting all these things to be true, what are the odds? What have the motives of the spellbinders got to do with the honesty of his cause? Most good causes, in truth, are maintained, at least in part, by hired and professional rhetoricians, whose personal interest in them is small. The most affecting sermon I ever heard was preached by a clergyman who read Rabelais and chewed tobacco. He was far from a pious man, and certainly not an ascetic, but all the same he was an extremely eloquent man, and so he did good service to a good cause.

All the other arguments against the extension of the suffrage strike as wholly puerile and unconvincing. For instance, the argument that the majority of women don't want it. What in the world has their wanting it or not wanting it got to do with it? Very few healthy children, at least of the male sex, want to wash, and yet we make them do so by terrorism and downright brutality, and so conquer their repugnance. Again, very few healthy mean want to work—and yet they have to do it.

The error in this argument against the suffrage lies in mistaking the thing itself for a privilege, an amusement, a sort of rude, manly vice, like alcoholism or faro. As a matter of fact, it is not a privilege or amusement or vice at all, but a duty—the highest duty, perhaps, laid upon human beings under a free republic. And women, if they are to take part otherwise in the business of democracy—for example, in its industries, its art, its moralizing, its crime and its witch-burning— must inevitably face that duty. The notion of a sex free to criticize the government and yet in nowise responsible for the government is obnoxious to justice and to decency.

The woman of yesterday, of course, was not free to criticise the government. It was regarded as vulgar for her to express any opinion, or even to have an opinion, about the organization and management of human society. That was work for men. In her nonage her father protected and thought for her; when she was married her husband took up the grim labor; when he, staggering under it, died of it the State appointed guardians for her. She was, in the eye of the law, a perpetual minor. Society asked nothing of her save that she keep her house habitable and her children full of camomile. In return for that service she was relieved of all necessity for ratiocination. The less her striving for originality—i. e., the greater her stupidity—the better she was esteemed. To think an absolutely novel thought was as dangerous for her as to drown her offspring. Her heaven was the home, and the home was her hell. [1 February 1912]

Discoursing yesterday upon the progress of the woman's suffrage movement I drew an affecting picture of the woman of today, marooned in her home, an idiot in the eye of the law, esteemed in direct proportion to her ignorance and childishness. I ran out of space before that picture, in all of its exquisite details, was complete, but there is no need, fortunately enough, to go on with it, for the woman of today is making a rapid escape from the famous three Ks of the German Emperor.[1] It is no longer considered pretty for a lady to be an ignoramus. She may acquire a considerable stock of political economy, of philosophy, of commercial acumen and even of physiology without being stoned to death. The decay of that melancholy indecency which once passed for propriety has restored to her her diaphragm and her legs, and the decay of that slavery which once passed for superiority has restored to her her cerebrum and her cerebellum.

Human society, as a condition of its swift economic progress, has had to draft her for multitudinous and complex labors, and in return for her acquiescence it has had to strike off her old shackles. She is no longer a lay figure, a cipher in the State. The lady, her supreme and perfect type, becomes as rare and as ridiculous as the sorcerer or the barber-surgeon. We expect a woman of today to show a certain alertness of mind, a certain practical efficiency, a certain originality and independence of spirit. It is no longer considered scandalous for her to work out a theology of her own, to have books of her own or to seek a trade or profession of her own. Not only do we admit her to such rights, but we actually insist that she exercise them, or, at any rate, some of them.

In millions of cases, for example, we make her go to work. Well, in going to work she inevitably comes into contact with those laws which regulate and condition work—that is, with the most important laws on our statute books. She must obey them; mold her desires to fit them; adapt her whole life to them. And thus giving them her support, she at once acquires the right to discuss their character, even to propose changes in them, and that right leads, by a short step, to the ballot. It is inconceivable, under a free democracy, that a citizen should have the right to debate a law and yet no right to vote upon it. Any land in which such an absurdity is permitted is no more a free democracy than Russia.

So much for the mere right to vote. The duty follows clearly from the right. A woman who obeys a law without reflecting, at some time or other, upon its wisdom and its justice, and without reaching, through that reflection, some notion that it might be better, is obviously a num-skull, and in consequence a mere cipher in the State. But a woman who does so reflect, and who does come to such conclusions, is under a plain obligation to voice and maintain them, for if they do not embody a plan to work her own good, then they at least embody a plan to work some other woman's (or man's) good, and in consequence she commits an offense against society when she keeps them secret.

We human beings are not creatures *in vacuo*. We cannot possibly live for two hours running without influencing, in some way or other, the lives of others. Nor can we so influence other lives without, by reflection and reaction, modifying our own. Therefore, it is our highest duty to so-ciety to engage, actively and incessantly, in that interchange and assaying of ideas which alone makes progress possible. To shirk that duty is as bad as to shirk any other duty—the duty of respecting the property of others, the duty of keeping clean. If we do shirk it, then we become mere slaves of the alert majority—slaves of the very sort that women were before the industrial process routed them out of their cages and laid upon them the necessity of adjusting themselves, alertly and intelligently, to the stimuli of a new and fluent environment. [2 February 1912]

Discoursing yesterday upon the proposed extension of the suffrage to women, I established amply, by six or seven different breeds of syllo-gism, that any woman who is forced to lend a hand in the industry of a democracy has a clear right to take part in its legislation also. Let us assume today that this has been proved. But even among persons who admit it freely a number of so-called practical objections to the suffrage are still raised. One of these objections, for example, is based upon the alleged fact that the natural refinement of women would be invaded and tarnished by participation in politics—specifically, that the fellows who go to political meetings and crowd into the polling places are so vulgar that mere contact with them would permanently soil and degrade a lady.

Well, let us look into it. That is to say, let us proceed from the theory to the fact. Make that journey—and the absurdity of the objection at once becomes apparent. For if you have ever been to a large political meeting, you must know very well not only that nothing goes on there that could possibly be obnoxious to a self-respecting woman, but also that many self-respecting women are commonly in attendance, and that they enjoy the proceedings immensely. It would be difficult, indeed, to imagine a more decorous assemblage than a big political meeting, say, at the Lyric.[2] True enough, there is a lot of noise and many lowly ward heelers are in the hall, but that noise is entirely harmless and those ward heelers are in their Sunday clothes and on their good behavior.

The ward meeting, of course, is less refined—particularly the ward meeting which groups and drapes itself around a keg of beer, as most of them do—but even here the ceremonies never descend to the scandalous. A few gentlemen may slip over that dim borderline which separates cold sobriety from golden mellowness, but with so many drinking and so little beer in a keg, it is commonly impossible for more than one or two to proceed to actual tightness, and these pigs are quickly thrown out. As for the rest of the ceremonies, they show vulgarity only in proportion to the general vulgarity of the neighborhood. And that vulgarity, we may safely assume, the women of the neighborhood are able to stand. It would be a harrowing experience, let us admit, for a woman living on Mount Vernon Place to attend a ward meeting on Chestnut street—but ward meetings on Chestnut street are for the voters of Chestnut street, and not for those of Mount Vernon Place.

The essential thing about a ward meeting, in brief, is its accurate reflection, not only of the political thought but also of the civilization and drinking manners of the immediate vicinage. If the neighborhood is uncouth, then the proceedings are uncouth—but the women of the neighborhood, if they were present, would not notice it. The wife of a man who habitually dines in his undershirt is not apt to be disgusted on seeing him drink beer out of his derby hat. Nor will it surprise her to discover that such drinking is followed by a paralysis of his higher cerebral centres and a considerable increase of his enthusiasm for Andrew

Jackson. Furthermore, and last of all, the woman voter herself, once she begins going to ward meetings, will tackle the keg as her husband does, and thus she will suffer a benign blunting of her sensibilities.

These same considerations are sufficient to show that the actual act of voting will involve no invasion of a decent woman's self-respect. At the polling place, as at the ward meeting, she will be among her neighbors—the very persons whose habits of body and mind are most familiar and most agreeable to her. If she lives among primitive folk, then she will find primitive folk around the ballot-box; if, on the contrary, she lives among polite folk, then she will find polite folk in line ahead of her. In neither case will she suffer, at the polling place, any psychic experience not already commonplace to her mind. In neither case will she encounter any style of raiment, display of tobacco juice or dialect of English not already established and dignified in her memory by innumerable precedents. [3 February 1912]

One of the objections constantly made to the extension of the suffrage to women is the objection that the right to make laws should be granted only to those able to enforce them—that since women are unable to serve on the police force or in the army they should not be allowed to vote. A moment's reflection is all that is necessary to reveal the imbecility of this argument. On the one hand, it sets up mere physical endurance as the test of a free citizen, and on the other hand it assumes gaily, and without the slightest evidence, that women would be unable to meet that test. Both the test and the assumption are fallacious. On the one hand, a citizen's talent for warfare is by no means a condition of his capacity for making intelligent laws, and on the other hand the belligerent genius of the modern woman, if it is actually in abeyance, is in abeyance only because it has been paralyzed by public opinion.

The truth is, of course, that the business of making laws and that of enforcing them are entirely separate and distinct enterprises, and not only separate and distinct, but even, in some sense, antagonistic. The experience of the race has shown that the man trained for one, or leading a life fitting him for one, is not ordinarily fitted for the other. No one, for example, would think of delegating the business of legislation to the police force, nor would any sane man advocate putting delicate matters of foreign policy into the hands of the regular army or militia for determination. Such duties and problems are best handled by men trained to the work—that is to say, by men accustomed to reasoning with their cerebre, stomachs and pocketbooks and not with their fists. And by thus neglecting their fists, these men naturally produce a certain atrophy of their fists. The average statesman, in brief, is a paunchy and cyanotic fellow, with distinct signs of arterio-sclerosis upon his face.

Nature, being a conservationist, breeds specialists. The man who can lift a barrel of flour is usually a man who cannot understand the binomial theorem; the man who can devise a novel get-rich quick scheme and so milk the public is usually a man who couldn't, for the life of him, milk a cow. And since no man is ever wholly without talents of some sort, large or small, it is pretty safe to assume, when he is found to lack one sort, that he possesses, in some measure, the other sort. Find a man who cannot distinguish between a rondeaux and a triolet and you will almost invariably see a man with an abnormal capacity for handling mules; find a man who shows a concave facade and translucent ears and you will al-most invariably see a man who has read Kant, Montesquieu and Balzac and is familiar with the theory of least squares. Such is nature's law of compensation. Such is the normal division of labor in the world.

For many centuries women have been forbidden, for reasons chiefly fanciful, to take a hand in the rough hacking and walloping of civili-zation, and as a result they have suffered a measurable degeneration of their muscles and sinews. Today they are generally smaller than men and generally weaker. But that very degeneration in one department has favored an enormous development in the opposite department. That is to say, women have come to possess an extraordinary stock of craft, of sapience, of prudence. Romanticists call it intuition—and praise it. Realists call it cunning—and damn it. But whatever its true name, there it is. The average man, in the prize ring, is a fair match for two women, but let him go into a contest of wits, and one woman will floor him with ease. For every Samson in the world there is a Delilah. Every creature who wears pantaloons is hen-pecked. Every one of us adapts his whole life to the behests and chicaneries of some woman or group of women.

This craft of women, true enough, has not been exercised, in the past, in the field of political intrigue, at least not directly. But that has been a mere accident. Once open the doors, and it will show itself to be just as wise and just as effective in politics as it has ever been at the domestic hearth. Craft is craft, whatever its fortuitous mode of display. Wherever and whenever women have been permitted to invade new fields of chicanery, they have at once demonstrated their capacity. I need only refer, for examples, to the fields of spiritualism, novel-writing, press-agenting and mental healing. Here they are now the full peers of men—and once they launch into politics they will quickly exhibit the same equality there. The notion that politics is a recondite and esoteric science, requiring extraordinary gifts for its comprehension, is a silly delusion, to be blasted by five minutes' talk with any politician. All it really demands is a reasonable alertness and craftiness—and these are the very qualities which all women possess.

So much for the political fitness of the dear girls. Let us consider tomorrow, in greater detail, the objection that their admitted physical inferiority would prevent them enforcing their own laws. [5 February 1912]

I referred yesterday, in soft and discreet words, to one of the objections most frequently made to the extension of the suffrage to women—the objection, that is to say, that it would be unjust to put the power to make laws into the hands of a sex too weak to enforce them. On its face, this objection seems sound enough, for it must be obvious to everyone that the average woman is measurably weaker than the average man. Her bones are smaller, her muscles are flabbier, her skin is less tough. What is more, she weighs considerably less, and has a gentler voice. Not only would she be at a disadvantage in an actual physical tussle with a man, but she would also be at a disadvantage in the antecedent bellowing and bluffing. She could not strike as devastating a blow as her opponent and she could not emit as appalling a whoop.

But nevertheless there is a fallacy in all this fine reasoning, and that fallacy lies in the assumption that physical combat among civilized peoples is altogether, or even chiefly, a matter of muscular and vocal strength. As a matter of fact, it is nothing of the sort. It used to be, true enough, but we are here considering, not what used to be, but what is. In modern warfare individual antagonists do not meet elbow to elbow and thus beat out each other's brains. On the contrary, they seldom come into physical contact at all, but face each other over long intervening spaces and conduct their contest, not with their mere muscles and lungs, but with their eyes and brains. In brief, war has become a combat of wit, of observation, of technique, and the advantage goes to that side which shows the greater virtuosity in cunning. In a battle between 10,000 longshoremen and 10,000 female bachelors of arts, fought with modern weapons of precision, it is altogether probable that the longshoremen would be drubbed and routed. Even a woman policeman, armed with a magazine pistol and a syringe of phosphine,[3] would do just as good service as any male cop in Christendom.

If, however, mere physical strength is no longer necessary to military efficiency, it is nevertheless true that physical endurance is still of value. Soldiers still have to march; they are still fed upon embalmed beef and other such victuals, and they are still exposed to the elements. But is the physical endurance of women appreciably less than that of men? Not at all. The experience of the race, indeed, teaches that it is actually more. Women, in brief, are able to face safely and with equanimity conditions of life which would soon destroy the average man. Their lungs need less air, their bodies need less food, they are more resistent to cold and damp. The clothing worn habitually by women would stamp out the so-called sterner sex in a year. Women more quickly accustom themselves to an unfavorable environment. A woman dipsomaniac, once she gets the knack of drinking, always lasts longer than a man. A woman can lose sleep with less damage than a man. A woman can go without meals with less damage than a man.

All these proofs of endurance, of dulled sensibilities, of toughness, would seem to give women a considerable advantage on the field of battle. And if we proceed from the theory to the recorded facts, we find that this is so. Wherever and whenever, in the history of the world, women have taken to warfare, they have invariably displayed an extraordinary capacity for enduring. The Amazons of Scythia and Libya were particularly distinguished for their long marches without commissariat. It was by such a march that they came to the relief of Troy. It was by such a march that they invaded and terrorized Attica during their last and greatest campaign.[4] And the French Revolution and the wars between the Italian republics furnish many other examples. If women have a defect as soldiers, it is the defect of abnormal and disconcerting readiness. To face them is to face a foe who needs no rest and takes none.

But many who oppose the extension of the suffrage while admitting all this, yet raise a further objection. That is to say, they argue that

warfare would still do great violence to woman's gentleness and delicacy—that she would succumb psychically if not physically—that the
spectacle of carnage would flabbergast and appall her. Rubbish! The fact
is, of course, that women are far less sensitive in such matters than men.
They make better nurses than men, not because they are more sympathetic, but because they are less sympathetic. A male surgeon, after cutting out an appendix, promptly disappears from the scene; it is a female
nurse who faces unflinchingly the subsequent bellowing of the patient.
In the presence of suffering, however horrible, women keep their heads.
Spectacles which would paralyze a man seem merely to quicken their
intelligence.

Therefore, it is ridiculous to allege that women are essentially unfit
for war—*i. e.,* for enforcing with arms their own legislative edicts and
follies. On the physical side, they are at least as fit as men, and on the
psychic side they are ten times as fit. But let us consider the woman
warrior at greater length tomorrow. [6 February 1912]

Considering yesterday the question of woman's fitness for war—a
quality ridiculously denied them by bilious foes of the suffrage—I ran
out of space before I could support my argument with appropriate examples. But that such examples are to be had in abundance, even without going to ancient history, must be obvious to every student of the
feminist movement of the past generation. The doings of the militant
suffragettes in England have plainly revealed, not only a high degree of
political sapience, but also a quite extraordinary capacity for military
enterprise. They have fought and they have endured, and what is more,
they have done both things enthusiastically, and without making any
maudlin appeals for sympathy.

If you want to get a glimpse of the warlike talents and callosi-
ties of women you can do no better than read "The Suffragette," by
Sylvia Pankhurst, an astonishing record of daring and fortitude. Miss
Pankhurst herself has shown military genius of a high order. She
planned and commanded some of the most effective attacks upon the
constabulary of London and was undaunted when the catchpolls wal-
loped her with their espantoons. Her eyes blacked and bleeding at the
nose, she was yet able to howl down the mob of circumambient scoffers,

and at the police station, later on, she flabbergasted magistrate and bailiffs with her caustic wit. The best the bravest men can do is to fight and run away. But women fight and *dance* away—a vast and revolutionary improvement in technique.

Behind prison walls, as in the thick of roughhouse, the English suffragettes have displayed an unconquerable spirit. Some of them, cast into dungeons, went on what they called hunger strikes, and so it became necessary to feed them by force. To anyone familiar with this process their sufferings must be evident. The victim, as I hear, is first strapped to a chair and then a section of gas stove tubing is rammed down her throat. The free end of the tube, to which a funnel is attached, is then elevated, and the funnel is filled with buttermilk, lentil soup or some other suitable victual. Respiration is seriously impeded, and speech, of course, is downright impossible. And yet the suffragettes bore the thing with supreme courage. One of the most impressive pictures I have ever seen, indeed, shows a middle-aged crusader in black bombazine, her arms and legs fastened to a chair, a gas pipe protruding from her face—and devastating epigrams flashing from her eyes!

In a hundred such ways the growth of the feminist movement has uncovered latent talents and capacities in women—not only for labor, intrigue and the dialectic, but also, and more especially, for what the anarchists call action. The woman of yesterday, when injustice crushed her, took refuge in tears. The crystal drop of moisture, trembling on her eyelash, was not only her anodyne, but also her weapon. With it she attacked and melted the hard heart of her male oppressor. But no more. The woman of today, disdaining tears, puts her trust in more valiant remonstrances. She has become familiar, indeed, with every weapon in the arsenal of aggression, from the knockout drop to the magazine pistol, and from jiu-jitsu to hydrocyanic acid, and she uses them all with skill and daring.

A friend in Denver sends me certain statistics which well exhibit this change. In the year 1889, as he shows, wife-beating was a common crime in that city—so common that no fewer than 716 cases were tried by the magistrates during the twelvemonth. But in 1893 the women of Colorado gained the suffrage, and at once there was a sharp decline. By 1896 the number of cases had dropped to 426 and by 1900 to 301. Last year there were but 116. Says my friend:

It is common to ascribe this decline to new laws passed by women legislators, but the truth is that the present laws are no more harsh or effective than those in force in 1889. The real cause is the increased courage of the emancipated woman. No longer held down, consciously or unconsciously, by medieval notions of her own inferiority, she now resists violence with violence, and the result appears upon the court records. In a few years, I fully believe, husband-beating will be commoner in Denver than wife-beating.

Returns from larger areas reveal the same change. Not only where women have actually gained the vote, but also where they are still battling for it, have the effects of that endeavor, and its consequent release from convention, shown themselves. The woman policeman, unknown five years ago, is now commonplace. Women now serve as bailiffs and jailers. They go in for games requiring hardihood and courage. They show an increasing talent for the more desperate and difficult varities of crime.

For example, homicide. In 1885, according to Dr. John J. Brewster, the distinguished statistician, but 2.3 per cent. of the murders committed in the United States were committed by women. But by 1900 the ratio had risen to 3.1 per cent. and last year it was nearly 5 per cent. Murder, of course, is a crime, but let us not forget that it is also an act requiring considerable enterprise and courage, and that its increase among women is thus good evidence of growing initiative and independence. No Lady ever harmed a fly. A woman, to achieve the assassination of her husband, or even to imagine it, must first throw off those false assumptions of weakness, of squeamishness and of dependence which have oppressed her sex for centuries. However much we may abhor her act, we cannot fail to recognize the warlike spirit and hardihood behind it.

Thus the argument that women are unfit for war, that they could not enforce their own laws, goes to pieces. Their fitness for war, if anything, is actually superior to that of men. As I have shown, they have the courage, they have the endurance and they are not appalled by carnage. All they need, to send them flocking to the battle field, is release from that purely fictitious qualmishness, that theoretical lack of mettle and fortitude, with which the sentimental imagination of man has endowed and cursed them. The Waterloo of tomorrow may be won, not on the cricket fields of Eton,[5] but on the soap boxes of the suffragettes. But of all this more anon. [7 February 1912]

THE WORKING WOMAN AND THE VOTE

The estimable Maryland Association Opposed to Woman Suffrage is seeking to inflame the rabble with a pamphlet entitled "The Wage-Earning Woman and the State," in which the thesis is maintained that the working girl doesn't need the vote. According to this pamphlet, her interests are so well looked after by the male voters that she couldn't possibly do better for herself. In all but three States, one of which is an equal suffrage State, there are laws "for the protection of women who earn, which laws are distinct from and in addition to the laws protecting all wage-earners, men and women alike." Basking in the sunshine of these humane enactments, she is a favored and coddled creature, the pet of sentimental and amorous man, the darling of the gods. No act of her own could ever make her lot more soft and rosy.

With all due respect to a camorra of earnest and pious ladies, Bosh my dears! No one denies that such laws are on the statute books: the thing denied is that such laws, as they stand, are worth a hoot. In point of fact, two-thirds of them are full of snakes, and the rest of them are not enforced. In every Southern State, I daresay, there is a law solemnly regulating the labor of women, and particularly of immature women, and yet every sane man knows that little girls slave away in the cotton mills, and that their slavery converts them into anemic invalids, and that their invalidism makes them bad mothers for the Southerners of tomorrow.

And so in all directions. Here in Maryland, if I make no mistake, we have an impressive body of law for the protection of the woman worker—and yet, no further back than two months ago, three little girls came to THE SUN office to ask me to help them in a strike. One of them, a puny, sickly little thing, said that she was 13 years old. Imagine a girl of 13 on strike! On strike for a better workroom, a reasonable lunch hour, bearable hours of labor, fair wages! Where were the humane laws of Maryland? Where were the benign enactments of the impeccable males—i. e., of the ward heelers, barroom bravos and professional job holders—at Annapolis? Of what value to these little girls were the statutes "for the protection of women who earn * * * distinct from and in addition to the laws protecting all wage-earners, men and women alike"?

But here, of course, my objection may show unsoundness: it is perfectly possible that laws passed by women would be ineffective, too.

Even so, however, our present system is full of injustice and evil. Why should the woman worker, laboring just as diligently as the man worker and just as painfully, and just as reluctantly—why should this woman worker have to go to the man worker, her rival and enemy, for her rights? Why should she have to beg, as a suppliant, what she has a clear right to demand? Why should she have to content herself with what is doled out to her, unwillingly and patronizingly? Why should she be kept from making that fair and equal bargain with the world which men make? Why should she be treated as a ward and an inferior? Why should the laws affecting her be framed in the spirit of the laws prohibiting cruelty to animals?

This conception of women as inferior creatures was sound enough when they *were* inferior creatures—when they were the mere slaves and parasites of men. In return for their docility and stupidity they were given valuable immunities; it was considered indecent to burden their minds with the more bitter problems of civilized society. They were protected, at least in some measure, from the struggle for existence. When they faced the world, it was from behind a sturdy rank of protecting males. They did not fall at the first fire. They were not tortured with the incessant dilemmas of tactics and strategy. Even the enemy tried to be kind to them.

But that arcadian day is no more. The average, the typical woman of today is a working woman, and she has to work hard and faithfully to get a living. The struggle for existence is no longer a tale from afar, brought to her by her protector: she is in the midst of it. The harshest problems of life are before her. She must be wary if she would survive and more than wary if she would get ahead. That little girl who came to see me was but 13 years old, but she was giving as much hard thought to a problem in political economy as ever Adam Smith gave to it, and her conclusion about it ten years hence will be just as much worth hearing.

Here, indeed, is the crux of the matter: our laws dealing with the woman laborer should not be based upon what some sociologist or political economist or ward heeler thinks would be good for her, but upon what *she herself* thinks would be good for her. She pays the piper in blood and sweat; she should have a free right to dance as she pleases. It is not alone benevolence that she demands, nor even chiefly, but freedom—the equal rights of a free citizen under a democracy—the right to make her own bargains, to get what she can for herself, to protect her own jaw in the clinches.

Men have fought for this right in the past, disdaining with great contempt the philanthrophy offered in place of it. There were Factory Acts in England so long ago as 1802, and by 1825 they filled a large book, but that didn't keep the workingmen of England from demanding the vote as well. Sop after sop was thrown to them; the Factory Acts were revised and mellowed in 1833, 1844, 1845, 1847, 1860, 1862, 1863, 1864, 1867, 1870, 1871, 1874 and so on down the years. But they kept on fighting for the vote—i. e., for the right to make Factory Acts themselves—and finally, in 1885, after two partial victories, they got it. The workingmen of England still have to work, and work is still unpleasant: the possession of the vote has not brought them the millenium. But they now have a direct and equal voice in the regulation of their work. They do not have to depend upon charity; they can fight for themselves, and on a reasonably fair field. [3 May 1913]

THE DEFEAT OF WOMAN SUFFRAGE

Now that the first soreness of defeat has begun to wear off and things may be seen in retrospect with diminishing emotional distortion, it is in order for the members of the Just Government League of Maryland to consider well the causes of their recent inglorious defeat at Annapolis.

The woman suffrage amendment was rejected in the House of Delegates by a vote of 60 to 34, almost a two-thirds majority. What is worse, it was rejected unceremoniously, lightly, almost mockingly. Two years ago its defeat was marked by a warm and intelligent debate, but this time the only member who thought it worth while to denounce it from the floor was the Hon. "Cy" Cummings, against whose renomination the suffragettes fought so violently and so vainly—and even "Cy" was content to poke a few idle jokes at it. Its sole defender was the Hon. Charles H. McNabb, of Harford county, whose speech was a burbling thing of the cross-roads Demosthenes type, and frankly amusing to a good many of the Delegates. The speech of the Hon. Lloyd Wilkinson was not a plea for the amendment at all, but merely a plea for common courtesy to its advocates.

I am no political coroner and profess to no skill at legislative autopsies, but none the less I venture the guess that two factors contributed very largely to this humiliating collapse of the suffrage propaganda. Both of these factors were tactical errors of the suffragettes. The first was the error of burdening the campaign for the suffrage with appeals and demands for all sorts of extravagant "moral" legislation. The second was the error of trying to make votes by threats and reviling, instead of by calm and reasonable persuasion. The two, taken together, disgusted and alienated enough Delegates to defeat the amendment.

The suffragettes, I am convinced, went into the contest with a sound case. They had reason and fairness on their side. They were opposed, in so far as they were opposed at all, only by stagnation on the one hand and stupidity on the other. They made an infinitely better showing, on the mere argument, than the so-called antis. But instead of being content with that argument, instead of appealing solely to reason and fairness and progress, their leaders proceeded to loose their program of grotesque and idiotic special legislation and to attack with the utmost ferocity all men who presumed to see nothing but buncombe in that legislation. The result was that they made far more enemies than friends, and that many men who were actually in favor of woman suffrage turned against them. The second result was their ignominious defeat.

It goes without saying, of course, that the leaders of the Just Government League acted in good faith, that they did what they thought was the best thing to do, that they were firmly convinced of the efficacy of their perunas. They deserve the highest credit, indeed, for playing the game so ardently: if they accomplished nothing else, they at least made woman suffrage a live issue temporarily. But inasmuch as the net effect of their undoubtedly honest effort was unqualified disaster, it is now time for them to give serious consideration to a revision of their methods, and failing that, for suffragists in general to seek other leaders.

The suffrage cause, it should be remembered clearly, is not the private property of the small group of persons who run the Just Government League. Thousands of other persons are also interested in it, and many of them are doing good work, in their various ways, in furthering it. When they see it ruined and made a mock of by a few hysterical fanatics, when it is sacrificed to private hatreds and infantile politics, when it is made a mere appendage to a campaign for "reforms" that not one intelligent man (or woman) out of fifty even dignifies with consideration, when it is given the aspect of a new peruna, another donkeyish cureall, a plaything of press agents and Munyons—when this happens, then it is high time for all suffragists who still retain their reason to call a halt.

Woman suffrage is never going to be put through in Maryland by browbeating and rowelling, and it is never going to be put through by burdening it with the advertising matter of all the mountebanks who choose to jump aboard. If it ever succeeds at all it must succeed on its merits, and the only way to bring those merits home to reasonable men will be to present them with courtesy and argue for them with intelligence. Not many votes are ever going to be made by bellowing that every man who refuses to get in line is a rogue, or by seeking to show that the chief boon of the suffrage will be to drive every "strictly male" man out of the State. [4 March 1914]

A TAX ON BACHELORS?

From the Washington *Post's* report of a recent vice meeting at the capital:

> Dr. W. C. Woodward, health officer of the District of
> Columbia, urged the encouragement of early marriage among
> young men as one of the remedies for the social evil. * * * He
> approved a suggestion by Senator Beall, of Illinois,[6] of laws
> placing a tax upon bachelorhood, a graduated tax between the
> ages of 24 and 42, providing that all men more than 32 years
> old should pay an annual tax of $100 as long as they remain
> unmarried.

A sane and just impost, despite the fallacy of its premise. The social evil, as every intelligent investigator knows, is not supported by bachelors. But all the same, they deserve to pay hard cash for their escape from the cares and burdens of marriage, and what is more, 99 per cent. of them are perfectly willing, and even eager to do so. I don't know a single bachelor, indeed, who is opposed to this proposed tax. The only criticism they make upon it is that it is too low. The majority of them think that a dollar a day would be better. [3 April 1913]

A few chance words, printed in this place the other day, in favor of a dollar a day tax upon bachelors have brought an unexpected flood of letters of approval. And strange as it may seem to anthrophobes of the baffled sex, the great majority of these letters are from bachelors. The writers, let it be remembered, do not hate money; they are not spend-thrifts; they like taxpaying no more than anyone else. But they realize to the full the value of the high liberties and immunities that they enjoy, and they are willing to make payment for them in cash. They ask charity of no man, not even of the community in general. As one of them says:

> I ascribe all my present prosperity to my lack of a rowdy wife and extravagant family, for on the one hand it has enabled me to devote my whole energies to my profession, and on the other hand it has kept my expenses moderate. I frequently lend money to married men with twice my ability, but, poor fellows! they can never get ahead in the world. Time was when I would have been forced into marriage by law, or at least by custom. The removal of that old necessity has been valuable to me. I am willing to pay a reasonable indemnity.

From another comes this curious and confidential revelation:

> I have a married sister somewhat older than myself. When I reached the age of 25, she decided that it was time for me to be married. Thereafter, for 10 long years, my life was a curse. Scarcely a week passed that she didn't trot out some new candidate. I was lured into scores of embarrassing situations. I was baited with widows, grass widows and maidens. Two or three times I made very narrow escapes, indeed. Finally, about a year ago, I decided to put an end to this persecution. I went to my sister, assured her on my word of honor that I was fully determined to remain a bachelor, and offered to give her $10 a week for letting me alone. Convinced at last, she accepted, and today I am a happy man. When I go to her house for dinner, all of the other guests are now either men, or married women with their husbands. I have no more nightmares. The $500 a year is a fine investment. My new found peace of mind has enabled me to lift my income by fully $2,000 a year. Incidentally, my brother-in-law is well pleased. He has a deuce of a time making both ends meet.

And here is a confession that is even more curious:

> So thoroughly am I in favor of a tax on bachelors, as a fair
> payment for their superior ease and happiness, that I have
> actually tried, in a modest sort of way, to pay it. That is to say,
> I have made a practice of sending $100 to the City Collector's
> conscience fund once each year. But I would be better pleased, of
> course, to make payment openly, and to have my resultant rights
> clearly understood. I think a dollar a day would be very fair. The
> money might be used to increase the pay of woman employes
> of the city, who are now underpaid and discontented, and so
> constitute a permanent menace to bachelors.

A fourth correspondent thus considers the practical bearings of the
proposed tax:

> The only sound objection I have ever heard to the tax is that
> it would cause thousands of bachelors to submit to marriage.
> This, of course, would greatly increase turmoil and conflict,
> and perhaps do serious injury to civilization. But it might be
> prevented by laying a heavy penalty on bachelors who marry—
> not on young bachelors, but on the old fellows. Let the marriage
> license for a man less than 25 be $1, as at present, but double it
> every year thereafter. At 35 it would be $1,000. Most men would
> rather pay $1oo a year than $1,ooo in a lump.

This difficulty is also considered by several other correspondents.
One of them, at least, is sure that no such epidemic of marriages would
result from the tax. Says he:

> The only bachelors who would marry to escape payment,
> would be (*a*) those who couldn't afford to pay, and (*b*) those
> who were too stingy to pay. If there are women willing to
> marry such rats, then let them do it, say I. The noble fraternity
> of bachelors—numbering, as it does, such men as Dr. Welch
> and the Hon. W. S. Bryan, Jr.—would be well rid of them.
> The tax would give us bachelors a definite and dignified
> status, just as the framed license behind the bar gives a
> definite and dignfied status to a kaif.[7] Today all bachelors are

in the humiliating position of speakeasies, as it were. They are *ferae naturae.*[8]

And so the letters run, with unqualified approval of the proposed tax as their dominant note. True enough, a few objections are offered, but not by bachelors. The following, from a suffragette, is a sample:

> Your proposal is pernicious, immoral and idiotic. But I would not be surprised to see it adopted. Under our present laws, men are grossly favored. All of the advantages of life are on their side. Not until women have the vote will they escape from the intolerable conditions which now oppress them.

Nevertheless, I don't see how the possession of the vote would give women much help in the present case. Certainly they cannot be nursing false hopes of forcing bachelors into matrimony by law! The day for that sort of thing has gone by. The more stringent the laws, the more savage the penalties, the more desperately all bachelors of the better sort would evade and defy them.

A more serious criticism is advanced by a widow lady. Says she:

> What about widowers? Why should they escape? It seems to me that all widowers should be forced to remarry within five years. They haven't the excuse that they have conscientious objections. They can't say they can't afford it. An unmarried widower constitutes a subtle criticism of marriage; bachelors are always glad to point him out as a sort of horrible example. Such things ought to be stopped.

Well, it mout be. But I do not venture to discuss these difficult subphases of the main problem. All I desire to do is to show that bachelors, as a class, are by no means opposed to special taxation. In all my acquaintances, indeed, there is not a single one who offers serious objection to the proposed tax. There remains, of course, the difficult business of working out its exact amount, manner of application and mode of collection. The one thing needed to determine these things is a frank and free public discussion. The views of such eminent sociologists as Bishop Wegg, of Havre de Grace, Dr. Donald R. Hooker, Dr. Zechia Judd, Clark d'Arlington, the Hon. William H. Anderson, Miss Alice

Hackett and Miss Jane Snookum[9] would be interesting and illuminating. [5 April 1913]

With the State expenditures increasing steadily on the one hand and the city of Baltimore trying to get relief from its excessive burden of State taxes on the other hand, the Legislature will soon have to look about for new means of increasing the revenue. The income from direct taxes and licenses, indeed, is now near the limit, and unless other sources of revenue are promptly found, the State will find itself hopelessly in debt. In this emergency, why have the lawmakers overlooked a tax upon bachelors? The State is full of them and they hold far more than their just proportion of its wealth. Why not make them pay a dollar a day apiece, and so solve the fiscal problem at one stroke, and without putting any new burdens upon householders and heads of families?

The present population of Maryland is about 1,250,000. According to the Census Bureau, slightly less than half of the State's inhabitants, or say 650,000, are males, and according to the same authority 48.4 per cent. of these males, or 314,600, are between the ages of 20 and 54. According to the same authority again, 39 per cent. of these males of marriageable age, or say 122,700, are unmarried.

Consider, now, how much money a dollar-a-day tax on bachelors would raise annually! Even supposing that half of those now living in the State should be driven into marriage to escape the impost, no less than 61,500 would remain, and, what is more, they would represent very accurately that portion of the population best able to pay taxes—*i. e.,* the most selfish, crafty and stingy portion. Paying a dollar a day, they would flood the State Treasury with the enormous sum of $28,447,500 a year, or more than six times the whole income of the State from direct taxes in 1913.

No need to point out that this princely income would convert Maryland from one of the poorest American States into one of the richest. There would be enough money in the treasury to complete the State roads system forthwith, and to put through a score of other necessary and invaluable improvements. After a few years, indeed, all imaginable improvements would be made and paid for, and the money piling up in the treasury would be available for investment in Government bonds and other securities. In the course of time, no doubt, the income from these securities would be sufficient to pay all the expenses of the State, thus making it possible to abolish all taxes, even including the tax upon bachelors.

I commend this plan to the attention of the hon. gentlemen of the Legislature. The most pressing of all the problems now before them is the fiscal problem: every one of the uplifting and forward-looking plans on their calendar involves the expenditure of money, and money is growing tighter day by day. They can't raise the direct tax upon property without starting a revolution, and they are near the end of their squeezing of automobilists, the banks, the liquor ring and Baltimore city. Let them turn to the bachelors, and so escape their woes. Everybody envies a bachelor, and hence everybody hates him. The more he protested against the dollar-a-day tax, the more the public in general would approve it. [21 January 1914]

THE FEMINIST KISS

Some anonymous suffragette contributes to the Philadelphia *Inquirer* a long argument in favor of what she calls "feminist kissings"—*i. e.,* the free bestowal of busses by the erstwhile party of the second part, without the traditional pretense of diffidence and reluctance. "The feminist kiss," she says, "is a thing of no dissimulation. It is the symbol of individuality, of freedom, and, given in the new spirit, it should be as precious to the recipient as the gems that fell from the lips of the enchanted princess." And then she goes on:

> The pale woman of the stage and of literature * * * could no more take the initiative in kissing than she could bring herself to propose marriage.

A subtle touch here. Notice how this shrewd suffragette puts the incapacity of which she speaks upon "the pale woman of the stage and of literature," and not upon any actually existent female creature. The truth is, of course, that no such female creature is to be found in the world. The legend to the contrary is no more than a sentimental fiction, a degrading superstition, a clumsy effort to soothe the vanity of men. Not only do women take the initiative in fully 75 per cent. of all kissing bouts, but they also propose marriage three times out of five. This is one of the hidden scandals of civilization. Every man above the age of 25 knows of it by embarrassing and alarming personal experience, but there is an immemorial convention that it shall never be mentioned. In exactly the same way it is the custom to say and assume that relatives by blood are on the footing of firm and intimate friends and allies, whereas the fact is that they seldom admire or even like one another, and are often scarcely acquainted.

How hard superstitions die! And how lamentably they befog the mind that yields to them! The average married man, asked point-blank, will tell you glibly that he proposed to his wife, and even show indignation if you question it. But a searching cross-examination, in the manner of Prof. Dr. Siegmund Freud, almost always drags the truth out of him. This truth is hidden away in the remotest subcellars of his consciousness, with 50 layers of falsehood covering it. His wife, by endless and dogmatic iteration, has convinced him that he proposed to her, and then she has put a clincher upon the action by machiavellian appeals to his vanity—the weak spot in all men. As a result, he is profoundly astonished when the actual facts are unearthed, and not only astonished but also pained and apologetic.

However, as women grow bolder, this ancient superstition tends to lose some of its old power. The modern suffragette disdains the petty chicaneries of the woman of yesteryear. On the one hand, she tracks down her victim in the open and proposes to him without any effort at concealment, and on the other hand, she boasts of it later on. Her own vanity is too great to permit her any disingenuous playing up to the horrendous male's. Thus the suffrage agitation adds one more to the debts that civilization owes it. It makes women more honest than they used to be and forces men to imitate them. This change must be regarded with sentiments of approbation by every venerator of the true, the good and the beautiful. [13 July 1914]

WOMEN WHO SMOKE

The *Evening Sunpaper's* thinly disguised defense of smoking by women, printed as an editorial article on Tuesday, seems to have escaped the notice of the rev. sanhedrin of baltimoralists. At all events, no roar against it has gone up from sanctified tracheæ. Can it be that Baltimore is so steeped in carnality that the advocacy of one more sin, however horrendous, passes without comment? If so, then the need of Dr. Sunday's ministrations is indeed made manifest, and the sooner he begins his exorcism of the local devils the better. Say what you will against Sodom and Gomorrah, there is at least no evidence that the ladies of those sinks of iniquity smoked cigarettes, nor do we hear of any such lascivious habit being recommended by the contemporary gazettes.

The spread of smoking among women is a phenomenon that has long given disquiet to the more austere and forward-looking division of moralists, of whom I have the honor to be one. Ten years ago the woman smoker was very rare, and usually somewhat dubious. If she was not actually a lady of levantine levity, she was at least one who monkeyed fatuously with the razor-edged blades of impropriety. But today the habit is so widespread that the unthinking may be almost excused for assuming that it has become respectable. On all sides one finds women smoking: it begins to seem almost as natural for them to light the little coffin-nails after dinner as for men to light cigars. Worse, they have ceased to effect the ænemic "ladies" cigarettes of yesterday, and now puff the regular brands. Still worse, not a few of them have begun to smoke pipes, and even cigars, in the seclusion of their boudoirs.

For this change, so disturbing to the moral mind, I put the blame—or lay the credit, if you will—upon feminism, that most insidious of all the uplifts. Women, striking off their old shackles, grow intelligent, and growing intelligent, they cease to regard the taboos which formerly set them off from men. The double standard of morality shows signs of Cheyne-Stokes breathing[10] and begins to pick at the coverlet. There are women today who smoke incessantly; there are women who drink cocktails; there are women who ride astride; there are women who go into politics; there are women horse doctors, saloon-keepers, newspaper editors, constables, white slave traders, surgeons, pastors, even soldiers; there are women who swear like pirates.

This last accomplishment is even more recent than smoking. I remember well when two estimable ladies of Baltimore shocked me almost out of my boots by asking me to teach them the rudiments of profanity. This was five or six years ago, and, as I say, I was dumbfounded by the request. But after much embarrassment I managed to explain to them the principles of the science, and one of them, at least, showed a great deal of native talent. How they are getting on today, I don't know; I haven't examined them for a long while. But the comforts that one gets out of a discreet and reasonable use of the staccato damn are so agreeable that it is almost impossible to stop, once one has begun. The heroin habit is no more ingratiating, and no more difficult to put away.

But what I started out to do was not to discourse on swearing, but to call attention to the *Evening Sunpaper's* astonishing apologia for smoking by women. It is surely a significant sign of the times, and one sufficient to fill the most light-headed with apprehension, that a journal professedly devoted to the promotion of virtue at the domestic hearth should give over its columns to any such propaganda. That way madness lies—madness and the decay of the republic. If we are to be saved from the fate of Ninevah, Babylon and Zion City, Ill., it is renunciation that must save us and not indulgence. The ideal before us is a nation in which no citizen, whether male or female, shall ever dally for a moment with the abhorrent machines and devices of happiness. Women must stop smoking and swearing, just as men must stop boozing and poker-playing, or the devil will presently have us in his inexorable meshes.

However, who is actually surprised—I mean by the *Evening Sunpaper's* betrayal of virtue? Is its pretense to rectitude, after all, more than a thin and revolting effort at deception? If it is so all-fired moral, then why does it employ me to fill this space daily with paralogical floutings of the sanctified men who sweat and suffer that all of us may be saved? Myself intensely moral, I certainly do not approach that business with anything resembling enthusiasm. If I had my free choice, I'd much prefer to preach an arctic and unyielding asceticism. And yet, taking advantage of the necessities of a man with a wife and eight children, the *Evening Sunpaper* forces me to hold to evil courses, and so betray my natural righteousness. Is it any wonder that a tear of self-pity slides down my nose? Is it any wonder that I snuffle? [12 February 1915]

VI

THE BANE OF RELIGION

RELIGION AND POLITICS

THOSE GAY YOUNG preachers who plan to launch an Ecclesiastical Wilson League[1] are playing with fireworks of a peculiarly dangerous kind. The American people, I believe, are not hospitable to politics from the pulpit. If this republic has any intelligible purpose at all, it is the purpose of opposing and stopping that sort of interference. In the present campaign, with smoldering religious animosities lying just beneath the surface, the scheme now under way is particularly perilous. No good can come of it.

Preachers, of course, have a right to their political views, but it does not follow that they have a right to become politicians. When they dedicate their lives to religion they give over many of the common rights of ordinary men, the while they take on rare and valuable privileges. One of those forfeited rights, I believe, is that of playing politics. Politics is a dirty business. It is inevitably and eternally contaminating. No man can touch it and not carry away his smear. As a profession it ranks with saloon-keeping and bookmaking. As a diversion it ranks with poker and cornet playing.

Preachers had better keep out of it. Let them vote as they please. Let them even, as private citizens, solicit the votes of their friends. But let them beware of going into active politics, *as* preachers. The public does not want to hear their political views in that capacity. Their training does not give them any appreciable fitness for judging politicians. Their opinions about the tariff, public expenditures and the trusts are no weightier than the opinions of other men. All the more danger, then, when they seek to give those opinions the false force of their ecclesiastical authority. All the more peril when they try to capitalize their good repute. [5 October 1912]

The Hon. Charles F. Hogue, wiskinski for the Wilson Clergy Contribution Fund, to the clergymen of Baltimore:

> The Christian Church * * * the Master's injunction. * * *
> Christian laws and Christian principles * * * men of Christian
> character * * * a clear call to the Church * * * our God's supreme
> purpose * * * the kingdom of God * * * opportunities for the
> Church * * * do battle in God's and His people's name * * * the
> Church's mission * * * our chosen Master * * *

And a lot more of that sort of soft and soothing stuff. The candidacy of the Hon. Woodrow Wilson, it appears, has the direct approval of the Most High. The man who votes for him will perform an act of exalted piety. The man who contributes to his campaign fund will help establish the Kingdom of God on earth. Woodrow is the modern Moses. He is an archangel battling with devils. All persons opposed to him are limbs and emissaries of Satan.

Could anything be more ridiculous? Could anything make the Wilson cause more ridiculous? As a matter of fact, there is no issue of piety in this campaign, nor even any issue of common morality. All of the candidates, including the Socialist, agree enthusiastically that virtue must prevail. All promise, faithfully and apparently sincerely, to protect the good against the bad. All give their solemn ratification, not only to the Ten Commandments, but also to a vast and miscellaneous host of deputy and sub-commandments. If there be any rule of morality that they do *not* indorse, unanimously and with sobs, it is only because they have never heard of it.

No, beloved, Woodrow has no monopoly of the piety now on tap, of the piety now drenching the country like a cataract of buttermilk. Every time he takes a hack at Sin, Theodore matches it with a complete laparotomy. Every time he re-enacts the Beatitudes, Theodore sets his calliope to playing "Onward, Christian Soldiers." And meanwhile, the Hon. William Howard Taft sings every hymn that is lined out and recites every Golden Text, and pledges his sacred honor to murder every little devil that bobs up between March 4, 1913, and March 4, 1917. Such unanimity, perhaps, was never before witnessed in the world. Such a wholesale ratification of the true, the good and the beautiful is unprecedented in profane history.

But what, then, is the issue in this campaign? If the three principal candidates are all agreed that virtue must triumph, that it is wicked to steal, that the tyrant deserves the knout, that graft must be put down, in what way do they stand apart? The answer is simple enough. Woodrow is against Theodore and William because he himself wants to be President. Theodore is against William and Woodrow for exactly the same reason. And William is ditto for the ditto ditto. Compared to this issue, no other issue is worth stating. It is the master issue of the campaign, as it is of all campaigns. And in order to prevail, the three candidates are prepared to whoop vociferously for any morality, however diaphanous and dubious, which seems to have votes behind it.

Here, perhaps, I may be doing injustice to one of the three—the Hon. William Howard Taft, to wit. So far as I know, he is the only one who has had courage enough to speak out against theories apparently held by large numbers of people. He alone gives his platform metes and bounds. But even so, it is not recorded that he scorns piety or questions morality. Like Theodore and Woodrow, he is magnificently in favor of the Ten Commandments, and not only the Ten Commandments, but also the Code of Hammurabi, the Rule of St. Benedict, the Memorabilia of Socrates, the Declaration of Independence, the Longer and Shorter Catechisms, and the bound volumes of the International Sunday-school Lessons. Angels could do no more.

Wherefore, and by reason of which, it seems to me that the Hon. Mr. Hogue has a hard task before him if he would establish a Messianic character for Woodrow. Woodrow, I dare say, is a decent fellow, an honest man of the second dimension, the sort of genial busybody who spreads intelligently the ideas of his betters, a person of indubitable integrity. But that he has anything whatever to do with "our God's supreme purpose," or that it is any part of "the Master's injunction" to vote for him, or that he makes "a clear call to the Church"—all this I doubt with a great, grave doubt. And, what is more, I believe that any effort to defend so preposterous and impertinent a proposition is bound to make many persons lawf ha-ha and to put the cross-marks of many other persons in trans-Wilsonic columns. [8 October 1912]

THE SUNDAY LAW

Down at Back river, on Sabbath evenings, the bar is wide open, but the dancing pavilion is dark. In brief, liquor selling on Sunday, which is specifically forbidden by law, is permitted by the county police, but dancing on Sunday, which is only indirectly forbidden, is prohibited. A quaint and humorous code of morals!

But halt! Standing upon the bluff at Hollywood, one sees to the westward the ghostly lights of Baltimore town, and there, too, a quaint and humorous code of morals is enforced by the police. In Baltimore the man who would presume, on a Sunday, to give a public performance of "Hamlet" or "Das Rheingold" or the Fifth Symphony would be dragged to jail as a common rogue—and yet the 200 disorderly houses of the town are open 168 hours a week, and it is precisely on Sunday evening, next to Saturday evening, that they enjoy their greatest prosperity.

Here is a point that the professional virtuosi of virtue apparently overlook. Their frenzy is for the appearance: they let the substance go. In laying the ghost of evil they foster evil itself. Against Sunday baseball they set their faces—and yet it must be plain to any sane man that Sunday baseball would keep thousands away from the second-rate suburban resorts, where no man may take his ease unless he pays a heavy rent to the bar. Against Sunday dancing they howl in horror—and yet it must be plain that the young man who takes his girl to a dance on Sunday night, even if it be above a livery stable, is measurably better off than the young man who is driven, by sheer ennui, to seek Sabbath divertisement in the tenderloin.

Attacked by reason, the professional moralists almost always seek safety behind the breastworks of piety. That is to say, they maintain that Sunday was ordained for churchgoing and that laws permitting merrymaking on the day would empty the churches. To this, of course, many obvious answers are possible. In the first place, it is ridiculous to maintain that that purely theoretical man who is driven to church in desperation, simply because no other and more attractive diversion offers, is appreciably benefited by his attendance. And in the second place, it must be admitted, even by the most earnest, that the whole of Sunday cannot be spent in church. The morning service consumes, let us say, two hours and the evening service an hour. That makes three hours. But the average man is awake 16 hours out of the 24. What is he to do during the remaining 13?

As a matter of fact, it is highly probable that a more civilized Sunday would encourage rather than discourage churchgoing. Our present barbarous laws, by prohibiting all rational amusements within the city limits, drive thousands out of town on every fair Sunday in summer. I should say that fully 10,000 Baltimoreans go to the fishing shores along the Patapsco and its branches every Sunday from May to October, and that 15,000 more spend the day at the suburban parks or in playing baseball or watching baseball games elsewhere over the border.

These folk make a day of it. They go out early in the morning and they remain until dark or later. Here are 25,000 potential churchgoers driven out of town every Sunday. Many of them, I admit, are not of the stuff of which churchmen are made—but if they were within reach it might be possible, nevertheless, to attract them. As it is, they are lost entirely.

The truth is that the argument that a reasonable and humane relaxation of the blue laws would ruin the churches is not supported by the probabilities. I speak, of course, of a reasonable relaxation, and not of a total wiping-out. It is undeniable that if a burlesque theatre were opened next door to each church in the city, and both were wide open all day Sunday, the burlesque theatre would do much harm to the church and to decency. But nobody advocates any such absurdity. All that the most impatient reformer asks is that the people, when they are not at church, be permitted to amuse themselves decently and in order and without breaking any law.

In Germany and France the theatres and summer gardens are open on Sunday—but not during church hours. That arrangement seems to work admirably. The people go to church in the morning and amuse themselves in the afternoon. I once tried to get into a church in Munich on a Sunday morning. It was the hour of high mass and the church was crowded to the doors. That afternoon I tried to get into a hall wherein a big Munich orchestra, led by some great conductor from Vienna, was giving a concert. It, too, was crowded to the doors.

The real objection to reasonable Sunday laws, in truth, is not that they are inimical to religion, for they are not, but that they are distasteful to those persons who hold that Sunday should be devoted entirely to meditation and self-torture. I know men—honest, earnest, estimable men—who so believe, and who exhibit their belief in their acts. But most of us, unluckily, are incapable of such sustained and arduous goodness. We insist that innocent merriment is not sinful—that a man must have some fun in his hours of ease—that it makes a better man of him—that Sunday afternoon is the best time for such relaxation—that, to thousands of hard-working men, it is the only time available.

We do not object to the asceticism of our more staid brothers, but we do say that they must not ask us to follow them when we think them wrong. Virtue, once it grows militant and tyrannical, tends to become a vice. It is perfectly possible, indeed, to go upon a debauch of goodness. The man who harasses and tortures his fellow-men in the name of morality is upon just such a debauch. It is not an excuse for him to say that no intent to do evil is in his acts, just as it is not an excuse for a drunkard to say that, when he beat his wife, his one thought was to make her respect him. The apple is the true test of the apple tree. Blue laws which send prosperity to the river resort, the disorderly house and the side-entrance saloon are certainly not laws that rise superior to all honest criticism. [1 June 1911]

A LETTER FROM SATAN

Office of

THE GENERAL MANAGER.

HELL, DECEMBER 12TH, 1911.

The Hon. H. L. Mencken, care The Evening Sunpaper, Baltimore, Md.:

My Dear Henry—Your letter of yesterday, inclosing the clippings from the Sunpaper, reached me this morning. My very best thanks for it. Needless to say, I am delighted to hear that Baltimore is to have another campaign for the enforcement of the Blue Laws, particularly since this one is supported by many gentlemen of undoubted probity and large influence, and so promises to be more or less successful. If you can manage, without attracting attention, to slip in a subscription for me, I shall promptly forward my check to cover it. Better credit it to "Cash" or "A. B. C." and make it about $10. If it's larger, it will cause too much gossip. I trust to your discretion in this delicate matter.

As you well know, I have long viewed with alarm the growing liberality of the Baltimore Sabbath, and if that alarm has been selfish, I can at least plead that it has also been very sincere. In particular, the Sunday concerts at Druid Hill Park, on Sunday afternoons in summer, have given me uneasiness. They seem to attract, year after year, larger and larger crowds. Well, the withdrawal of those crowds from what one may call the normal sedentary debaucheries of a Baltimore Sunday makes serious inroads into my business, and so I am against it.

I send 20 of my best inspectors to Druid Hill whenever the band plays on Sunday, but they seldom come back with any reports worth entering on my books. Five or six hundred young jackasses caught smoking cigarettes, a few score caught kissing their best girls behind oak trees—and that's about all. The business doesn't pay me. In self-defense I have had to make a rule excluding all cigarette smokers until they have done their 20,000 boxes, and all calf-love osculators, no matter what their records. I can't afford to have the notion get around that going to Hell is child's play.

I have always feared that these Sunday concerts in summer might pave the way for Sunday "sacred" concerts in winter—i. e., for vaudeville shows disguised as concerts. The Police Board, I have reason to suspect, has been in favor of such an extension. It authorized the concert to raise funds for the Fifth Regiment's frolic in Atlanta—a frolic, by the way, regarding which I have received interesting reports—and it has lately authorized a number of other concerts, under the auspices of various pseudo-charitable organizations. That sort of thing, as you well know, might easily get beyond bounds, and do a lot of damage to my business. Therefore, I rejoice to see a strong organization formed to combat it.

What I really want, of course, is the old-time Baltimore Sunday, with everything tightly closed save the side-door saloons and disorderly houses. It is in such places that I really do trade, and so I am opposed to everything that will lessen their patronage. In that category I reckon Sunday concerts, Sunday golf, Sunday walks in the country, Sunday card parties, Sunday trolley rides, Sunday moving-picture shows, Sunday theatres, Sunday organ recitals at the Peabody,[2] the Sunday opening of the art galleries and libraries, the Sunday sale of soda water and candy, and the damnable custom of reading novels on Sunday, so eloquently denounced by one of the orators at the recent McCoy Hall meeting, as I see in the Sunpaper.

Such things must and shall be stopped, if Baltimore is to keep up its old representation in Hell. I look back to the last virulent enforcement of the Blue Laws, 10 or 11 years ago, with a sentimental longing for an encore. At that time, as you know, for you were a reporter then and had your eye on the town, the Baltimore Sabbath kept my inspectors busy and gave me unmixed delight. All decent forms of amusement were rigorously prohibited by the constabulary. Candy stores and soda fountains were ruthlessly raided. The delicatessen dealers of East Baltimore street were pinched by the score. Even the sale of Sunday newspapers was forbidden. As for giving a concert or a dance on Sunday, it was unthinkable.

Well, the result was enormous prosperity for the side-door saloons and disorderly houses. The former were packed from dawn to dark; the latter were so prosperous that they multiplied enoromously. The two together offered the only visible hospitality to strangers in the city. What is more, they offered the only visible public entertainment to resident young men. It was a poor Sunday, in those days, when I didn't gobble a couple of hundred recruits. Drunkards were being manufactured faster than I could put down their names. The police, busy with their chase of soda clerks, delicatessen dealers and newsboys, had no time to devote to the Red Light district, and so the red lights burned brightly. I grow mushily sentimental whenever I think of it. *Eheu fugaces!*[3]

But don't get the notion that I am a pessimist, a croaker! Far from it! The truth is that my business in Baltimore, even in the face of the park concerts and other such scandalous inventions, has always been good. My inspectors all know that the place to hunt for trade is in a moral town. Well, Baltimore is a moral town. The Baltimore Sunday, for all the efforts of the Sabbath-breakers, is still beautifully depressing. And the consequence is that the good old custom of getting drunk every Saturday night and of sleeping all day Sunday still flourishes in your midst. Every Sunday morning, when I go over the weekly souse reports, I notice the name of

Baltimore over and over again. Once, out of curiosity, I had my chief clerk tabulute the reports for one Saturday night. They showed 37,750 drunks in Baltimore alone, not counting in Highlandstown, Woodberry or Sparrows Point. Not so bad, you must admit.

Room remains, however, for improvement. The thing to do is to stamp out all competition. Those Sunday organ recitals at the Peabody give me constant uneasiness. In the first place, they attract a lot of people who might otherwise spend Sunday reading novels, playing poker or beating their children, and, in the second place, they pave the way for Sunday orchestral concerts. From Sunday orchestral concerts, kind fates, deliver me! I frankly fear them. Imagine a band playing in each of Baltimore's 17 theatres every Sunday afternoon and evening! No more solitary boozing in hotel rooms! No more crowding into side-door bars! No more gay doings under the red lights! I shiver whenever I think of it!

Well, my letter grows overlong, and so I must chop it off. In closing, my dear Henry, I sincerely hope that you will do whatever you can to help the proposed enforcement of the Blue Laws.

Meanwhile, my best wishes for your health and prosperity, and my regards to all the boys.

Faithfully yours,

NICHOLAS SATAN.

Dict. N. S.—M. R.
[13 December 1911]

PROHIBITION, CHRISTIANITY, AND ISLAM

The Rev. Dr. Carlton D. Harris, editor of the Baltimore *Southern Methodist*, continues to xanthiate his estimable gazette with vague and sophistical attacks upon my theological talents, in particular upon my theory that prohibition is not a Christian doctrine, but a Mohammedan one, and that the Hon. William H. Anderson, in consequence, is one of the noblest old Moslems that ever garroted a Giaour. In his current issue, for example, he essays to dispose of this theory in two ways—first, by trying to show that there are direct prohibitions of alcohol in the Bible, and secondly, by arguing that the Anti-Saloon League, a supposedly Christian body, is not actually opposed to it, but merely seeks "the destruction of the legalized saloon."

The discerning will notice a plain contradiction in these two arguments, but let it pass. I take up the second first, and quote from the learned Doctor:

> The Anti Saloon League *does not* stand for the prohibition
> of alcohol. * * * In the second section of * * * the prohibition
> resolutions delivered to Congress by the Anti-Saloon Committee
> of One Thousand December 10, 1913, *provision is made for*
> *Congress to manufacture alcoholic liquors for necessary purposes.* The
> section reads: "Congress shall have power to provide for the
> manufacture, sale, importation and transportation of intoxicating
> liquors for sacramental, medicinal, mechanical, pharmaceutical or
> scientific purposes, or [for] free use in the arts. * * *"

The italics are the Doctor's own. Obviously, there is nothing but nonsense here. If the Anti-Saloon League is really willing to allow the manufacture and sale of "intoxicating liquors" for "medicinal purposes," then all it asks is that the present trade of the licensed kaifs be turned over to the drug store (as has actually happened in all the so-called "dry" States), and, therefore, it cannot call itself a foe of alcohol. To that extent, one may grant at once, it is wholly Christian. But if, as Dr. Harris hints, it is genuinely (though secretly) opposed to the sale and use of alcohol as a beverage, even in drug stores, then it is wholly Mohammedan, or, at least, not Christian, for there is not a single direct prohibition of alcohol, whether as a medicine or as a beverage, in the whole New Testament, and on the only occasions when it is mentioned at all in the historical books the sacred writers refer to it with either tacit or undisguised approbation. For example, in John, ii, 1–11; in Matthew, ix, 17; in Mark, ii, 22, and 1 Timothy, v, 23.

Thus it appears that the Anti-Saloon League, viewed from one angle, is Christian but wet, and from another angle, dry but Mohammedan. I am inclined to take the latter view of it, not because of anything that Dr. Harris says, but because of what the league itself says. Turn to the pamphlet upon "The Effect of Alcoholic Drinks Upon the Human Mind and Body," prepared by the burlesque "Scientific Temperance Federation," of Boston, for the use of the league in Baltimore, and you will find what I allude to. On page 18 there is the unqualified statement that "alcohol *increases* liability to sickness"—obviously, an insuperable objection in a "medicine." And on page 30 you will find a whole paragraph cunningly devised to leave the impression upon the immature mind that alcohol has no medicinal virtue whatever, and that "all physicians" have lost their old faith in it. Certainly an organization which holds such unfavorable notions of the "medicinal" value of alcohol cannot actually favor its use as a medicine! For the purposes of deceiving Congress it may *say* that it does, just as the Hon. William H. Anderson says that he loves saloonkeepers and wishes them well, but certainly it is too much to ask reasonable men to *believe* that it does.

So much for the Rev. Dr. Harris' attempt to make it out that the Anti-Saloon League is not opposed to alcohol as such, but merely to the licensed kaif, and that, in consequence, it is a Christian organization. In the matter of his second, or, rather, his first argument—*i. e.,* that there are direct prohibitions of alcohol in the Bible—I am in consultation with fellow-theologians of special gifts, and shall present my answer in due course. In the meantime, I may as well inform him that all of these experts, after a preliminary examination of the three texts he quotes, are of the tentative opinion that there is nothing in them forbidding a decent and reasonable consumption of fermented beverages. [24 January 1914]

The Rev. Dr. Carlton D. Harris, in the Baltimore *Southern Methodist:*

> Quoting Scripture does not make a man a theologian, for the devil has quoted it as accurately as some others. But he has never *interpreted* it correctly.

By one of the jokes of fate, this is precisely the objection to Dr. Harris himself, for in the very same article he quotes Holy Writ with the most laudable accuracy—and then proceeds to misinterpret it with hideous zeal. His quotations are as follows:

> Wine is a mocker, strong drink is raging: and whosoever is deceived thereby is not wise.—*Proverbs, xx, 1.*

> Look not thou upon the wine when it is red, when it giveth its color in the cup, when it moveth itself aright. At the last

it biteth like a serpent, and stingeth like an adder.—*Proverbs, xxiii, 31, 32.*

Woe unto him that giveth his neighbor drink, that puttest thy bottle to him, that maketh him drunken also.—*Habakkuk, ii, 15.*

These extracts from the Old Testament are brought forward by Dr. Harris in support of his contention that the use of alcoholic beverages, *as* beverages, is inherently immoral and unchristian, and hence should be prohibited. But a brief inspection of them is sufficient to show that no such implication is actually in them, nor can it be read into them by rabbinism without straining the meaning of words beyond all endurance. The first of the three, interpreted in the light of reason, becomes no more than a piece of sound and homely advice to drinkers—a primeval copy-book maxim. What it says is simply this: that the man who uses alcohol as a beverage must be careful to use it moderately and prudently. In its milder forms—*e. g.,* wine, cider, ale, beer—it is apt to deceive the novice or the fool into overestimating his capacity; in its stronger forms—*e. g.,* forty-rod, peppermint extract, apple-jack, the whole repertoire of "dry" town drinks—it is downright dangerous. "Whosoever is deceived thereby is not wise."

But note clearly that the charge brought against "whosoever is deceived thereby" is *not* that he is immoral or irreligious, *but merely that he is not wise.* Nothing could more plainly indicate the abysmal difference between the Christian view of alcohol and the Moslem (or Anti-Saloon Leg)[4] view. All that Christianity says here (or anywhere else, for that matter) is that the man who uses it must exercise due care—in the common phrase, must mind his p's and q's. But what Mohammedanism says of it is that the man who uses it is guilty of mortal sin, an enormously different thing. On the one hand, we have a mere rule of conduct, a piece of good advice, a paternal warning; on the other hand, we have an unqualified commandment and coupled with it a threat of eternal punishment. It is my contention that the Anti-Saloon Leg joins the Moslem side as against the Christian side, and that it is therefore a Moslem and not a Christian organization, its pharisaical protestations to the contrary notwithstanding.

Dr. Harris' second text is even less a prohibition of drinking in general than his first. A reference to the context shows plainly that the thing aimed at is not the use of alcohol at all, but the violation of the Seventh Commandment. It is the argument of Solomon—*cf.* verses 27–30, immediately preceding—that excessive drinking, involving a loss of prudent inhibitions, conduces to such violations—a thing obvious to all observant persons. But Solomon clearly refers (verse 30) to "they that tarry *long* at the wine, they that go to seek *mixed* wine," and not at all to those that confine their drinking to moderate amounts and stop short before their faculties are in any sense obscured. In point of fact, there is not a single word in Proverbs xxiii which may be reasonably interpreted as an attack upon alcoholic beverages in general. Even verse 31 plainly distinguishes between *red* wine—probably the most potent of the varieties known to the ancient Jews—and other wines.

As for Dr. Harris' third text, its failure to sustain his case must be patent to all. The thing prohibited here is not the use of alroholic beverages *per se,* but their use for the purpose of debauching and degrading the innocent. The last clause of the verse, discreetly suppressed by Dr. Harris, makes this as plain as day. The scoundrel who plies his neighbor with drink in order to strip him and make a shame of him—"that thou mayest look on their nakedness"—this scoundrel is righteously denounced by Habakkuk. But there is not a line in the whole chapter arguing that the use of wine in moderation, as the Jews used it then and as they still use it to this day, is an offense worthy of prophetic denunciation. Even toward the actual drunkard Habakkuk's attitude is that of pity (i, 10) and not that of reproach. All his ire is reserved for the man who seduces another to drink for the deliberate purpose of making a spectacle of him.

So much for Dr. Harris' extraordinarily inept and disingenuous perversions of the plain letter of the Old Testament. The texts that he quotes are not new. They have been studied and expounded by Jewish rabbis of the highest scholarship for centuries, and so it may be reasonably presumed that their exact meaning is now known. As a delicate indication of that exact meaning, let me call Dr. Harris' attention to the fact that not a single Jewish rabbi in the United States today is a prohibitionist, and that the moderate use of alcoholic beverages, both for ritualistic and for social purposes, is still well-nigh universal among the Jews, as it was on Habakkuk's day and in Solomon's. [30 January 1914]

THE SIGNIFICANCE OF BILLY SUNDAY

That pseudonymous *littérateur* who filled this space a week or two ago with proofs that the Rev. Dr. Billy Sunday and I are spiritual *corpsbrüder* might have saved his parts of speech for some more useful and difficult enterprise. The facts he sought to establish by salvos of beautiful words I admit without argument. More, I have been admitting them openly for at least two years past. In point of fact, I am the original Billy Sunday man in Baltimore, for I can prove by the evidence of no less a dignitary than the Hon. William H. Anderson, LL. B., that it was I who first suggested bringing the rev. dr. to our fair and sinful city, to shake up the whited sepulchres of pulpit and pew and flood the tablernacle with tears and mirth. Do I seem to boast? Well, remember that I have cause. It is no small thing to save Sunday-school superintendents from hell, even vicariously.

The Rev. Dr. Sunday is by no means the naif roughneck that jealous preachers and imaginative newspaper reporters make him. On the contrary, he is a man of sound education and considerable culture, and if he tries to put the dogmas that he preaches into language comprehensible to the vulgar, then he does no more than Martin Luther did before him. The difference between Bill and the average whooping cleric of our own vicinage is simply that Bill is a far more intelligent and hence a far more efficient whooper. In brief, he does very well what the rest of them do very badly, and his superiority is all the excuse he needs. Expertness is a virtue in itself. It is creditable to a man to do anything well, no matter how dubious that thing may be. It is discreditable to a man to do anything badly, no matter how pious that thing may be. This is why I venture to admire Rabelais, Dr. Welch, Beethoven, the Hon. D. Harry and General von Kluck. And this is why I venerate the Hon. Dr. Sunday.

In our theological principles, of course, we are scarcely at one, though we come together on our common distrust of Sunday-school superintendents, elders, deacons and other such *blattidae*[5] of the house of God. Bill, I take it, is a true believer in the singular balderdash that he spouts from his battlements, and would rejoice sincerely if the New Puritanism were to prevail in the world. I, on the contrary, regard that New Puritanism with sentiments of the utmost aversion, and hope and believe that it will eventually blow up and bust. But, by a favorite trick of the gods, Bill's campaign of slush and piffle gives satisfaction to both of us, for Bill himself sees only the long lines of frauds and numskulls who march up to be greased with his holy oils, whereas I see only the long lines of more intelligent folk—not quite so long, perhaps, but vastly more significant—who flee from the tabernacle in the grip of a spiritual *mal de mer,* and are so cured forever of all those hatreds and hallucinations which come together in what I have here called the New Puritanism, but which its advocates usually denominate by the simpler term of "true Christianity."

This style of "true Christianity," improperly so called, is an emanation from the decaying corpse of evangelical Protestantism. The old gladiator is dead! May his soul R. I. P.! He fought a good fight in his day and Christendom will never forget him, but he took to dissipation in his old age and so the salts of calcium began to accumulate in the walls of his arteries and finally he went down with a crash. Today he lies pathetically upon the field of battle, and lay and clerical saphrophytes concern themselves with his tissues. The result is a vast emission of gases, chiefly high in sulphur. One sniffs unmentionable things. The air grows rank. All that remains is to apply a match to the inflammable mixture. The result on the one hand will be a clearing of the polluted atmosphere, so that self-respecting men can once more breathe it. And on the other hand it will be the decent cremation of the cadaver.

Meanwhile, let us hold our noses and be patient. Such august proceedings are not put through in a day. It will take years, perhaps many of them, to achieve the business. But possibly not so many as some persons think. Bad boys are already scratching matches upon the seats of their pants. The Rev. Dr. Sunday is one such. The long-haired whoopers of the pulpit who imitate him feebly are others—and they are not few. Every time such a gentleman of God rises up in his pulpit (or breaks into the newspapers) to make an ass of himself (which is almost every day) he helps the benign process along. He "converts" and "saves" a boob, perhaps, but he loses a man. Eftsoon the New Puritanism (or, if you choose, "the only true Christianity") will be represented by a rabble of button-heads led by a General Staff of whirling dervishes. And then, to go back to the old figure, the time will be ripe for the torch, the flash and the Sis! Boom! Ah!

Wherefore and by reason of which, Hoch, Bill! For the life of me I can't see why there should be any opposition to him. The Puritans should welcome him ardently, for he will offer them a far more thrilling and satisfactory orgy than their customary pastors have ever been able to provide, even with copious lay help. And the anti-Puritans should hail him as one who reduces Puritanism to a screaming absurdity. He is the ideal perunist. He is himself, in fact, a perfect peruna, for he both pleases the patient and encourages the undertaker. The first effect of his jehad will be to fill the churches that employ him with a horde of inflamed sub-men, for it is the easiest thing in the world (for a man as intelligent as Bill) to light up the emotions of such anthropoid creatures. And the second effect will be to empty them of all men of intelligence. The net result, perhaps, will be a numerical gain in membership—but what a gain! How joyously and confidently the anti-Puritan sharpshooters will tackle that huge, stupid mob when the great day comes!

To sum up, gents, the joke is on the Puritans. Let us not revile them, but snicker over them gently. We can afford to bide our time. They are not only putting the rollers under that strange amalgam of hate and imbecility which passes among them for Christianity; they are also, and more importantly, putting the rollers under democracy. A nation dominated by the vicious and unintelligent is just as unhealthy as a religion believed in by the vicious and unintelligent. There will be a blood-letting anon, and after the blood-letting there will come a revision of axioms, a transvaluation of values. The truth is mighty and shall prevail. Puritanism is a biological fiction, the negation of truth. It cannot last much longer. [1 February 1915]

Several kind friends, one of them fair, write in to protest against the essay upon the Rev. Dr. Billy Sunday and his holy works that I printed in this place last Monday, the chief of their objections being that it was, in effect, an attack upon evangelical Christianity, and hence a naughty and contumacious thing, and probably *ultra vires*. With the highest imaginable respect and affection, Pish, my dears! I have no present quarrel with evangelical Christianity *per se*, nor shall I have one so long as any part of it retains any appreciable measure of sense and decency, but if the Puritans who now feed upon its vitals ever succeed in their pious work of making it wholly unsightly and obscene, I shall take a crack at it with the utmost ease and elegance, and what is more, with a very clear conscience. What is still more, the business will expose me to no risk, for though the Puritans themselves will make faces at me, I shall have the hearty approval and support of that minority of reflective men which offers the only body of opinion worth a moment's attention.

The old ban upon religious discussion in the United States is fast lifting. The Puritans themselves, by carrying their grotesque theological ideas into politics, have thrown away the immunity that they formerly enjoyed. Their clergy now take to the stump with the utmost assiduity, hectoring candidates, inventing platforms and demanding all sorts of nonsensical reforms, and whether they like it or not they must submit to the cross-examination which goes with that sort of sport. What they say, in substance, is that the Word of God is behind their vast yearning to defame and punish their fellow-men. Well, here is a proposition that is open to debate, and any citizen is perfectly free to take part in that debate. And being so free, he is also free to examine the Puritan theology underlying the Puritan politics, and to denounce it openly when he finds wormholes in it.

In brief, the Puritans are no longer favored by the one-sided rules that once gave them a free license to damn all their opponents to hell, but protected them against excoriations in return. The growing sense of their intellectual irresponsibility, and particularly of the ignorance and chicanery of their clergy, has knocked out all the old presumptions in favor of the sacerdotal rabble-rouser. A clergyman of today, at least in the Unted States, is no longer assumed to be a holy man *ex officio*, and hence inviolable. He may be so in point of fact, and if he is, and gives evidence of it by his words and acts, he is accorded the highest attention and respect. But if, on the contrary, he is seen plainly to be nothing more than a hollow-pated jackass, a roaring mountebank, a tin-horn press-agent, then his cloth does not protect him in the slightest from the disgust and antipathy that all decent men feel for such muckers of the house of God.

The only difference between the Rev. Dr. Billy Sunday and the lesser dervishes who imitate his matter and his style is that Bill is far more expert than they are, and hence far more successful. Such methods as he uses are by no means his private inventions. On the contrary, they go back to the Great Awakening of 1734–44, and were early brought to a high state of efficiency by the star performers at negro camp-meetings.

Certain white churches, in the last few generations, have reborrowed them from the blackamoors, and ever and anon they are tried out on a large scale. Their net effect has invariably been to fill the tabernacle with the feeble-minded and empty it of the intelligent. A few more campaigns of the Sam Jones-John Alexander Dowie-Billy Sunday type, and Puritanism will be reduced automatically to the intellectual level of obeahism, palmistry and Christian Science. That is to say, a belief in it will be confined wholly to the stupid, the ignorant and the dotty.

Such persons, true enough, constitute an overwhelming majority of the population of the United States, and so Puritanism will probably continue to make a show of strength for a good while, and its pathological aberrations (often distinctly sexual, and of much interest to the psychopathic specialist) will continue to be embodied in the laws of the land. But soon or late the civilized minority will begin to see clearly the grave danger of allowing the ideas and ideals of the mob, whether political, politico-theological or purely theological, to prevail in the republic, and the result will be a concerted effort to put the mob back in its place. That effort, I believe, will be attended by bloodshed, as was the effort to put down the enfranchised negro mob-man in the South, but it will succeed just as surely. The notion that the majority is irresistible, that its mere size protects it from overthrow, is just as absurd as the notion that the majority is wise. A few genuinely intelligent men, once they have rid themselves of the pruderies of mob morality, will be sufficient to do the business.

Meanwhile, the more plainly Puritanism can be hooked up with admitted extravagance and imbecility—that is, the more plainly it can be demonstrated that the mental processes of its great prophets and gladiators are identical, or nearly identical to those of cornfield negroes—the more quickly will come that alliance of thoughtful men which must eventually end it. It is the capital merit of Dr. Sunday that he makes this identity almost unescapable. Once he has "saved" a city, its understanding of the theories for which he stands is vastly more accurate than before. The anthropoid majority of such a city may continue whooping for him for a space, and for the puerile pulpiteers who attempt feeble imitations of him, but the minority has been definitely aligned against all that sort of balderdash, and awakened to the menace it presents to civilized, orderly, efficient and honest government.

Here in Baltimore the rev. gentleman will do a lot of good. The trouble among us at present is that our more intelligent men greatly underestimate the horsepower of the New Puritanism. Knowing it to be nonsensical, they assume fatuously that it can be disregarded. The result is that they hang back from opposition, leaving the brunt of the losing fight to a few volunteers and mercenaries. But when they see that sweating, frothing, baying mob sweep up like a tidal wave around the Sunday pulpit, and when they see the Legislature stampeded by the uproar and the statute books stuffed with a mass of new and super-idiotic "moral" legislation—when this spectacle unfolds before them they will begin to understand at last that the time is fast approaching for the counter-attack, and that it had better be directed, not at superficial symptoms, but at the outworn fallacy at the bottom of all mob-rule. It is an insult to God for the mob-man to have any theology. It is an offense against civilization for him to have any politics. His business in the world is not to think, but to obey. [5 February 1915]

THE NEW CHRISTIANITY

The Rev. Dr. Charles Fiske's protest against the jamming through of a Prohibition resolution at the recent Episcopal convention is sound and apposite, but it is highly unlikely that it will bear any profitable fruit. Don Carlos has seized the throne. The de facto chorepiscopus, Mgr. Cochran, is in full control of the situation, and whatever his deficiencies otherwise, he is at least enough of a politician to make effective use of his advantage. Besides, there is his bar'l. It is no light thing to attack and overthrow a gentleman whose ardor for good works is supported by so much capacity and willingness to finance them. Therefore, I renew specifically the prophecy I have hitherto made in general terms. The worst is yet to come. The declaration for the bald principle of prohibition will be followed anon by a declaration for snoutery in all its lovely forms. The Protestant Episcopal Church in Maryland is climbing up the Golden Stair.

Meanwhile, the neutral in theology may pleasantly divert himself by observing the way that so-called Christianity in the United States is heading. Theoretically a means to salvation and a way of life, it is fast becoming a sort of glorified mixture of rough-house and kaffeeklatsch. The ideal Christian of today, as the current mullahs depict him, is not one who turns upon his brother a smiling and forgiving face, but one who pursues his brother with clubs and artillery. His piety is measured, not by the degree of his own goodness, not by the extent of his approximation to Christ-like patience and forbearance and to loving kindness, but by the eagerness and ferocity with which he pursues the erring, and by his skill at uncovering and denouncing new classes and orders of sinners, and by the number of them that he gets into jail. The public hangmen is the archetype of this new pseudo-Christian. He is always ready for his relentless office, and it is always performed in the name of God.

Obviously, if it be the first duty of the neo-Christian to punish the sins of his brother, it is his second duty to search them out with the utmost assiduity. In other words, the right to punish involves the right to examine. This explains the enthusiasm of neo-Christianity for sumptuary and inquisitorial laws. The supply of victims must be kept up; there must be a constant feeding of the fires; hell must never shut down for lack of orders. And if, perchance, the number of violators of existing laws shows a falling off, then new laws must be made to rope in fresh recruits. The ideal will be reached when every man, woman and child is unceasingly guilty—when the number of punishable sins coincides exactly with the number of normal human acts. This ideal will be attained in the United States about the year 1925. There is yet a good distance to go, but we are on our way.

But what of the neo-Christians themselves? Who is to hang the hangmen? Tush, tush, dear hearts! Do not ask foolish questions. Neo-Christianity offers every man his free choice: he may elect to be a sinner and so lay himself open to pursuit by the saints, or he may elect to be a saint and so win his own salvation by rowelling and butchering sinners. If he makes the latter choice, his post-mortem security is taken care of. All he has to do, to insure it absolutely, is to crack the head of some other sinner every time he himself commits a sin. Thus the benign system of cracks and balances. Does the devil tempt you, O saint? Are you inspired, by that lost collar-button, to a vagrom damn? Do you sneak a glance at a pretty girl? Is there sherry in the pumpkin pie? Then hasten forthwith to the nearest boarding house and accuse the startled landlady of keeping a brothel, or rush to the Police Board with the news that this or that cop missed Sunday-school last Sunday, or denounce the Hon. Spot Mitchell for allowing working girls to be murdered by the dozen in his beer-garden,[6] or accuse the Germans of hanging Belgians for the wearing of the green.

Such is the technique of the new Christianity. Its fundamental principle is that salvation is to be won in one way only, and that is by exposing and punishing the other fellow. It has been purged of all mysticism, of all inner experience, of all renunciations. It has become a system of jurisprudence, straight-forward and clear. It posits the law as the measure of all things, including even souls. It is stern, inflexible, infallible, inexorable, merciless. What Christ himself thought of it you may find by consulting the Book of Matthew, Chapter XXIII, beginning at the thirteenth verse.[7] [12 November 1914]

VII

THE VICE CRUSADE 1

General Notes

THE FOLLY OF CRUSADERS

From "Temperance Torchlights," by Matilda Erickson, quoting one Dr. Brewer, given name unknown:

> It can be asserted with great certainty that the boy who begins to use cigarettes at 10 will drink beer and whisky at 14, take morphine at 25 and spend the rest of his lifetime alternating between cocaine, spirits and opium.

Why is it that all moral crusades, practically without exception, run to just such childish absurdities? I am a constant and copious reader of all sorts of moral tracts, and in every one of them I find the same wild tendency, to overstatement, the same grave piling up of false and ridiculous charges. The prohibitionists, not content with submitting the actual evidence against alcohol, invent testimony so obviously bogus that it must inevitably make them more foes than friends. The anti-vivisectionists, as I have more than once shown, deliberately garble evidence to suit their holy purpose. The anti-vaccinationists manufacture libels with such amazing fluency that mendacity, with them, may be said to constitute a fine art. And all other breeds of militant moralists are as bad—whether their butt be the cigarette, divorce, carnivorism, Sabbath-breaking, dancing, poker-playing, polygamy or the stage. It is difficult, indeed, to find a single performer who can stick to the plain facts for 10 minutes running.

In part, of course, this habitual exaggeration may be considered a natural symptom of enthusiasm. Any man, when he goes crusading, is apt to lay it on a bit thick. But there is a distinct difference between the mere virulization of actual facts and the deliberate invention of "facts" that are not facts at all. That difference the moralist does not sense. He comes, after a while, to hold that any charge or statement which helps his cause, however widely it may depart from the plain truth, is sound and fair. His constant tendency is to convert suspicions into direct allegations, theories (and even hypotheses) into laws, possibilities into probabilities, and then into downright certainties.

How are we to account for this? How is it that persons who profess such an ardor for morality are, at bottom, so incurably unmoral? Perhaps, the answer is that morality, in itself, is in sharp antagonism to common honesty—that its one effort is to make true, everywhere and at all times, something that is true only in part and on occasion. The moralist is simply a man who is blind to that fact—one who knows nothing about morality. If he did, he would know that the particular moralic axiom he advocates is as heavy with exceptions as a rule of German grammar—and so he would lose his eagerness to advocate it. In brief, a certain ignorance, or rather stupidity, is essential to the business of moral crusading, and that stupidity reveals itself as an utter inability to distinguish between what is true and what isn't true.

The anti-tobacco crusaders show this failing to full flower. The actual facts in support of their jehad are very few and not very impressive. It has been proved that the use of tobacco by the young has a tendency to interfere with normal growth; it has been proved again that the excessive use of tobacco by adults works various minor injuries; and it has been proved, finally, that the use of tobacco, in various conditions of disease, tends to retard and even to prevent recovery. Beyond that the evidence does not go. The British Royal Commission appointed to investigate the subject found that the use of tobacco in moderate quantities by a healthy adult had no effect whatever, one way or the other. It did no good and it did no harm. Not the slightest physical difference, organic or functional, separated smokers from non-smokers.

Do the anti-tobacco fanatics present these facts and have done with it? Of course they do not. On the contrary they proceed to the manufacture of an enormous stock of additional "facts," without the slightest regard for the truth. Because it is notorious that all bad boys smoke cigarettes—just as they turn naturally to all other forbidden things—the argument is launched that cigarette-smoking causes their badness. Because it so happens that most (though by no means all) drinkers also smoke, it is solemnly charged that smoking is the cause of drinking. And because an occasional drinker—perhaps one out of every 20,000—proceeds from alcohol to worse drugs, tobacco is denounced as the advance agent of cocaine and opium.

Such are the laws of logic as applied to the vice of moral crusading. Just as there is a transcendental logic for the private use of psychic researchers, whereby 40 frauds make a fact, so there is a moral logic for the use of moralists, whereby the plain denial of a fact becomes itself a fact. It was by this logic, no doubt, that Dr. Bailey arrived at this axiom that all smokers are moral lepers, and it was by this logic that Dr. Brewer attained to his certainty that the boy who smokes cigarettes at 10 will be a sot at 14 and a drug-fiend at 25. [8 September 1911]

HAVELOCK ELLIS ON VICE

With moral crusades going on for our benefit in each of three busy rings, not to mention the animal tent and the elevated stage, most Baltimoreans, I believe, will find much nourishing and suggestive stuff in Havelock Ellis's new book, "The Task of Social Hygiene," just issued by the Houghton-Mifflin Company. In particular, I recommend the work to local optionists, vice crusaders and toreadors of the Blue Laws, for it is precisely of such earnest folks that Mr. Ellis discourses most copiously and profoundly. But I give them fair warning that he is against them, and so I doubt that they will ever read him, for it is a peculiarity of all that class of men that they don't want to hear any evidence in rebuttal.

But, meanwhile, there are thousands of other persons whose convictions, however they may lean, are less rigid and perfect, and it is to these waverers that the book will bring most instruction and, I hope, most conviction. The essential thesis of Mr. Ellis, as you will find it in his chapter on "Immorality and the Law," is that any legal interference with the personal habits of man, no matter how well-intended, is unwise and pernicious, and that its ultimate effect must inevitably be a flouting of the law. So long as our peasant and barroom lawmakers confine themselves to prohibiting acts which involve the direct injury of one human being by another they are on safe ground and public opinion is with them, but once they begin to prohibit acts which involve only the self-injury of the individual, or the mutual injury of *participes crimi-nis,* then they interfere with that freedom which every man values as his life, and the greater the penalty they lay upon the offender the less it will ever be inflicted.

At the moment it is the war upon the social evil that most inflames the vulgar in Baltimore, and so it is of special interest to hear Mr. Ellis upon the subject. What he has to say of it chiefly takes the form of a warning that the ecstatic campaign of repression, far from affording a remedy, actually makes the evil worse, and must, in the long run, result in putting it altogether out of bounds. In brief, it essays to stamp out by law something that can never be stamped out so long as civilization remains what it is, and thus it leads from one hypocrisy to another, and the end must be, as in the case of Sunday laws, a *reductio ad absurdum* of the whole enterprise, or, as in the case of laws against gambling, a general and ineradicable corruption of the police.

Here Mr. Ellis is at one with Mayor Gaynor of New York, Mayor Harrison of Chicago, Director of Public Safety Porter of Philadelphia,[1] Frederic C. Howe, director of the New York People's Institute, and nearly all other serious and unemotional students of the problem. The trouble with our American police, he points out, is not that they are inherently more corrupt than the police of other countries, but that they are constantly under greater temptation to corruption. The laws that they are called upon to enforce are, in many cases, laws wholly unenforceable, and so it is no wonder that they occasionally strike compromises with chronic violators. In direct proportion as repression is honestly attempted, the profits of successful evasion increase. And in direct proportion as those profits increase the burden of temptation upon the police increases. No wonder they sometimes fall. If a policeman getting $20 a week has on his post a gambling house or a clandestine brothel which can afford to pay him $100 a week for looking the other way, he must indeed be an exceptional man to resist the temptation forever.

The European policeman, as a general thing, is under no such fire. In the matter of prostitution, for example, he is never given the hopeless task of stamping it out altogether. All he is expected to do is to regulate it according to a program determined by his superiors, and that program, as a rule, not only frankly admits the existence of the thing, but also gives assent to its necessity. Even in London, which the local vice crusaders are so fond of citing as a city free from disorderly houses, prostitution itself is by no means prohibited. On the contrary, it is elaborately regulated and segregated, and thus, having a lawful outlet and being relieved of hounding and blackmail, it removes itself voluntarily from prohibited areas and offers no appreciable nuisance to the general population.

But let us go from London to New York. What do we find? We find a hypocritical law prohibiting prostitution altogether—and a general dispersion of the evil from end to end of the city. The London policeman, meeting a woman in Piccadilly at night, does not arrest her on the spot, for the English law forbids him to touch her unless she actually breaks the peace. But the New York policeman, meeting a woman on Broadway, is in duty bound to arrest her if she speaks to a man. No wonder his self-respect is gradually undermined by that inquisitorial and unsavory job! No wonder his decent disinclination to do his work is transformed into a crooked disinclination! No wonder he passes from a rebel into a grafter!

But this is precisely the system that the vice crusaders would introduce in Baltimore. As things stand today, there is no reason why the more orderly prostitute should pay any graft to the police, and as a matter of fact, she pays none. The law, of course, commands him to drive her out, but a wise interpretation of the law, approved by our judges, forbids him to molest her so long as she obeys rules laid down extralegally for her behavior. But if those rules were abandoned and the law itself were enforced, in all its mediæval stupidity and cruelty, she would have to fight for life with the weapons of the outlaw. That is to say, she would have to seek to elude the police, and, failing that, to bribe them. And the net result would be a police force corrupted and disgraced, and a condition 10 times worse than that we have now.

All these arguments, however, I have rehearsed before. What I ask you to do today is to get Mr. Ellis' book and read carefully his chapter on "Immorality and the Law." There you will find the ripe conclusions of a man who has devoted all of his life to the study of the complex and disheartening problem. He is, by universal consent, the greatest living authority upon the subject, as he is upon several associated subjects, and I fancy that not even a vice crusader would venture to question either his knowledge or his good faith. It seems to me a significant thing that a man so well equipped should stand squarely against practically every proposition advanced by our volunteer rescuers, and I think that, while the matter is under public discussion, it is the clear duty of every thoughtful Baltimorean to give him attention. [22 November 1912]

VICE AND THE LAW

The Hon. Charles J. Bonaparte, arising in his accustomed place this day, reads me a severe lecture upon the mortal sin of law-breaking, and pleads eloquently that full faith and credit be given to each and every enactment of the Legislature of Maryland, however boozy the Legislature and however idiotic the enactment. A virtuous doctrine, surely, and I am certainly not one to dispute its theoretical soundness. But the trouble with this wicked old world is that it forces us to make constant compromises between theoretical virtue and bitter necessity, and this happens no less in the domain of public duty than in the domain of private conduct. In brief, we must often choose between our duty to the fools who rule us and our duty to ourselves, and if we sometimes perform the latter rather than the former, that is only saying that our patriotism is benignantly mitigated by a globule or two of common sense.

In the case now before the house, the Legislature of Maryland has adorned the statute books with a law which is as completely unenforceable, in the last analysis, as an act forbidding the smoking of cigarettes. If any attempt were made to put it into full effect tomorrow the only result would be a public scandal. Most of the persons who now violate it would continue to violate it, and many of them would try to buy immunity from the police. In the face of such temptation, I daresay, not a few policemen would fall, and so we would have the condition of affairs that now exists in New York, and, in less measure, in Chicago and other cities.

But fortunately for the public security, the men charged with the enforcement of such laws—*i. e.,* the members of the Police Board and of the Supreme Bench of Baltimore City—are usually men of considerable experience in the world, and in consequence, men with small respect for platitudes. And so, at the risk of being denounced by purists, they strike a sagacious compromise. That is to say, they enforce to the letter those parts of the law which happen to be enforceable, and let the other parts go unenforced. The result, I freely admit and they themselves admit, is a lamentable defiance of the Legislature of Maryland, that camorra of Solomons. But the excuse for the said defiance is that the theoretical damage it does is vastly less costly than the actual damage that would be done by any attempt at complete compliance. In brief, it is better for a few judges to risk their hides and souls by overlooking one form of lawbreaking than it would be for them to practice virtue and so bring about a larger and worse form of lawbreaking.

The Hon. Mr. Bonaparte, however, sticks to his sterling silver guns. Any violation of the law, no matter how benign, brings before him an appalling vision of the decay of the republic. And why? Because he regards every law as an expression of the people's will. The fact that it is on the statute books proves to him that the people who are charged with obeying it, or a majority of them, are actually in favor of it. And so, any violation of it appears as the contumacious act of a lewd and lawless minority, and that act heralds the end of free government among us.

Unluckily for the Hon. Mr. Bonaparte, an appeal to the facts fails to give support to his fears and his prophecies. The laws which govern the people of Baltimore are not actually made by the people of Baltimore, nor even by a majority of them, but by a majority of the politicians assembled at Annapolis, and two-thirds of those politicians are countrymen who have little more understanding of the needs and hazards of life in a large city than so many Esquimaux or Zulus. In all their law-making they proceed constantly upon the fallacy that what is workable in the country is also workable in the city, that what the farmers want the city folks will think nice, and so the statutes they pass, particularly in the department of morals, are often hopelessly and ineradicably stupid and ridiculous.

Because a farmer, for example, is physically tired on Sunday and wants nothing more than a chance to snooze by daylight, they pass a

Sunday law forbidding any exercise or other recreation by the city man, who is commonly tied to a desk or work-bench all week and wants activity beyond all things on Sunday. And because it is an easy matter in a small and isolated community, where strangers are few and every resident knows all other residents, to track down and tar and feather any frail lady who strays in, they assume that the benevolent enterprise is equally simple in a large city, where strangers are innumerable and most persons do not even know their next-door neighbors. Thus they saddle us with Blue Laws, and thus we are afflicted by the vain effort to enforce such laws.

It is true enough, of course, that city members of the Legislature often vote for such laws, or at any rate, that they make no effort to repeal them. But that is only saying that the average city legislator, if he is not an unspeakable ass, is very apt to be a coward—that he is afraid to carry out the wishes of the majority *pro* because of the superior violence of the minority *con*—that he would rather be wrong than submit to attack by moralists, the most cruel and uncharitable of all men. As Havelock Ellis says:

> No public man likes to take up a position which his enemies may interpret as favorable to vice and probably due to an anxiety to secure legal opportunities for his own enjoyment of vice. This consideration especially applies to professional politicians. A member of Parliament, who must cultivate an immaculately pure reputation, feels that he is also bound to record by his vote how anxious he is to suppress other people's immorality. Thus the Philistine and the hypocrite join hands with the simple-minded idealist. Very few are left to point out that, however desirable it is to prevent immorality, that end can never be obtained by law.[2]

And if this is true of the English member of Parliament, who is commonly an educated and self-respecting man, how much more true it must be of the Maryland legislator, who is commonly no more than a man-like member of the *pediculidæ!* Are we to obey this clown when he sets us tasks that are not only evil and repulsive, but also downright impossible? I think not. Let the Court of Appeals decide all it pleases that his acts, however asinine, are legal. Most sane men knew it before the Court of Appeals ever decided it. But most sane men also know that a vicious and unrepealable law is dangerous to peace and security, and that the only way to maintain civilized government is to draw its teeth.

Let the Hon. Mr. Bonaparte have done with his platitudes and get to the truth. He must know, as all of us know, that if we suffer acutely from the social evil in Baltimore, that suffering is chiefly caused, not so much by the prostitute herself as by her political brothers and fellow-craftsmen at Annapolis. [23 November 1912]

THE CRUSADING SPIRIT

Consider, beloved, the fruits and usufructs of crusading. The vice crusaders start their mad chase of the scarlet woman—and send her scurrying North, East, South and West. For years and years we have kept her in a gilded cage, out of sight of the chemically pure. But now she is to be turned loose in our midst, to favor us all with her genial neighborliness. The crusaders have gained an affecting victory—but who is ass enough to say that vice has been overthrown?

Consider, again, the suffragettes, and how their whooping has hurt their cause. Two or three years ago, as the result of a long campaign of education and persuasion, that cause was prospering in Baltimore. Hundreds of Baltimoreans were beginning to believe in its justice. The newspapers, once indifferent and then jeering, were coming over to affability. Shrewd politicians were doing their best to look pleasant. But then appeared the crusading spirit, and with it came extravagance and posturing, sophomoric panacea-preaching and shrill scolding. What is the net result? The net result is that the suffrage jehad is once more a nuisance and a joke.

'Twas ever thus from childhood's happy hour. The crusader is always a clumsy and unintelligent reformer. Now and then, true enough, the cause he advocates may seem to prosper, but not often does its apparent prosperity work the genuine good of humanity. The local optionists, I dare say, have made fully as many drunkards as they have saved; the private jug, in the last analysis, is a good deal more dangerous than the public bar. And in the same way the vice crusaders of the world have done far more actual damage than the white-slave traders.[3] And the shrieking sisters, not to be forgotten, have chiefly "helped" their cause by solidifying and enraging the opposition.

But all this, of course, doesn't daunt the crusaders. Even in the presence of overwhelming evidence that they are defeating the very ends they profess to serve their ardor does not diminish. And why should it? The truth is that they care nothing about results: what they are interested in is the chase. In brief, they are sportsmen first and reformers afterward. Their one hot desire is to pursue somebody, to injure somebody, to lock up somebody, to ruin somebody. A state of universal grace is not the aim of their safari, but merely its excuse. Nothing would distress them more than complete and permanent success, just as nothing would distress a lion-hunter more than the unanimous massacre of all the lions in the world.

Fortunately enough, no such complete and permanent scccess is possible. Even if the various crusaders who now raise such a din were to stamp out all the sinners in Baltimore tomorrow, a new crop would appear the day after. The sinner, in other words, is not a distinct species of man, as the lion is a distinct species of animal, but merely an ordinary man turned sinful. All of us are born virtuous. You never hear of a babe in arms breaking the Sabbath or playing poker or being heaved out of a kaif. But the storms of life gradually weaken this pristine purity of character, and so it is difficult to find a grown man who is wholly without sin. Even accepting the unsupported and dubious evidence of those who claim to be, it is probable that not more than one-half of one per cent. of the adult males of civilization can qualify.

Therefore, crusading has an unlimited and inexhaustible supply of shining marks. If all the lions in creation were murdered tomorrow, lion-hunting would cease forthwith, for it is impossible for a rabbit to grow into a lion; but if all the sinners of today were led to the gallows, the new crop would begin to blossom in 10 days, and within a year it would overrun the earth. Thus crusading is the most satisfactory of all forms of the chase, for it never diminishes the supply of game. If it were not for that fact, we should no doubt hear demands for some sort of artificial protection. That is to say, the more intelligent crusaders would ask for game laws, just as the duck-hunters have asked for them, and there would be open and closed seasons for the pursuit of saloonkeepers, tobacco-chewers, dope fiends, wine-bibbers, Sabbath-breakers, poker-players, crap-shooters, theatregoers and the ladies of vermilion.

However, all this is no reason for holding crusaders in horror. The most I say against them is that they are human, that they enjoy the same diversions which all of us enjoy, that they are moved by the same sporting instinct which urges the small boy (already a hardened sinner at 5 years!) to hunt the vagrant tomcat with air-rifle and cobblestone. I myself, though far above the average in virtue, have the same weakness. That is to say, I enjoy baiting crusaders almost as much as crusaders enjoy baiting bartenders. It is amusing to see them blush and hear them bark: they make good game because they *are* game. At any moment they are likely to turn on one and bite one in the ankle—and such a bite may cost one one's leg. Four ones are four, which is one more than a crowd.

But what would you? Who would give a hoot for a perfectly safe pastime? Or for a perfectly safe life? Those theologians who argue against hell are sad and bilious fellows, and no wonder! If they had their way, they would rob this earthly existence of its hazard, and hence of its joy. The self-respecting man seeks a risk; he wants a run for his money. Which brings us, by a circuitous route, to the one indubitable virtue of crusaders; they promote deviltry by exaggerating its dangers. The local optionist, depicting the villainies of the Rum Demon in words that make the eyes bulge and the flesh crawl, challenges the courage of every young man. To retreat in the presence of so horrendous a foe would be womanish and disgusting. And so the majority of us take a nip now and then, if only to show that we are not caitiffs. [27 December 1912]

THE ADVISABILITY OF VIRTUE

How I am quoted by the furious and inaccurate *Suffrage News:*

> The red light district is a necessity.

Have I ever said anything of the sort, or even thought anything of the sort? Of course, I haven't. The red light district is no more a necessity than Bright's disease or astigmatism. It is perfectly possible to imagine a city without it. But it would be very difficult, I believe, to *find* a city without it—in some form or other, gathered in a clot or spread out thin. In brief, it seems to be inevitable, but a thing that is inevitable need not be a necessity.

What the inflammatory suffragettes try to convict me of is the crime of arguing that vice has a use—*i. e.,* that it is necessary to the well-being of man. But I fall into no such error. I am too accomplished a hypocrite to be so ensnared. All I say of vice is that it exists, and that no human war upon it has ever disposed of it, or even appreciably diminished it. The one thing we can hope to do with it is to ameliorate its effects. But what the moralizing suffragettes propose to do is to intensify its effects. That is to say, they propose to add imprisonment, mutilation and hanging to the already terrible consequences of the particular vice they denounce. I regret that I cannot follow them. I find it impossible to view human weakness and suffering with so jaundiced an eye.

The loose use of the word "necessity" is one of the chronic crimes of these singularly savage girls. In the same issue of the *Suffrage News* I find the following:

> What the vice crusaders mean to teach the public * * * is the *necessity* of clean, moral lives. * * *

More balderdash. As a matter of fact, morality is no more a necessity than immorality. A man may dabble in a score of vices for years and years, and yet suffer no noticeable damage thereby, and die eventually to the sweet sound of public lamentation. It has been done over and over again. If the suffragettes question it, I shall be glad to give them names and dates—of course, in the strictest confidence.

But this possibility, I grant freely, does not attain to the virulence of a probability. That is to say, the chances are always against the experimenter. He may get through in safety, true enough, but then again he may come to sudden grief and suffer irreparable damage. Persons who perform upon the B flat cornet are sometimes murdered by the neighbors; tobacco chewers have been known to choke to death at minstrel shows or on the judicial bench. Which brings us to the real truth about virtue: if it is not necessary, it is at least *advisable*. The good man, taking one thing with another, is more to be envied than the bad man. He is more apt to win public respect while he lives, and his mind is likely to be more tranquil when he faces death. In brief, he makes a more prudent bargain with life than a bad man, for he gets more than he gives up.

But prudence, it must be obvious, is not a universal human trait, nor even a common one. The average man is an ass. The average woman has little more sense than the average trained sea lion. Of all the men I know, not one is without gross and incredible follies. I myself play the fool at least 10 times a day, and sometimes as much as 100 times. No honest man, reviewing his day at bedtime, can help feeling like a donkey. The result is that all sorts of vices, some of them mild enough, but others very dangerous, flourish in the world. [1 January 1913]

THE METHODS OF THE VICE CRUSADERS

The ferocity with which the current vice crusade is being carried on by its gladiators is no proof of an unusual lack of charity in those gentlemen, but merely one more indication of the eternal incompatibility between militant morality and the fairness commonly prevailing among civilized white men. Upon all other subjects under the sun, including even faith, it is perfectly possible for two men to meet in friendly dispute, but once a moral issue is raised they tackle one another in the fashion of hyenas, and the loser reaches the coroner in the form of an attenuated emulsion. Hence the peculiar fascination of the combat.

And yet it must be plain to everyone who has given any thought to the matter that the rules of morality are far from fixed—that there is often room for a legitimate difference of opinion regarding the rightness or wrongness of a given action. Even the Decalogue, by long odds the most satisfactory code of morality ever subscribed to by man, is not complete. The whole science of morals, indeed, is no more than an organized attempt to improve it, by adding to it on the one hand, by interpreting and developing it on the other hand, and by explaining it away, as it were, on the third hand. Many actions which we now regard with virtuous indignation—stuffing the ballot box, going naked, using cocaine and bribing legislators, for example—are not forbidden by the Decalogue. And some things that we regard with great toleration— the invention and propagation of new and preposterous religions, for example—seem to be specifically prohibited by it.

Even when the Decalogue appears to retain its old validity unchallenged there is commonly a violent difference of opinion as to the exact extent and bearing of its prohibitions. Consider, for example, the sin forbidden by the Seventh Commandment.[4] The language of the Commandment is admirably direct and unequivocal, and yet the Public General Laws of Maryland presume to qualify it. That is to say, they provide that only a violation involving an innocent third person shall be considered a violation at all. In case no third person is involved, directly or indirectly, no punishment is provided. And this same qualification appears in the penal codes of almost all the other States of Christendom. To that extent, at least, the Decalogue has been amended.

It is precisely in this field—the debatable ground of amendment and interpretation—that the most sanguinary moral battles are fought. On the general validity of the Commandments practically all civilized white men are agreed, but on the subtler questions of meaning and implication it is difficult to find two thoughtful men who agree entirely. And when we pass from meanings and come to means—when we begin to consider how given interpretations are to be enforced—then we plunge into a battle so vociferous and so fierce that the wars of Zulus and tomcats pale beside it.

The present mad whooping and bellowing over the so-called social evil affords an admirable example. So far as I can make out, all the sluggers engaged are agreed upon two points: (*a*) That the Seventh Commandment is sound in principle and (*b*) that it is impossible wholly to enforce it in practice. But upon the remaining points, (*c*) how far it may be enforced and (*d*) by what means, there is an irreconcilable difference of opinion, and that difference of opinion reveals itself in the form of a desperate combat with clubs, poisons, cobblestones and curses, in which all the other Commandments are torn to flinders.

I say all, but I mean especially the Ninth: "Thou shalt not bear false witness against thy neighbor."[5] It has been violated constantly since the beginning of the controversy, and not only constantly, but also lightly, nonchalantly, with no thought of sin. The last offender was an eminent clergyman—a gentleman whose piety and good faith I haven't the slightest reason to doubt. And yet he violated it openly and shamelessly, and when I called him to book he made his escape by violating it again! And I myself, in the midst of my virtuous denunciation of him, adorned the tale by violating it as boldly!

Such is moral endeavor. Such is the combat of the pure. Two-thirds of the energy of the vice crusaders is devoted to attacking the men who do not believe in their panacea—not by argument, mind you, but by threats, slanders and reviling. For example, every police official who has presumed to stand against them has had to meet the abominable charge that he shares the profits of prostitutes. And they have made a systematic and relentless effort to scare off all other critics and opponents,

either by direct attack or by back-alley appeals to supporters and superiors. I could a tale unfold—but not yet, not yet!

The joke is, of course, that the persons who draw the fire and ire
of the vice crusaders are all quite as earnest and intelligent as they are
themselves, and quite as eager to reduce vice to a mininium. The dispute, in brief, is not over principles, but over means. And it is precisely
that dispute over means which provokes the worst passions of militant moralists. The Anti-Saloon League, pledged to one scheme for
reducing drunkenness, spends four-fifths of its energies bawling against
the advocates of other schemes. The Lord's Day Alliance, setting up
as infallible its own narrow, pecksniffian definition of a decent Sunday,
condemns the adherents of all other definitions to the stake.

And so on and so on. Once the issue is joined over the means of
enforcing a moral law the law itself is forgotten. The warring armies
of its supporters attack each other more savagely than they attack the
common foe. And the result, of course, is the prosperity of that common foe. Vice crusading makes vice romantic and prosperous. Local
option multiplies bootleggers and promotes drunkenness. The Lord's
Day campaign turns thousands of decent citizens into determined and
habitual lawbreakers. [17 February 1913]

VULGARITY AND INDECENCY

Just what the Police Board will accomplish by its current campaign
against vulgar dances is one of the things that only the future can reveal.
That it has the power, at least physically, to repress any frisk or wriggle
that outrages its sense of propriety is plain enough, but that this forc-
ible, and perhaps extra-legal repression will bring about any genuine
improvement in the morals of the vulgar is not so certain. The cell,
as Haeckel once observed, does not act, it *reacts*—and this is true, in
particular, of those cells which afford pasturage to the moral sense. The
surest way to make a given action attractive, indeed, is to prohibit it and
put a penalty upon it. Almost the only charm about smoking cigarettes,
to the average healthy boy, lies in the assurance that he will be whaled
if he is caught doing it. He smokes, in other words, because he wants to
be brave, and not at all because his system craves a narcotic.

In the present case, the problem is complicated by a considerable
uncertainty as to the Police Board's powers under the law. It has a clear

right, of course, to proceed against open violations of public decency, and a clear duty to exercise that right, but it is not always easy to show that a vulgar act is actually indecent. Here, in fact, we enter the trackless Bad Lands of personal morality, and those Bad Lands are peopled by many fearsome lions and tigers ever eager to spring upon the unwary. What seems an intolerable indecency to the professional moralist, with his raw nerves and hypersensitive nose, may appear to be only harmless clowning to the lowly sinner. It is certainly a dangerous thing to set up policemen as judges in such delicate matters. Their proper business is with gross and unmistakable violations of decency. Whenever they attempt to establish more subtle distinctions, they make asses of themselves and bring the laws into ridicule.

Particularly is this the case when they work under the lash of over-trained specialists in immorality. A policeman, as a general thing, is a man of sturdy common sense, and his natural impulse is usually to be honest and fair. But it is easy to corrupt his judgment and even his honesty by threatening his job. It is by this process that politicians make him connive at undoubted violations of the law. And it is by the very same process that professional moralists, with their great talent for bullying, make him take a hand in unlawful and intolerable tyrannies. It seems to me just as bad to have him do the second thing as to have him do the first. In both cases he arrays himself against the very good order he is sworn to uphold.

That vulgar persons are fond of vulgar amusements is not a matter in which the police can have any proper interest. It is not competent for a civilized government to prohibit vulgarity, nor would it accomplish any actual reform if it did. We think of Germany as a police-ridden country, with harsh and inquisitorial laws, but there is no law in Germany prescribing how and when a young donkey shall hug his best girl. If he wants to hug her on the public street, he hugs her there and then, and no one dares interfere with him. He is free to kiss her and chuck her under the chin. He may sit with her on a park bench and put his arm around her. And so in England, in France and elsewhere.

It is only in free America that a Puritanical minority devotes itself savagely to regulating the conduct of the vulgar mass. It is only here that a police captain would dare prescribe the exact manner in which two free agents shall dance. The Germans and other Europeans are just as inhospitable to open indecency as we are, but they are civilized enough to understand that mere vulgarity is not necessarily indecency. They know that poverty and ignorance are not productive of the reserve which we call refinement, and they do not attempt to improve matters by calling its lack a crime.

Let those Baltimoreans who are wholly civilized keep a sharp eye upon this growing passion for browbeating the poor. Let them not forget that the very moralists who now denounce the tango, the growler and the moving picture so violently would go even further if they had the courage. You and I read Rabelais, chuckling with joy; these hyenas of virtue would snatch the book away from us if they dared. We go to see "A Doll's House;" these fellows would ban it if they could. Our women go to the opera with necks and shoulders bare; these snouters would send them to the House of Correction if it were possible. Let us not forget these things.

But is all war upon vulgarity therefore in vain? Not at all. What violence cannot do, good example may accomplish. The average human being is easily led upward; progress is in the blood of the race. Put good music into direct competition with bad music, and good music will always win. Put decency beside hoggishness, and hoggishness will grow ashamed. Let us combat vulgar dancing, if it exists, by providing opportunities for decent dancing. Let us try to give the poor and ignorant cleanly recreations, as we have tried to give them clean water. Let us call off the policeman and go to them as fellow human beings eager to help them upward and tolerant of their weakness and blundering. [22 February 1913]

REFORMERS AS AGITATORS

The learned Maryland *Suffrage News*, in the course of an able editorial in its current issue, defends the suffragettes against my late charge that they are agitators pure and simple, with far more enthusiasm and hydrogen in their souls than common sense. The argument of the *News*, in brief, is that agitators, whatever their failings, are necessary to the progress of the world. They march ahead of the mass, spying out the land, clearing the way, slaying the immemorial dragons. This work requires a degree of faith which few human beings have. It requires, too, mental and physical toughness, disvulnerability to assault and treachery, and a great talent for whooping. An agitator must have the hide of a rhinoceros and the vocal reeds of a calliope.

Let me agree with the *News* in all it says, and even in all it doesn't say. Let me go further, and praise all agitators, and particularly all suffragette agitators, in a voice of brass. They are, without doubt, the true saviors of the world. They are the heralds of progress, the advance agents of the enlightenment. And if, as usually happens, they proceed to the business by making themselves personally obnoxious, if they try to wake up the world by prodding it, cowhiding it, bellowing at it and blowing it up, then their sufficient defense lies in the fact that this is the only workable way to arouse it from its hoggish slumbers. Once their hullabaloo passes the maximum of bearable unpleasantness the world will treat with them in order to get rid of them. And the ensuing compromise—between the hot haste and eagerness of the agitators and the chronic sloth of the world—is what we call progress.

It is by this process, as everyone knows, that every important reform of history has been brought about. For example, the introduction of Christianity. The preaching of the early Christian pastors was extremely disagreeable to the luxurious Romans, and they showed it by setting fire to the pastors. But the preaching kept on, and even increased: ten volunteers took the place of every martyr. By and by the Romans decided that the easiest way to get rid of this disagreeableness was to compromise with it—and the more they negotiated to that end the more they were won over. In the end they became Christians themselves—not Pauline Christians, of course, but compromise Christians who carried over into the new faith many notions and habits of their own. Many of these elements still persist, to the satisfaction of most of us, but to the intense horror of various agitators. The progress of the future, like that of the past, will be made by compromising with these agitators, and with those who object to other doctrines and practices.

So in all other fields of human thought and custom. The essential thing about the agitator is that he is unquenchably obnoxious, that he offends and tortures the public with his yammering, that his agitation finally becomes intolerable, just as the blowing of a steam siren would become intolerable. Then it is that he gains his point, or, at all events, a part of his point. The public offers to compromise with him, not because he has converted it, but simply because he has worn it out. Later on, it may become actually converted—as a matter of practice, it usually is—but at the moment of surrender it is moved almost solely by a desire for peace. It can't stand the whooping a moment longer. It is at the end of its endurance.

But all of this, of course, does not indicate that the agitator is wrong. On the contrary, he is usually partly right—if not in his promise and prediction, then at least in his complaint. Thus it is, for example, with the suffragettes. They may be wrong when they argue that the disfranchisement of women is the cause of war, measles, high taxes and the social evil, and when they argue that the vast majority of men are lewd and soulless scoundrels, but they are right when they argue that women should have the vote. The excuse for their method lies in the fact that the public will never grant their rightness until it has been clubbed into despair by their wrongness—that it will never give them the vote until they have taken away its civilized peace and security. In brief, they must fill it with something resembling terror before ever it will treat with them.

The same excuse justifies the extravagances of most other agitators, including, for example, the vice crusaders and the boozehounds. Considered casually, the campaign of the vice crusaders seems to be wholly unsound and preposterous. They exaggerate undoubted evils beyond all reason, piling on horrors until the eyes pop and the liver turns to water. And they propose remedies so violent and so impracticable that the veriest idiot must laugh at them. But at the bottom of all this mountebankery there is a perfectly valid idea, and that is the idea that the world would be better off if prostitution were abolished, that the thing is evil in itself and the mother and father of innumerable other evils. It is not nearly so bad, of course, as they say it is, but all the same it is bad enough, and no sane man is in favor of it.

So with the boozehounds. When they try to show that all crime and wretchedness are caused by drink, that without it there would be no need for police, that its abolition would stamp out disease, that it is the one curse of man—when they argue thus, they merely make the reflective man snicker. He knows better: it is impossible to convert him to so naif and illogical a doctrine. But beneath all their campmeeting eloquence and bogus statistics there is the undoubted fact that alcohol is injurious to thousands of human beings, that it makes for disorder, that its evils are many and vicious, that its use ought to be strictly regulated.

In brief, they are right at bottom, as the vice crusaders and suffragettes are right at bottom. Their whole error lies in extravagant and donkeyish exaggeration, in telling the truth so violently that it becomes a lie, and not only a lie, but also a nuisance.

But the value of such agitators lies in this very weakness. If they argued in a dignified manner, sticking closely to the facts, no one would listen to them. Their one sure way of attracting attention is by snorting and yelling. If they keep it up long enough, and do it vociferously enough, the noise they make will become intolerable to the public. And then the public, pursuing its immemorial custom, will offer to compromise with them. And the essence of that compromise will be the residuum of sound sense in their illimitable cream puff of bosh. [23 April 1913]

WHAT VICE CRUSADERS ACCOMPLISH

Some earnest moralist, characteristically anonymous, took me to task in the Letter Column the other day in these pained terms:

> Those who have stood for more than a generation for the highest civic righteousness embodied in character, conduct and unstinted public service are not legitimate butts to be sneered at and jeered at by a passing professional jester wagging his fool's cap and jingling his bells.

Sincere words, and thus worthy of a respectful hearing, but unluckily enough, there is a fallacy in them, and that is the fallacy of assuming that the bogus pieties of a self-consecrated archangel are identical with "the highest civic righteousness" and that his eager display of his own virtue constitutes an "unstinted public service." The fact is, of course, that both assumptions are false. The "righteousness" preached by the archangel is commonly not righteousness at all, but merely an inhuman conspiracy against innocence, happiness and joy. And his "public service," nine times out of ten, consists wholly of a diligent endeavor to get honor and publicity for himself.

It seems to me that such men are not public benefactors, as they try to make us believe, but public nuisances. It seems to me that their effort to make large numbers of people do as they say, against the inclination and honest belief of those people, is an outrage upon liberty and a menace to public security. It seems to me that their constant assumption that they are perfect and infallible, that they alone know what is best to be done, that all persons who presume to disagree with them are ignoramuses and scoundrels, that the world will go to the devil unless their pet perunas are rammed down every throat—it seems to me that this assumption is intolerably unsound and idiotic, and that it is the duty of every good citizen to combat it with all his might.

Such men spend a great deal of time boasting about their piety and try to make it appear that their evil enterprise is inspired by a great yearning to save the erring, but I am thoroughly convinced that no such lofty motive is in them. What actually *does* move them, or, at any rate, most of them, is our old friend, the Nietzschean *wille zur macht*—the will to power. In other words, they want to boss and control their fellow-men. They are moral bosses, just as Mr. Mahon is a political boss and Mr. Morgan was a financial boss. They get their thrill out of exercising compulsion. Their aim is not so much to save the sinner as to *compel* the sinner. And so they concentrate their efforts, not upon undoubted evils, but upon things that most men do not regard as evils at all. In other words, they seek out opposition, and get their fun by battering down that opposition.

Thus it was, for example, that a pack of moralists attacked and disposed of the plan that was made three or four years ago for giving Sunday orchestral concerts at the Lyric. This plan was made by honest and decent men, with no desire for gain in them, and they hoped to make their concerts elevating and useful. They made sure of the highest ideals by engaging Mr. Hemberger as conductor. Their aim was to offer the people of Baltimore cheap and civilized entertainment on Sunday afternoons, when four-fifths of the churches are closed and thousands have nothing to do. They thought that they were doing a public service, and they *were* doing a public service.

But their series of concerts got no further than the first. A mob of professional moralists—old practitioners! familiar names!—descended upon them and put them to rout. They were denounced as bitterly as if they had proposed to give a series of burlesque shows. The police were called upon to suppress them. They were threatened with imprisonment if they went on. Imprisonment for giving first-class orchestral concerts on Sunday afternoons—such concerts as are given in every other civilized city in the world: London, Paris, Berlin,

New York, Chicago, St. Louis, even Washington! Imprisonment for giving Beethoven's Fifth Symphony or the "Hallelujah" chorus on the seventh day of the week!

Was this attack an act of morality? Was it even a thing of common decency? I don't think so. On the contrary, it seems to me that the men who made it committed an offense against good order as serious as any ever committed by a Back River saloonkeeper. They struck at the contentment, healthy recreation and sound aspiration of the people. They made it measurably more difficult for the average Baltimorean to get through Sunday in a civilized and cleanly manner. They turned trade into the suburban beer gardens and dance halls. They delivered a blow at the public security by delivering a blow at decent amusement. They did something typical of whooping moralists. They played their evil game according to its evil rules.

With such men, however pious their pretenses, I have no patience. When they pry into the private morals of their fellow-men they commit an offense against that toleration and charity which should prevail between man and man. When they bully the police into enforcing bad and oppressive laws they range themselves with the politicians who try to bully the police into abrogating good laws. They accomplish no permanent good: their schemes never work. The one sure effect of their eternal snouting, posturing and browbeating is to curse the community with enmities and clog the wheels of intelligent progress. They are a dangerous bunch, believe me. [29 April 1913]

VIII

THE VICE CRUSADE 2

Prohibition and Other Panaceas

THE PLEASURES OF ALCOHOL

As is usual in all public discussions in America, the current local option controversy is bringing forth paralogy and false pretenses from both sides. On the one hand, the local optionists argue that all they ask for is freedom for every neighborhood to decide the saloon question for itself, whereas everyone knows that they would oppose bitterly any effort to substitute local option for prohibition in the neighborhoods now dry by legislative fiat. And on the other hand, the foes of local option argue eloquently that the abolition of the saloon in any given ward would plant a crop of blind tigers,[1] whereas every Baltimorean knows that this has not happened in Roland Park, Woodberry and Walbrook, to cite but three examples.

Again, when it comes to discussing the effects of alcohol upon society and the individual, both sides exaggerate shamelessly. On the one hand, the foes of alcohol blame it for 80 per cent. of all diseases, for 85 per cent. of all domestic discord and for 90 per cent. of all crime, and picture a rumless world as a sort of tinsel heaven. On the other hand,

A SATURNALIA OF BUNK

the friends of alcohol undertake the vain task of proving that it is a food, that its effects upon the drinker are beneficial, that it meets a natural need of man.

Both, of course, are wrong. It is not true, as the drys constantly assume, that every man who drinks alcohol is a drunkard, or that, even under the most vicious license system imaginable, any large proportion of sane adults would stand in any danger whatever of so becoming. And it is not true, as the wets constantly assume, that alcohol is necessary to human welfare, or even to human happiness. Thousands of men and women get along without it and are none the worse, just as other thousands consume it and are none the worse.

Any truly honest and intelligible defense of alcohol must be based, first, upon the frank admission that its use is a vice, and secondly, upon the argument that every human being is free to practice that vice if he chooses. An untenable and ridiculous position? Not at all. Once rid yourself of moralistic fustian, once get away from the notion that certain acts are inherently and invariably right and others are inherently and invariably wrong, once put aside all timeworn formulæ and go to the real facts of life, and you will quickly see that a man's right to choose his vices is just as sound as his right to choose his occupation or his dwelling place.

What is a vice? Merely a device for relieving the monotony of existence, for making life more bearable. So long as the consequences of a given vice are chiefly on the credit side, so long as the enjoyment it produces is not outweighed by the injury it does—just so long it may be assumed to be harmless, and even beneficial. Such is the case with the use of alcohol, in the vast majority of cases. The man who drinks himself to death is, after all, very rare, and the chances are that he would go to the devil in some other way if there were no alcohol to the world. The average drinker, the normal drinker, certainly doesn't drink himself to death. He may get an overdose once in a while, but he always stops short of suicide.

But the foes of alcohol argue that even this normal drinker is injured, that his life is appreciably shortened by his vice. Well, suppose it is? Before that argument can have any weight the drys must first prove that mere length of days in itself is desirable. Most intelligent human beings, whether they say so in so many words or not, are scarcely convinced that it is. They believe that a few months, or even a year or two, at the end of life can be well spared—that it is better to enjoy life while it lasts than to drag it out ascetically to the lean and slippered pantaloon. And even the most bitter enemies of alcohol admit that those who drink it enjoy the drinking.

Mere enjoyment, of course, is not happiness. It is not fair to say that a man with four seidels under his chest is happy, in the sense that Balboa on his Darien peak and Washington at Yorktown were happy. But enjoyment, after all, is a pretty fair substitute for genuine happiness, and what is more, it is the best substitute that most human beings ever encounter. Life, to the average man, is a gray day. His soul seldom soars. He is a stranger to ecstasy. Therefore it is a kindness to him to touch the gray, from time to time, with rose and gold, however bogus the dyes. And that is just what alcohol does. It is the cheapest, safest and most convenient of orgiastics. It produces the maximum of glow at the minimum of cost, either to the pocketbook or to the arteries.

But there are horseshoe nails in its mitt! On occasion it kills! Well, well, so it does. But all other agents of joy have the same defect. To brush one's teeth gives true pleasure, but to brush one's teeth 400 times a day would wear them down to the gums and cause death by starvation. And by the same token it is not alcohol itself, but excess in its use, that is dangerous. The normal man does not yield to it: he knows nothing whatever of its alleged tendency to produce an irresistible craving for itself; when he has drunk enough he stops drinking. And as for the man who can't stop, the weak man, the man whose appetites master him, the natural drunkard—as for him, what philosopher will maintain that the world is not benefited by his exit? [11 March 1912]

LIQUOR AND CRIME

And so, the mood of greasing being on me and Christmas being but four days off, I turn to my old friend, the Hon. Satan Anderson, and praise him without restraint. Can you imagine a more wily, a more resourceful, a more devilishly ingenious and pertinacious fellow? He has been murdered at least 40 times, and yet he always bobs up serene and smiling, and with all his lacerations healed overnight. I have myself, on 75 separate occasions, blown up his alleged facts, shot his statistics in the foot, and heaved dead cats through his pathos—and yet he always comes back, he is always ready with fresh sophistries, he never lets go the tail of Demon Rum. Going further, I have sought to seduce him from his madness by tempting him with genuine Muenchener. I have sent barrels of it to his lair in the Towel Building,[2] and have led him past thousands of kaifs when the wind was offshore, and have hidden bottles and seidels and steins of the best brews in every nook and corner of Annapolis, hoping that he would stumble upon them and fall. But no: he keeps the faith. He is bulletproof and factproof, Hofbraeuproof and Pschorrbraeuproof, Spatenbraeuproof and Franziskanerbraeuproof, Salvatorproof and bockproof.

Especially factproof. Consider, for example, this extract from a letter he contributed to yesterday's *Evening Sunpaper:*

> Will the Free Lance answer why it is that the police * * *
> always search the saloons first for men who are wanted for
> holdup or some similar offense, if there is no relation between
> liquor drinking and these things?

Here we have (*a*) a false statement of fact, and (*b*) an erroneous deduction. The truth is, of course, that the police do *not* search the saloons first. What they actually do first is to go to the suspected felon's boarding house and inquire of his landlady if he is in. If she answers yes, they enter at once and proceed to manacle him. If she answers no, they enter anyhow and search all the cupboards. And if they do not find him by this process they go to the houses of his friends, his relatives and his best girl, perhaps in distant cities, and there keep watch. Meanwhile, some other crook, eager to curry favor, usually comes forward with *pianissimo* news of the fugitive's whereabouts, and so, by the exercise of their characteristic sapience, the cops collar him. If that doesn't happen, how do they get him? Well, if that doesn't happen, they seldom get him at all.

But even supposing it were true, as the Hon. Mr. Anderson alleges, that every crook proceeds at haste from the scene of crime to the nearest kaif, what would it prove? So far as I can make out, nothing. A crook naturally desires some refreshment after a successful felony, just as a surgeon desires refreshment after cutting off a leg, or a judge after handing down a long and unintelligible opinion, or a newspaper editor after composing a racy editorial. The surgeon, the judge and the editor go home and drink out of their private jugs, but the poor crook, being, as a rule, a stranger in the city, is forced to use a public kaif. Is this misfortune of his to be held against him? I think not.

But I wander from the point, which is this: that what a man does *after* a given act is obviously not the *cause* of that act. If I get up in the morning and shave myself, it is certainly no proof that shaving makes me sleepy. And if a bridegroom, at the wedding feast, lets his rejoicing augment to the point of inebriety (as so often happens, alas, alas!), is it fair to charge that drunkenness brought him to the altar? I hope not—and even the Hon. Mr. Anderson must agree. Time and time again, fugitive bank cashiers have been found in the bosoms of their Sunday-school classes, eloquently expounding Ephesians iv, 28,[3] but would my learned friend argue thereby that the International Sunday-School Lessons promote embezzlement?

No, my dear sir; you will have a deuce of a time proving that alcohol, that slandered boon, is the cause of crime. The truth is, and every policeman knows it, that crooks as a class are very sober men. When they drink at all it is periodically and as a pleasing recreation; in the heat of professional endeavor they eschew the wine cup. In brief, they are intelligent men. They know when to go to alcohol for its comforts and they know when to avoid its snares. And that knowledge they share with 99 per cent. of all truly civilized white men, including Congressmen, musical composers, City Councilmen, the judiciary and the vast majority of the clergy. [21 December 1912]

WHAT PROHIBITION WOULD MEAN

The renewal of the Hon. William H . Anderson's threats to bring in a prohibition amendment to the State Constitution in case the local option bill is rejected next winter shows how little truth there is in the local optionists' constant allegation that they are in favor of home rule, that they plead only for the inalienable right of every community to decide the liquor question for itself. It is with this claim in their mouths that they tackle all candidates for public affairs. Let a candidate but refuse to indorse the local option bill, and they are full of tartuffian[4] accusations that he is a foe to the fundamental principle of democracy.

But as a matter of fact, they themselves are not in favor of any such principle. The thing they actually are in favor of is the despotic and anti-democratic principle of prohibition. They want to abolish the legal sale of liquor in Maryland, and to introduce in its place that surreptitious sale which now makes a hog-pen of every dry State in the South. In brief, they are typical militant moralists. They put whooping above honest reform, sound above sense. They are in favor of prohibition because it is melodramatic and violent, and not at all because it is effective. They get more joy out of damning the brewers than they would ever get out of making the State dry. That lust to revile and punish which is at the bottom of all other enterprises of militant morality is at the bottom of this one too.

No professed local optionist in Maryland is actually in favor of local option. If you want to test any of them, propose to him that the question of Sunday selling be submitted to the voters in each election district. He will be against it. Or propose to him that the people in the areas now dry by legislative fiat be given a chance to decide the thing for themselves. He will be against it again. No honest enthusiasm for self-government is in him. He has none of that respect for common fairness and square dealing which you will find in most of the men he denounces as scoundrels. He doesn't want to make his fellow-men secure in their rights: his one aim is to take away their rights—and not only the right to drink, but more especially the right to decide about drink, one way or the other, for themselves.

What has the local option fight accomplished in Maryland, after all these years of bitter accusation and abuse? On the one hand, it has made fine pickings for the politicians, it has thrown the saloonkeepers into their hands, it has created and prospered that "liquor ring" of which the local optionists bellow so tragically. And on the other hand, it has stirred up hatreds that will continue to make trouble for a generation to come. It has loosed the worst passions of humanity. It has destroyed that reasonable tolerance and good will which should prevail between man and man, even when they disagree. It has put a premium upon the most hysterical excesses of professional moralists, those insatiable foes to peace, to sound progress and to Christian charity.

Does any sane man believe that the passage of the local option bill would improve matters? Certainly not. On the contrary, it must be plain that the resultant local fights would only serve to make matters worse. In probably a half of the election districts there would be a new election every two years. These incessant elections would make fortunes for the ward bosses. The sale and delivery of votes would become an organized industry. A regular tax would be laid upon the saloons, and that tax would be as heavy as the traffic would bear. And by the same token, a staggering tax would be laid upon the foes of the saloon—a tax collected in the name of God by professional rabble-rousers and tear-squeezers, devoted frankly and enthusiastically to stirring up hatreds between neighbor and neighbor.

The passage of a prohibition amendment, if anything, would be worse. True enough, it would not carry with it any pestilence of ward fights, but it would establish the blind pig from end to end of the State, and if you want to know what the blind pig means just ask anyone who is familiar with conditions in Georgia. The saloon is bad enough. It has a lot to answer for. The local optionists, whatever their follies, have at least brought that fact home to all of us. But every evil that the saloon works is also worked by the blind pig, and a hundred others follow after. It is one of the most powerful agents of corruption ever set up in Christendom. It makes drunkards, it fosters the spirit of law-breaking, it debauches the police, it gives excuse for hysterical raids, it multiplies animosities, it reduces civilization to barbarism.

All this we are asked to face in the name of piety and virtue. Every man who protests against it is denounced viciously as an atheist and a rascal. The local optionists assume a monopoly of rectitude. They try to make it appear that they represent Christianity, that they *are* Christianity. But I doubt that many fair men are going to be deceived by that bumptious and gratuitous pretense. The people of Baltimore, in general are getting tired of the whooping of self-consecrated archangels. They are beginning to see clearly how much of all this bawling is good-will to men and how much of it is mere yearning to make somebody sweat. They are beginning to understand the difference between that real Christianity which strives sincerely to lift up and dissuade the erring and that bogus Christianity which is no more than a debased and savage form of Mohammedanism. [29 March 1913]

YELLOW FEVER AND THE SALOON

The Rev. Dr. Romilly F. Humphries, rector-elect of Grace and St. Peter's Protestant Episcopal Church, to a reporter of the estimable *Evening News:*

> Can we make men good by legislation? * * * The answer
> to that question is Panama. By legislation, which is enforced

community action, you can make conditions wholesome and pure. You can make men live in cleanliness and decency, and you can reduce to the minimum the ravages of yellow fever. * * * In the realm of morals we need not hesitate to enter. * * * Experience has shown that the ubiquitous saloon, etc., etc. * * *

A shining example of that seductive super-logic which is at once the delight and the quagmire of uplifters. Is it reasonable thus to liken yellow fever to the saloon? Is it even ordinarily intelligible? I doubt it. No two things, indeed, could be more assertively unlike, despite their common corroding of the liver. Yellow fever is something that every sane man flees instinctively. In the whole world there is not a single man who feels that he needs it, or who argues that he gets any good out of it, or who regards it as a source of recreation or pleasure, or who wants to have anything to do with it. Its chief and only character is it obnoxiousness. It hasn't a friend in Christendom.

Is the saloon similarly hated and dreaded? Of course it is not. The chief mark of the saloon, in truth, is not its disagreeableness at all, but its charm. The reason why it is insidious and dangerous is precisely that it serves a universal human need, that it gratifies an ineradicable instinct, that it is no more repellant, in itself, than the lodge-room or the church. No sumptuary law, however harsh and barbarous, will ever take away its attraction. Whatever the penalties laid upon saloonkeepers, a vast majority of healthy men will still feel the impulse to meet their fellows over a social glass, and so long as that perfectly normal and decent impulse survives in them, the saloon itself, in one form or other, will also survive. The effect of repression, however determined, will not be to make it better, but merely to make it worse. The one practicable way to dispose of it will be to invent something which meets its uses without presenting its dangers. So far, as we all know, that something has not been invented.

The loose and shallow thinking of the current uplifters would be amusing if its consequences did not threaten to be so serious. The air of profundity with which they announce the obvious puts them in the front rank of moralists. It is truly affecting to hear them publish the epoch-making discovery that prostitution is an evil or that the saloon is far from perfect or that starvation wages make for sin. But what good is accomplished by all that solemn mouthing of platitudes? How is the world benefited by such laborious proclamations of the indubitable?

The thing the truly thoughtful men of the nation are trying to determine is what is to be done about it—and here the uplifters have nothing better to offer than the policeman's club. But the policeman's club, alas, will not destroy the impulses which lie at the bottom of these evils, and so long as those impulses remain they will inevitably work their way to some sort of satisfaction. Destroy the saloon and you set up the blind tiger. Destroy the brothel and you give us something worse.

The thing to be remembered constantly in dealing with all these pet targets of the chemically pure is that the human appetites and impulses behind them, whatever their occasional perversions, are essentially healthy and normal. The desire to drink a seidel of beer or a high-ball or two in congenial company may conceivably lead a man to a drunkard's grave, but in itself that desire is not unhealthy, nor is it even immoral. On the contrary, it is actually a sign of normality, and the man in whom it is present, all other things being equal, is apt to be a more tolerant and useful member of society than the man in whom it is not present. And so with the impulses which lie at the bottom of the social evil, and of all its fearful consequences. Those impulses, in themselves, are so thoroughly normal that their absence is universally recognized as a sign of disease.

And yet our moralists constantly proceed upon the assumption that all these desires, instincts and impulses are shameful and criminal, and that society is bound to oppose them and stamp them out. For example, I once heard Dr. Howard A. Kelly argue for the militant suppression of the social evil, despite its admitted failure to suppress, on the ground that civilized societies have always combatted homicide in the same way. The doctor, as always, was perfectly serious and very much in earnest—and yet it would have been difficult for any man, I fancy, to have devised a more dubious syllogism. The impulse to do murder is not only very rare in man, but also essentially pathological. A sane and healthy man, at least in civilization, does not kill his enemy. But the other impulse is the very reverse of pathological and the very reverse of rare. As well compare pyromania and laughter, or treason and patriotism.

So with Dr. Humphries and his pointless parallel between yellow fever and the saloon. The only imaginable opposition to measures against yellow fever comes from the ignorant—for example, Christian Science healers, chiropractors and the lower classes of negroes. The sufficient remedy for that ignorance, supposing it to be uncomplicated by downright imbecility, is education. Show any sane man how the destruction of the mosquito stamps out yellow fever, and he will immediately approve that destruction. He has nothing to gain by opposing it. He has no desire or instinct or impulse contrary to it.

But it is impossible, by any conceivable process of education, to rid man of his social instinct. Nor is it possible, by any marshaling of unimpeachable evidence, to convince him that the moderate use of alcohol either kills him or makes a brute of him. As a matter of fact, the more competent he is to examine into the matter, the more sure he grows that no such results need be feared. Such bogus experts as the Hon. William H. Anderson are full of proofs that alcohol is the cause of all human ills. But such genuine experts as Sir William Osler are convinced that it is nothing of the sort. As for me, I prefer the opinion of Dr. Osler, on a question of physiology or pathology, to the massed opinions of all the Andersons on both sides of the Styx. And on a question of civilized government and the social relation, I prefer the net experience of mankind in all ages to the well-intended but vacuous sophistries of my good friend the Rev. Dr. Humphries. [17 June 1913]

MENCKEN CAUGHT IN A RAID

The Hon. Charles L. Mattfeldt, M. D.,[5] is a man of sense and has an accurate understanding of the moral mind. He knows that the thing the malignant moralist craves is roughhouse, that the raiding and rowelling of harmless folk is the chief end and aim of "social service," and so he turns his catchpolls loose and exhorts them to bring in scalps. Hence the buffoonish doings at Back River last night, so eloquently described in the *Sunpaper* of this morning. One pictures the machiavellian Uncle Fred gritting his teeth today. Or perhaps grinning. After all, Uncle Fred has a sense of humor. He has been up against the archangels himself. He has seen raids at Back River for 20 years, and he knows them for what they are worth.

It so happens that I was personally snared in one of last night's raids, and in consequence I witnessed the whole affair, from beginning to end. It was one of the most inept and donkeyish in all my experience. The county cops came bouncing in like rubber balls, and seemed a great deal more scared than the persons raided. (Cops do not relish such a job; at best, it makes them look foolish.) As they gathered up a few half-empty bottles of alleged malt liquor and proceeded to manacle two or three waiters, the crowd favored them with a large buzzing snicker. This was at the Hon. Spot Mitchell's. Then they crossed Back River and tackled Hollywood, finding nothing. Meanwhile, they missed seven 10-cent paddle games within 20 yards of their sunburned, bucolic noses.

It is interesting to relate, by the way, that I was refused all alcoholic stimulants at Mitchell's, and this before the catchpolls heaved in sight. I arrived at the place in a state of exhaustion, after a grand tour of the nearby games of chance, and called for a modest, medicinal dose of malt. Two separate waiters refused to serve it. Then I sent for the proprietress, and she too refused, offering me the alternative of a bottle of sarsaparilla. I was doing some very earnest refusing myself when the *rurales* burst in, tripping over their own feet. Let the county grand jury take note of this interesting circumstance: I was *refused* a drink four minutes before the raid.

Mitchell's large pavilion was crowded at the time, and the crowd was quiet and well-behaved. The snouters who work the Sunday-schools tell horrible tales of the doings in such places. The innocents who listen to them conjure up pictures of lewd, levantine debaucheries, with murderers and white slave traders smoking opium in corncob pipes, naked nautch[6] girls dancing on the tables, and the dead body of a fresh victim going overboard every 10 minutes. Nothing could be more idiotic. There is no more debauchery at Mitchell's than at Emory Grove.[7] No form of vice or disorder is tolerated. I have been there half a dozen times this summer, and I have seen but one drunken man—and he was being refused admittance by the head-waiter.

But the folks drink beer! Well what of it? They enjoy that innocuous recreation, and they have the money to pay for it. What right have old maids, male and female, at Towson and Wetheredsville to complain? Why should these entirely harmless and well-meaning persons submit themselves to the dictation of a bunch of absurd fanatics, egged on by fifth-rate politicians? Why should their legitimate comfort be made a pawn in a tin-horn game of wirepulling? They are honest, everyday people, even as you and I. They mean no harm. They do no harm, not even to themselves. Why should they pay any attention to insane and oppressive laws, advocated by nickel-plated saints and passed by cowardly and crooked Legislatures? Is this the United States, or is it Russia?

I argue, of course, academically. As a matter of practice, the said laws are incapable of enforcement, and they always will be. Dr. Mattfeldt is well aware of it. He knows that he couldn't enforce them permanently with less than 500 men. But he also must know that the Sabbatomani-acs, like the vice crusaders and the boozehounds, esteem the raid a good deal more than they esteem the enforcement—that their one dearest delight is to see some one jump—and so he turns his gendarmes loose. He is an honest and sensible man. Give them what they want! No actual harm is done. Back River will be wet again in two weeks, probably in one week. It will be still wet, beloved, after you and I are dry, dry clinkers. [21 July 1913]

THE FANCIED EVILS OF ALCOHOL

All the Anti-Saloon League's preposterous rumble-bumble about the physical effects of alcohol is blown up in the current issue of *American Medicine*. The editor of this paper, facing the fact that the per capita consumption of alcohol is increasing in the United States, while the death rate is steadily falling, boldly casts aside all sophistical explanations, and proceeds to the truth—*i. e.*, that the damage suffered by drinkers, provided they exercise a reasonable discretion, is vastly less than the virtuosi of virtue, or even than the majority of physicians, have hitherto assumed. Says he:

> We are driven to the conclusion that *alcohol is not as bad as we have painted it.* We physicians * * * ought not to be ashamed to confess that we have been mistaken. We have long acknowledged that we were wrong in blaming alcohol for all the hardened livers and arteries and kidneys we saw, and we have even confessed that healthy, heavy drinkers may have less of these conditions than abstainers with bad digestions. So we ought not to be afraid to tell the world that our increasing consumption of alcohol is not an indication that the people are going to the deminition bow-wows. They are getting healthier, happier, wealthier and more moral every year. Could a little alcohol have contributed to this end? There now! We have made the awful suggestion.[8]

The writer goes on to show the small value of the discovery, so vociferously touted by the boozehounds, that alcohol is not a stimulant, but a depressant. Suppose it is? What of it? Isn't it reasonable to assume that a depressant may have quite as much value as a stimulant? I think so. When I have finished a hard week's work and foregather with my friends to relax and expand, it is certainly not a stimulant that I want. I am stimulated enough already; my nerves are on edge; I am tired of reacting to stimuli. What I want is a gentle sedative, something conducive to good humor, a mild soothing syrup. That thing is to be found in small quantities of very dilute ethyl alcohol.

A drug? True enough. But is the use of a mild drug an act of immorality *per se?* I deny it. The discreet use of drugs is one of the greatest arts of civilized man. If he limited himself to actual foods, his feeding would still show the primal simplicity and unimaginativeness of that of hogs in a pen. Instead, he adds useless but pleasant drugs to the fundamental mineral salts and carbohydrates—to wit, such things an alcohol, caffeine, tannic acid, acetic acid, piperine, theobromine, eugenol, myrosin, allyl iso-sulphocyanate and a multitude of other terpenes, ethers, aldehydes, ketones and phenols. Not one of these substances is nourishing; not one of them is necessary to life. And yet they are all used incessantly by civilized men.

There is no evidence whatever that the ingestion of small quantities of alcohol is dangerous to the healthy man. On the contrary, all the evidence that is worth hearing—for example, that of Sir William Osler— is on the other side. The current balderdash upon the subject is based upon loose reasoning, chiefly by medical men whose pious enthusiasm is greater than their talent for ratiocination. On the one hand, they make the capital error of assuming that whatever large quantities of alcohol will do small quantities will also do, and on the other hand they merely shoot in the dark, blaming everything on the nearest bystander.

It is time for that sort of booming sophistry to be halted, and the editor of *American Medicine* seems to be qualifying for the job. It is also time for a protest to be made against that moral buncombe which seeks to make the use of alcohol an act of immorality. In point of fact, it is no more an act of immorality, in itself, than the act of drinking coffee. A man may make a swine of himself by the use of either drug, but that is no argument against him if he doesn't. The science of morals deals with acts, and not with mere possibilities. A man might conceivably make a pauper and a public charge of himself by taking 50 baths a day, but certainly no sane man would argue thereby that he is to be eternally damned for taking *one* bath a day.

The whole alcohol question has fallen into the hands of quacks and mountebanks. Like the vice question, it is discussed endlessly by self-constituted "experts" who know nothing whatever about it and whose logic would shame a Christian Scientist. That there are conditions of disease in which any amount of alcohol, however small, is dangerous to life is easily demonstrated, and that large quantities are highly deleterious, even to the perfectly healthy man, goes without saying; but to say that the drinking of an occasional glass of wine, or even of hard liquor, is an act of suicide or of immorality is to say something so preposterous that it scarcely deserves a polite answer. [18 November 1913]

VICE AND CIGARETTES

In the midst of all our torquemadan crusading, how is it that no moralist has dedicated himself to the extinction of the cigarette, that coffin nail, that debauchery, that father of crime? Elsewhere in this fair land it has been dealt staggering licks by the chemically pure. In Kansas, Iowa and Missouri the children in the public schools are taught to fear and abominate it; in Nebraska, Michigan and Alabama there are hot campaigns against it; in Indiana its sale is forbidden by law. But here in Baltimore not a single voice is raised against it. Our moralists are the most virulent in Christendom—their ardor, indeed, is often far more Mohammedan than Christian—and yet I have not heard a word from them about the licentious and diabolical cigarette.

Certainly this cannot be due to ignorance of its deadliness. It is a matter of common knowledge, indeed, that the cigarette is one of the most insidious of all agents of sin. The boy who inhales its noxious fumes today will be a drunkard tomorrow and a murderer next week. The woman who smokes cigarettes is sinister and unspeakable—a dangerous companion for the young. The man who pursues the corrupting vice is a shifty, blear-eyed rascal, with the complexion of a bilious jonquil and a liver that plots treasons. All criminals smoke cigarettes. So do all paranoics. It is the unanimous pet and comfort of felons condemned to be hanged.

On the medical side the evidence against it is irrefutable and overwhelming. In Dr. Osler's great work on "The Principles and Practices of Medicine" (lib. XIV, fol. 324) there is the direct statement that the cigarette is one of the most potent causative agents in influenza, cancer, diphtheria, ophthalmia, beri-beri and senile dementia. Dr. Osler there describes an experiment with guinea pigs made by Prof. Dr. Hugo Bier-fisch, of Leipzig. Two sets of guinea pigs, one of which had been trained to smoke cigarettes and the other of which had been kept pure, were exposed to virulent cultures of the *bacillus typhosus*. The virtuous guineas at once leaped out of the window, but the cigarette smokers, besotted by nicotine, snouted the fatal germs and at once fell into convulsions. By next morning all of them save one were dead of arterio-sclerosis, and that one was a babbling maniac.

This experiment was confirmed with trained rabbits by Dr. H. von Schweineshaxen, of Jena, and with Siberian wolfhounds by Prof. Dr. Max Donau, of Vienna. Dr. Donau is of the opinion that the disease commonly called hydrophobia is really a form of ptomaine poisoning caused by the use of inferior glue on cigarette wrappers. This theory, it should be stated in fairness, is disputed by Dr. Donau's distinguished colleague, Prof. Dr. Adolph Spatenbraeu, but Dr. Spatenbraeu agrees that cigarettes often cause jaundice, lumbago and housemaid's knee. He is also of the opinion that the delirium tremens sometimes encountered in temperance lecturers is more often caused by devotion to the seductive coffin nail than by secret dalliance with the confidential jug.

And all this medical evidence is amply supported by the statistics of our prisons and almshouses. Of the 226 murderers confined in Sing Sing prison between January 1, 1900, and December 31, 1910, no less than 207 ascribed their downfall to cigarettes. Of the 1,987 forgers imprisoned at the same place during the same time 1,562 blamed cigarettes. From Charleston Prison, near Boston, come reports that are even more impressive. Every one of the yeggmen now serving time there is a cigarette fiend. The late Dr. Clarence Richeson was another. Dr. Harvey H. Crippen, hanged in London for the murder of his wife, smoked 15 packages a day. Johann Hoch, the celebrated Chicago murderer, went to the gallows with a cigarette in his mouth and a glass of fake Pilsener in his hand.[9]

But there is no need to go on. Everyone knows that the cigarette is the father and mother of felony, as it is of Bright's disease. The boy who succumbs to it ends invariably as a profligate and an invalid. Like the boy who monkeys with the wine cup, he shoots the moral chutes, dying horribly and in two places at once, the almshouse and the gutter. The cigarette is the badge of the white slave trader, and not only of the white slave trader, but also of the following rogues and rascals:

Acrobats,
Atheists,
Bandits,
Barbers,
Bartenders,
Bigamists,
Blackhanders,[10]
Blackmailers,
Boomers,
Boozers,
Burglars,
Camorrists,[11]
Chorus girls,
Chickens,[12]
Child stealers,
Congressmen,
Cornetists,[13]
Counterfeiters,
Critics,
Dips,[14]
Dog-catchers,
Dope fiends,
Eagles,
Elks,
Firebugs,
Forgers,
Fortune-tellers,
Gamblers,
Ganovs,[15]
Garroters,
Grafters,
Grave robbers,
Hangmen,
Horse-thieves,
Job hounds,

Journalists,
Kidnappers,
Labor leaders,
Medical students,
Moll-buzzers,[16]
Mormons,
Murderers,
Musicians,
Phrenologists,
Piano tuners,
Pickpockets,
Pilsenerists,
Pirates,
Poets,
Politicians,
Press agents,
Reporters,
Revolutionists,
Road agents,[17]
Robbers,
Schnorrers,[18]
Seducers,
Shoplifters,
Spiritualists,
Suffragettes,
Swindlers,
Tenors,
Touts,
Violincellists,
Voluptuaries,
Ward heelers,
Whisky drummers,
Wire-tappers,
Xylophone players,
Yeggmen.[19]

And yet, as I have said, the deadly cigarette goes uncombated in Baltimore. Not a single moralist bawls it out. Not a single wiskinski goes among the pious taking up a collection for its extinction. Not a single brave fellow defies the sinister camorra of its victims and apologists. [19 February 1913]

CAFFEINE AS A DRUG

An anonymous defender of the Hon. Eugene Levering, in the Letter Column:

> Let the Free Lance show that coffee hurts the people as much as rum. How many homes does coffee break up? How many murders does coffee cause?

An apparently sound defense, but one, alas, that goes to pieces on inspection. I have never maintained that coffee causes murders or that it breaks up homes, though I suppose I could get moral evidence to that effect if I tried. All I *have* maintained is that coffee contains an alkaloid called caffeine, and that the use of caffeine is deleterious, and that the sale of it, in consequence, is as immoral as the sale of any other drug.

Caffeine and alcohol differ in degree, but not in kind. Both are drugs. Both poison the body and corrupt the mind. In the very same way, beer and whisky differ in degree, but not in kind. Every schoolboy knows, for example, that a single pint of beer could not conceivably cause a murder or break up a home, whereas a single pint of whisky might do both. But do the Hon. Mr. Levering and his friends therefore make a distinction between beer and whisky—*i. e.,* between a mild and probably harmless poison, and a powerful and obviously dangerous poison? They do not. Less than two weeks ago they were printing a flaming advertisement reviling brewers as well as distillers, and expressing astonishment that any man engaged in the manufacture and sale of alcohol *in any form* should be admitted to decent society.

Well, if the sale of alcohol is thus sufficient to make a man an outlaw, why shouldn't that outlawry extend to the sellers of other drugs? For example, caffeine. What ground is there for believing that the sale of one drug is more moral than the sale of another drug? If caffeine leaves the hands lily-white, why should alcohol stain them? Is there, perhaps, a graduated scale of drugs, ranged in the order of their morality? Then what is the position of caffeine? Is it above or below cocaine, above or below Peruna, above or below nicotine? If it is below, why is it below? In what essential is it more grateful to the moral sense than any other drug? In just what way does the man who sells it become a great moral leader, with an unlimited license to denounce and excommunicate the lowly rum-seller? [15 March 1913]

IX

THE VICE CRUSADE 3

Prostitution

ON PROSTITUTION

Dr. Donald R. Hooker, that earnest and romantic man, devotes an article in the Maryland *Suffrage News* of this week to a refutation of my occasional criticisms of the current Vice Crusade, in which he takes a part second only to that of Dr. Howard A. Kelly. Unluckily enough, Dr. Hooker does not quite understand what my objections are, perhaps because I have stated them with too great a regard for prudery, nor does he see clearly why I advocate some sort of segregation, *i. e.,* some sort of frank recognition of the social evil.

Let me, therefore, be a bit more explicit, at the risk of boring the unregenerate and outraging the pure. I do not argue, nor do I believe, that segregation would reduce materially the total number of unchaste women in Baltimore, nor do I believe that it could ever be made so perfect as to bring all offenders within its areas, nor do I believe that, either with or without medical inspection, it would lead, in itself, to any very marked diminution of the so-called social diseases. All I argue for it is that it is honest, and all I argue against repression is that it is not honest.

Prostitution, in brief, is not a mere bugaboo, to be sent fleeing by wind music, but a highly material fact, and what is more, a fact that seems firmly rooted in ineradicable human weakness. I do not say that the world will never see the end of it, nor do I say that its good effects counterbalance its bad effects, nor that its abolition would work a genuine hardship on anyone. All I do say is that it will never disappear so long as human beings, in the mass, remain as weak as they are today, and human society retains its present constitution. And in support of that contention I point to its survival down to our own day, in spite of centuries of attack so influential and so furious that the current campaign in the United States seems puny and ridiculous by comparison. In brief, I do not believe that Dr. Hooker and his friends will succeed where popes and emperors have failed, and on that doctrine I hang my case.

But what, then, is to be done about it? The thing is undoubtedly evil, and in the presence of evil honest men do not like to sit silent. At the moment two divergent plans are proposed and behind them are two theories of morals. The theory of the Vice Crusaders is that the way to deal with prostitution is to drive it under cover, to make it furtive and an outlaw, to combat its appearance and conceal its substance, to give it, in brief, a specious and deceptive air of non-existence. The theory of less virtuous and more tough-minded men is that the right way is to admit the inevitable without parley, to keep the thing itself naked and unashamed, to take away from it all romantic glamour and mystery, to ameliorate as much as possible its bad effects upon the individual, to separate it from associated and contributory evils—in a word, to try to make the best of it.

I am well aware that the former theory appeals strongly to many pious men, who argue eloquently that all compromise with evil is wrong, but all the same I believe that it is unsound, pernicious and nonsensical. Say what you will against it, we must constantly compromise with evil in this imperfect world. In the presence of the bitter facts of life, all the more idealistic forms of piety go to pieces. Nothing has ever been accomplished in Christendom by proceeding upon the theory that sin is a purely volitional phenomenon, to be stamped out by invective. All the moral progress we have made has been based upon a frank acceptance of human frailty, and a common-sense endeavor to diminish the evil in its inevitable effects.

Here, I believe, is where the Vice Crusaders run aground. In so far as they confine themselves to combating the costly sequelæ of prostitution—for example, the physical damage to the individual—nobody, I take it, is against them. But when they pass from their purely remedial role to that of critics and doctors of human weakness, when they set out to destroy a cause as deeply rooted as the cause of life itself, then they pass from the field of practical reform and become tedious and irritating idealists, and dangerous to the public security. Whatever progress is ever made in reducing the evils of prostitution will be made by men who have intellectual courage enough to admit openly that the facts of life are such and so, and who do not waste their time figuring out how much nicer the world would be if human beings were not as they are.

To repeat, I do not think that the Vice Crusaders are honest, and by this I do not mean honest in the sense of sincere, but honest in the sense of accurate in observation and frank in report. The best that you can say for them is that it would be nice if what they prophesy could come true, but every time you say that you must also admit that the probabilities are overwhelmingly against it. Why waste time arguing for the unobtainable when effective work lies so close at hand? Why denounce the weather as immoral—as it undoubtedly is—when it is so much easier to build a house?

I have read the pamphlets of the Vice Crusaders with great care, and I have also listened to the arguments of their chosen spokesman. The result of this inquiry is positive amazement at the inaccuracy of their data on the one hand, and at the fallaciousness of their reasoning on the other. Not long ago I heard an earnest clergyman, prominent in the Crusade, give an account of the social evil in the Western district so full of false premises and ridiculous deductions that I almost slid under the table. It seemed truly incredible that any adult male, interested in the subject, should be so ignorant of the actual machinery of vice. And from time to time, more in sorrow than in anger, I have called attention to the intolerable inaccuracy of reports made by touring crusaders from other cities, and by the chief field agent of the local crusade. Not even the local optionists have manufactured facts more industriously, or shown a more pious delight in the business.

Again, the logic of the crusaders, from end to end, is full of holes. For example, Dr. Kelly, more frank than some of the others, is disposed to admit that the complete stamping out of prostitution is impossible, but yet maintains that the effort should go on. It is also impossible, he argues, wholly to stamp out murder, and yet who would repeal the laws against it? What is the fallacy here? Don't you see it in the vain attempt to range an act based upon a pathological state beside a weakness based upon a normal state? The two are no more related, in truth, than suicide and laughter, despite their artificial juxtaposition in morals, and no intelligible conclusion can be brought out of any assumption that they are.

Then there is Dr. Hooker, with his magnificent argument, in this week's *Suffrage News,* that the social evil is not necessary, that its absolute abolition would not do material damage to anyone. A beautiful demonstration—as any self-evident demonstration must be. But physiological necessity, it must be obvious, is by no means the only causative agent behind the acts of man. In point of fact, it is a good deal less potent, in the everyday affairs of the world, than mere caprice and weakness—and it is precisely upon such weakness that the social evil is grounded. I do not say that it is good and I do not say that it is necesary. All I do say is that it is, that the weakness underlying it is. And while deploring that weakness as much as any other hypocrite, I do not carry my objections to it to the point of making impertinent protests against the laws of nature. I am a critic here of men, and not of the Creator.

So much for the causes of prostitution. Its effects, on the one side, at least, are a part of its causes, and hence equally immutable. It uses up, so to speak, a certain number of human beings every year. Innocent girls have to be debauched in order to supply it with recruits. Well, so far as that attack upon virtue is real all decent men are against it, if only because of their general detestation of deceit. But to what extent is it real? Perhaps to one-fiftieth of one per cent. As for the rest, it is the weakness of the so-called victim far more than the rascality of the seducer that diminishes so lamentably the average virtue of the world.

In other words, the current talk about the White Slave Trade is nine-tenths buncombe. All of the evidence pro is supplied by fanatics whose habit of magnifying small facts is almost pathological and who usually have a personal and financial interest in scaring the public to death. The evidence con you can get from any intelligent policeman. He will tell you, first, that not one prostitute in a thousand is under the slightest duress, physical or psychic, and, secondly, that not one in a hundred labors under any pressing sense of degradation. The vast majority of them, in truth, are women who would go wrong under any conceivable state of society, however benign, and many of them actually made a step upward when they adopted the life so copiously wept over by persons who are themselves sweetly caressed by fate and so can't understand the temptations and motives of the chandala.[1]

Such persons have little understanding of the world's unfortunates and little genuine sympathy for them. On the one hand they picture the Magdalen as a helpless victim of human treachery, and on the other hand they picture her as the worst of criminals. As a matter of fact, she is neither. If she is helpless, it is only in the sense that all of us are helpless. Her inherent character and her early environment, working together, have cast her for a degraded role in life, just as the character and environment of certain Vice Crusaders have fitted them for the parts of Tartuffe and Sganarelle.[2] Her means of escape are many, despite the efforts of the bombardiers of virtue, and whenever she is so inclined she duly escapes. In romantic literature she dies horribly, after five short years of repining. In real life she often marries.

But meanwhile, she does damage to civilization, and the effort of every good citizen must be to reduce that damage to a minimum. In this work the physician, of course, must be to the fore, for it is the physical ripple from her noisome bog that goes furthest and splashes most innocent persons. What is to be done here? The answer is simple enough. It is the duty of the physician, in his laboratory and in his practice, to combat all of the so-called social diseases, intelligently and unemotionally, until they yield to his science and are stamped out. And the very first condition of that combat, if it is ever to be successful, is that he put aside, as irrelevant, all thought of their moral implications and confine himself wholly to their aspect as purely physical phenomena.

Dr. Kelly, Dr. Hooker and other such earnest men frequently make mention of that revolution in medicine which has substituted the prevention of disease for its cure, and they commonly defend their vain effort to stamp out the social evil on the ground that it is genuinely prophylactic, that its high aim is prevention. But let them not forget, in the midst of all this fine enthusiasm, another and more important revolution in medicine. I mean that revolution which finally separated, I hope for all time, the physician and the moralist. No change ever made in human thought and custom was of more value to humanity. No divorce has ever done more to augment the prosperity and respectability of both parties.

The function of the physician of today is to relieve human suffering, and not to fix the moral blame for it. His business is with the facts before him and not with theories of human conduct. Once he essays to divide his patients into the just and unjust, he will find, if he pushes the inquiry honestly, that two-thirds of all who come to him belong to the latter category, that two-thirds of all human ills are the product of human weakness and error, that it is civilization and self-indulgence that fill our hospitals. But when he goes beyond the physical cause, he goes beyond his province, and when he does it habitually, he works a greater damage to sound and humane medical progress than the worst quack unhung.

But why segregation, admittedly imperfect? To repeat again, simply because of the two plans now before the public of this town, it is vastly the more honest. Simply because it admits frankly a condition we cannot wholly remedy, and seeks to make the best of it. Simply because it tends to destroy that romantic glamour, that alluring mystery, that charm of the forbidden, which is the chief attraction and danger of furtive, outlaw vice. Simply because it is grounded upon the facts of life as they are, and not upon some fanciful dream of life as it should be.

"The Vice Crusaders," said Rabbi Rubenstein at Har Sinai Temple the other day, "will end by scattering broadcast an evil which today we can at least locate, and against which we can yet, in a measure, guard the young and innocent." And as they scatter it thus, they will increase its enchantment tenfold, and so multiply enormously its menace tomorrow. The open brothel, however red its lights, offers little temptation to any save very young, or very lonely, or very drunken men. But the clandestine prostitute, detached from her proper and disgusting stage settings and taking on thereby the charm of the difficult and romantic, is a temptation to all men, old and young, drunk and sober, vicious and decent. [7 November 1912]

MR. BONAPARTE AND SEGREGATION

The Hon. Charles J. Bonaparte, vice-president of the Society for the Suppression of Vice, on the gentlemen, lay and clerical, who are opposed to his pious scheme for chasing prostitutes from pillar to post:

> "Segregators" * * * seek two ends. Their aims are, first, to
> promote the prosperity of keepers of houses of prostitution,
> * * * and, secondly, to assure the men who frequent those houses
> uninterrupted opportunities for vicious indulgence.

A shining example of that amazing impudence which character-
izes all of the Hon. Mr. Bonaparte's moral pronunciamentos. If these
words mean anything at all, they mean that every man who opposes the
woman hunt is either a friend and attorney of brothel-keepers or an
open procurer for their customers. He makes no exception; he allows no
room for a third "aim." *All* men who stand opposed to him, regardless of
their pretensions, are rogues and scoundrels.

Well, let us see what this means. On November 18, 1911 the Supreme
Bench of Baltimore City adopted a minute describing and defending
the system of segregation then in vogue in Baltimore, and containing
the following remark:

> Out of much reflection, study and comparison of views, this
> court has come to [the] conclusion * * * that to impose in all cases
> a sentence of imprisonment or heavy fine upon keepers of bawdy
> houses, *with the intent to entirely suppress such houses,* * * * is not, at
> this time, wise.

So far as is known, every member of the Supreme Bench agreed
to this minute. It was read from the bench in the Criminal Court by
Judge Duffy, a former State's Attorney. Does the Hon. Mr. Bonaparte
now maintain that these judges were animated by the two "aims" he describes—that they were either trying to make prostitutes prosperous or
seeking to afford "uninterrupted opportunities for vicious indulgence"?
To ask the question is to answer it. And to answer it is to reveal the utter
vacuity, impertinence and imbecility of the Hon. Mr. Bonapate's chief
argument.

He must know very well, if he knows anything about the matter
at all, that a great many men whose motives are wholly beyond suspicion are unalterably opposed to the woman hunt. He must know, for
example, that at least three-fourths of the members of the Medical and
Chirurgical Faculty are opposed to it. He must know that it is opposed
by all of the police captains, by all of the Federal white slave agents,

and by scores of clergymen, including many of his own faith. He must know that it has been publicly attacked by such men as Havelock Ellis, Mayor Brand Whitlock, Mayor Gaynor, Dr. Frederic C. Howe, Dr. J. R. Kean, of the Army Medical Corps, the Rev. Dr. William T. Russell and the Rev. Dr. W. S. Rainsford, and, to come nearer home, by Justice Eugene E. Grannan, Mr. Grgurevich and Capt. John Logan. To say that these men are either boosters of disorderly houses or advocates of debauchery is to say something so stupid, so ridiculous and so false that not even the Bonaparte "Progressives," I daresay, will ever swallow it without gagging.

When the Hon. Mr. Bonaparte raises this question of the relative dignity and responsibility of the vice crusaders and their opponents, he does a bad day's work for the crusaders. Here in Baltimore we all know the men at the back of the vice crusade. We know that they are few in number and that they are all professional agitators and extremists. The roll is easily called: the Hon. Mr. Bonaparte, Dr. Howard A. Kelly, the Hon. Eugene Levering, the Rev. Dr. K. G. Murray, Dr. O. Edward Janney and Dr. Donald R. Hooker. (The Hon. Samuel E. Pentz, formerly grand master of the lodge, has lately retired.) I have no grievance against these men: with some of them I am on very friendly personal terms. But I ask every sane man to answer for himself whether their opinion on any matter involving prudence and common sense is to be put above the opinion of the Judges of the Supreme Bench, or that of the police captains, or that of the great majority of physicians, or that of such experienced and honest men as those I have called by name.

No one questions the Hon. Mr. Bonaparte's right to oppose segregation. It is an admittedly defective system, and I, for one, am disposed to admit most of the evils urged against it. But to argue against it is one thing, and to try to dispose of it by bluff and bullying is quite another thing. The people of Baltimore, unless I err greatly, are getting very weary of the uproar raised by vice crusaders. They are willing to hear any reasonable argument against the system in vogue here for so long, but they are not going to be influenced by idle charges and threats against the men who are honestly in favor of that system, as something measurably better than dispersion. They are not going to submit to the browbeating of a crowd of busybodies who meet in a private room, and there issue orders to the police, the grand jury and the courts.

At the risk of tedious repetition I call attention again to the Hon. Mr. Bonaparte's personal unfitness to discharge any such despotic function. As vice-president of the Society for the Suppression of Vice he was one of the officers in command of a squad of police placed at the society's disposal (entirely without warrant in law) by a complaisant Police Board. I charge that the said squad of police was employed by the chief agent of the society for the purpose of harassing and disgracing an innocent public official, the motive being private revenge. I charge that the Hon. Mr. Bonaparte and his chief associates have so mismanaged the society that it has become a public joke and a public nuisance. I charge that their participation in hypocritical crusades and their stupid partnership with bogus crusaders have brought humiliation upon all the subscribers to the society, robbed it of the public's confidence and destroyed the real usefulness that it once had.

Let the Hon. Mr. Bonaparte remember clearly that the office he holds involves responsibilities as well as privileges. The presumptions are always in his favor: he is a man who has "done the State some service, and they know it." But when he seeks to argue his case in the terms of a campmeeting exhorter belaboring the devil, it is high time to haul him in. And when he is shown to be a responsible officer of an organization so suspicious in its practices that it has attracted the attention of the grand jury, then it is time to examine into his competence as a specialist in law and virtue. [2 September 1913]

THE VICE COMMISSION AND PROSTITUTION

When the Police Board takes up its grim job of carrying out the recommendations of Dr. Goldsborough's Vice Commission, the chief difficulty before it will not be to close the brothels and assignation houses, but to keep a restraining hand upon the eager and impatient pack of vice crusaders. Nothing is easier than to close a brothel—that is to say, a brothel of the tolerated, regulated sort so long existing in Baltimore. All that the police need do is to go to the door and order the keeper of the place to close. Nine times out of ten, if she is convinced that they mean what they say—as she must be in the present case—she will close at once, and without offering the slightest resistance. And in the unusual event that she refuses, it is a simple matter to take her into custody for maintaining a disorderly house, and to station a policeman before her establishment, thus putting an end to the egress of patrons.

But when a regulated brothel has been closed, there still remains the problem of disposing of the women who have lived in it. A few of those women—chiefly the older and more hopeless portion—sometimes show a disposition to reform, and these, perhaps, may be taken care of by such agencies as that maintained by Capt. John Logan of the Volunteers of America. But the vast majority, far from coming into camp so docilely, are only made fugitive and defiant. It is these who set the police a task that all the police forces of the world have hitherto failed to perform with anything even remotely approaching success, and it is these—and the clandestine army into which they slope by such easy stages—who offer the professional vice crusader his chief sport and livelihood.

That professional crusader, when he is before a Vice Commission, is always full of protestations that his sole concern is with what he calls "commercialized" vice. That is to say, he maintains that his one aim is to pursue and dispose of the persons who make their livings trading in the shame of women. But the moment any power to that end is put into his hands, he at once proceeds to tackle, not only the merchants of the redlight district, but also their victims, and not only their victims, but also all other women, however little they may be actual prostitutes, whose mode of life does not meet his notions of what is nice. In brief, he becomes a general censor of female morals, with a firm belief in the theory that every woman not obviously under male protection is guilty until she proves herself innocent, and it is upon this theory that he undertakes his relentless espionage of suspects, his incessant raidings of second-class hotels and lodging houses, and his ecstatic spying upon all that goes on in apartment houses.

Baltimore, so far, has never had such a whole-hearted, super-satisfying vice crusade, but it must be plain that the vice crusaders have made plans for one, and that they will soon be in the midst of it if the Police Board gives them a free rein. The fact that the laws of Maryland do not countenance a moral orgy of that sort will be of no importance unless the Police Board makes a deliberate effort to protect the innocent in their rights. The pursued themselves will be in no position to offer effective resistance. If they are of dubious virtue, they will not care to go to trial upon the question whether or not they are actual prostitutes, and if their virtue is beyond a doubt they will be equally disinclined to make known the devastating fact that even a dishonest doubt has been raised against it. In this emergency it is up to the Police Board to see that the ordinary processes of law are observed by the snouters, and that the ordinary rights of all women, even including prostitutes, are not invaded.

Its opportunity to do this service to public order and decency is unhappily only temporary. At the last session of the Legislature a committee of eminent vice crusaders attempted to secure the passage of measures that would have much facilitated the business of spying and relieved the hired snouter of the penalties which now threaten him if he carries his extravagances too far. Those measures were defeated at the request of the chairman of the Vice Commission, his argument against them being that their consideration was premature. But that they will be reintroduced at next winter's session of the Legislature is certain, and that they will be passed is highly probable. Their central purpose, as I say, is to increase the powers and diminish the responsibility of the snouter. They give him what amounts to a free license to snout and spy as he will. They take away many of the common and immemorial rights of the citizen and householder. But it is the clear duty of the Police Board, so long as those rights remain, to safeguard them vigorously and jealously.

The thing to remember about a vice crusade is that its management is always in the hands of ladies and gentlemen who derive direct and often lucrative incomes from it—that the armed pursuit and prosecution of the erring has become a recognized profession in the United States. These prehensile bell-wethers stir up the so-called moral element, from whom their revenues are then derived. It is not to be expected, of course, that such a profession would attract persons of much ethical responsibility or delicacy, and a reference to the facts supports the lack of expectation. But the Vice Commission, however good its motives, has turned Baltimore over to just such a pack of crafty whoopers and mountebanks, and its members must take the full blame for the useless, cruel and dishonest monkey-shines that impend. They had a chance to contribute something new and sensible to the solution of an ancient and difficult problem. They chose to give weak, rubber-stamp assent to a scheme that is based upon buncombe, hysteria and a denial of the plain facts, and that has failed miserably and ludicrously at all times and everywhere. [12 April 1915]

HOW TO DEAL WITH FALLEN WOMEN

The Hon. Alice B. Montgomery to the local suffragettes:

> I want all girl cases to be tried before a jury composed of half women and half men; the woman viewpoint and judgment is [*sic*] surely needed here if anywhere.

With the highest respect, Bosh! Sorry, indeed, would be the lot of that recreant working girl who had to face a jury of fat and virtuous dames! One and all, they would be hot for burning her at the stake, and the six men would have to save her at the risk of their own hair, eyes, whiskers and lives. In all human history there is no record of a woman who championed an erring sister. The voice of the gentle sex is always raised for the extreme limit of the law. It is man, the scoundrel, who preaches and practices mercy and forgiveness.

And why? Because a man is inherently more merciful than a woman? Scarcely. The real reason lies in the fact that a man is better able to withstand the attack that Puritans always make upon the person who ventures to speak up for the so-called fallen woman. That attack invariably takes the form of an accusation, either open or by innuendo, that it is not mercy at all, but a community of tastes and habits, that inspires the defender. The average man is not substantially damaged by this attack, for even when he is virtuous—which is usually—no one believes it. But the average woman has to avoid it as the pestilence, for the simple accusation is enough to ruin her just as effectually as if she were actually guilty—and perhaps even more effectually, for to be innocent and accused, in this department, is substantially equivalent to being guilty, whereas to be guilty and unsuspected is substantially equivalent to being innocent. Here I could offer many instructive examples, but refrain upon the advice of counsel.

This fact explains the utter failure of most of the current efforts to reclaim the fallen woman. The Puritans who engage in that salacious enterprise are afraid of each other, and so they approach their prey gingerly, fearfully and with prophylactic denunciations in their mouths. The result is that they seldom take a scalp, and then only when it is loose before they grab it. Ten times as many fallen woman would be saved if their rescuers approached them with genuine charity and good will. When a poor prostitute, run to earth by barking, foaming snouters, reaches dolefully for the bichloride bottle, an arm around her neck will not only save her life, but also probably bring her back to a reasonable rectitude. What she wants, in brief, is a kind word from some one who is honestly sorry for her and not afraid to prove it at his personal risk. The moralist, for all his pretensions, is never honestly sorry for her; he believes that she will go to hell, and that she will deserve it. And he holds her at arm's length while he exhorts her, for fear that his pious brethren will begin whispering in the Sunday-schools that they saw him hugging her.

Here we have the secret of the success of Capt. John Logan of the Volunteers of America, the only local merchant of salvation who has won the confidence and respect of the red-light ladies, and the only one who has, in any true sense, saved any of them. Logan's system is simple and honest because the man himself is simple and honest. He does not whoop for the blood of the women he professes to rescue; he does not ask the Police Board for cops to help him chase and persecute them; he does not fill the newspapers with threats, prophecies and theological treatises; he has no staff of hired snouters, lawyers, bogus "experts" and press agents. But when a poor prostitute grows ill and despondent, and her mind begins to fill with maddening pictures of the black future before her, she knows that she may go to Logan and get a hearty, human welcome, and that he and his wife will take her in without asking her questions, and without preaching at her, and without shrinking from her, and without exhibiting her in the Sunday-schools as a captive, and that he will send her somewhere where nobody knows her, and try to get a decent job for her, and protect her against the abominable attentions of the snouting brethren, and so set her on her feet again.

This method, as I have said, lays inevitable penalties upon its practitioner, and these penalties Logan has to pay. The vice crusaders, one and all, are against him, and they do their best to discredit him. He is pursued by sneers, innuendoes, moral liftings of the eyebrow. A few weeks ago, before the Police Board, it was openly hinted that his interest in the women of the Tenderloin was financial—that he concerned himself with them in order to shake money out of them! But there is nothing feminine in the composition of this Logan. He has the tough hide of an authentic male, and so he faces the music without flinching. If you want to find out the truth about him, go ask any of the women in the western Tenderloin. And then ask them about the consecrated fellows who whisper against him. [25 May 1915]

X

SUNDRY FORMS
OF QUACKERY

THE NEW THOUGHT

Wouldst be, O toiler, an astrologer, and get the coin of the true believer? Nothing could be simpler. Just send $10 to the College of Esoteric Sciences and by return mail will come a series of nine lessons. Master those lessons and you will have old Merlin floored. "The study of this science," says the college prospectus, "gives an understanding of the varying moods, fancies and tendencies of the individual, also how to blend with these different astro-aspects rather than be controlled by them: a knowledge which will be found to be worth many times the price of tuition and the time necessary to learn."

Thus the New Thought, borrowing the machinery of the correspondence schools, carries its blessing into every hamlet of the land. Not only astrology but also a score of other occult and subtle sciences are to be had in bulk for modest bank notes. The college teaches spiritual theraputics (therapeutics?) for $5 cash; name numbers, whatever they may be, for $5; Biblical symbology for the same sum, and palmistry, that delight of the romantic, for $3. Spiritual theraputics is so easy that it may be mastered in six lessons, and if you don't want to send the $5 in advance, you may send $2.50 with your application for matriculation and the rest when you receive your third lesson.

Spiritual theraputics, it appears, is based upon the "recognized fact" that "one's health is directly affected by one's mental attitude, and as the mentality is subject to and can be controlled by self these lessons instruct how to develop and maintain a mental attitude which will result in a healthy body, a happy mind and success to the individual." A rival to the Emmanuel Movement,[1] and much simpler and cheaper. No need to sweat for hours in a darkened room. No need to hire a string quartet to play Mendelssohn's "Spring Song."[2] Just make up your mind as to what you want, and you will straightway have it, whether it be a complexion like Lillian Russell's or biceps like Jack Johnson's. And for $5 cash.

Better still, there is psychic healing, which the eminent Professor Gore, of Florida, teaches for the extremely modest sum of $1. If, after you have received his six lessons, you are not willing and even eager to admit that you have got your money's worth, he will not only return your dollar, but also give you a bonus of 25 cents. Professor Gore's announcement appears in all of the New Thought journals, but a study of his first lesson convinces me that he is no true New Thoughter. There is, in fact, a lot of heresy in him, for he openly admits that there are diseases which the mind cannot heal. Says he:

> No system ever devised can cure a man of indigestion—not even God—who persists in swallowing chunks of half-masticated fat pork, and drenching them down with four or five cups of strong "black coffee." The man or woman who tells you he or she can heal you under such conditions, deceive you, for they KNOW better. Because they know that God has made Natural Laws, and he who does not respect them MUST suffer—even if only a babe. The child who puts its hand into fire will SURELY get burnt.

Tut, tut! Don't you believe it! The child may get burnt, but the burn will be purely imaginary, and as an imaginary injury it will quickly yield to an imaginary remedy. The professor himself should be well aware of this, for he testifies that he has cured cancer, epilepsy and diabetes by the psychic power within him. What is cancer? Cancer, according to the New Thought, is a delusion of cancerousness. Remove the delusion and the cancer will evaporate. That is what happened in the case of Mrs. J. E. Ray, of Conifer, Col. She had a cancer that had "baffled the leading specialists of the country," and yet Professor Gore exorcised it in four days by the clock.

But to return to his actual technique. Here is his first lesson to the student:

> At any convenient hour lie down with your head toward the North, or sit in an easy position facing the North, and take ten or a dozen deep, long and even inspirations, and exhale slowly, at the same time concentrating on the weak and ailing parts or organs, holding the STEADY INTENTION to send the Sub-Conscious Mind, with ALL your vital forces, into them, to stimulate, rebuild and regenerate them to a Newness of Life.

The effect of this will be to stimulate the flow of secretions "in any organ or part of your body," and those secretions will do the work. Do you doubt it? The professor has an answer for you—an answer that will floor you. "That you can do this," he says, "even the small boy who wishes to drown some poor insect (with saliva) or to clean his slate when a sponge or cloth is not handy, KNOWS. There is no 'guess so' about it. His supply of saliva is unlimited and equal to ALL his demands and intentions." What a pity that cows cannot be taught the New Thought!

But the drawing in of wind, the concentration of mind, the summoning-up of the Sub-Conscious—all this must be reinforced by other exercises. After concentrating, relax. Thus:

> Let the mind—the Objective Mind—roam around lazily at its own sweet will—fall asleep if you feel an inclination. You must not, however, try to force the mind in any certain channel, or on one certain thought, for to do this is to make you POSITIVE when you should be PASSIVE—or receptive. A positive mind does not receive, but rather sends out, and for the time being is insulated. You should remain in this passive attitude for at least 15 or 20 minutes—an hour if you like.

In other words, the mind is both a servant and a master. On the one hand, it may be whipped up and driven headlong into a cancer—but, on the other hand, it must be handled very gingerly. Obviously, a dangerous thing to have in the head. Imagine it running amuck. Fancy it gobbling, not a cancer or a bunion, but a lung, a leg! No doubt Professor Gore tells the student, in later lessons, how to keep it on the track. Meanwhile, beware of that monster sloshing 'round in your skull! [11 August 1911]

THE CURSE OF PATENT MEDICINES

The Supreme Court's recent decision in the so-called Patent Medicine case[3] opens a clear way, it appears, for the prosperity of any swindler who chooses to go into the trade of manufacturing bogus nostrums. By the terms of that decision it is now perfectly lawful to call any mixture of borax and water a "sure cure" for cancer or hydrophobia and to sell it as such. The prohibitions of the Pure Food and Drugs act, we are told, apply only to the contents of patent medicines. It is illegal for a manufacturer of soothing syrups to put opium in his decoctions without giving plain warning of that fact, and it is equally illegal for him to say that opium is in them when it is not in them. But if he says that they are certain cures for any disease, however incurable it may be, he is within his rights.

Just how the reverend seigneurs of our Aula Regis arrived at their judgment does not appear, for the Pure Food and Drugs act clearly says that "the term 'misbranded' * * * shall apply to all drugs * * * the package or label of which shall bear *any statement* * * * *which shall be false or misleading in any particular.*" The italics are supplied by the Journal of the American Medical Association, which marvels upon the mysteries of juridical logic. Certainly the statement that a watery solution of common salt will cure Bright's disease is "false and misleading," and yet, by the court's decision, it is held to be not so.

A lesser tribunal—to wit, the United States Circuit Court for the Eastern District of New York—has lately gone the Supreme Court one better by deciding that a patent medicine manufacturer shall have great latitude in stating the contents of his nostrum. The defendant before it was a man who made a so-called "peroxide cream" in which "the amount of peroxide was so insignificant that it could have no practical therapeutic effect." Despite this fact, which seems to have been demonstrated beyond a doubt, Veeder, J., decided that any amount of peroxide, however infinitesimal, converted common cream into genuine peroxide cream. In the same way, no doubt 1–100th of a grain of quinine converts a lump of clay into a genuine quinine pill.

These decisions indicate the need for prompt action by Congress. The Pure Food and Drugs act, by requiring the plain labeling of patent medicines containing narcotics, wood alcohol and other poisons, has already sounded the doom of many once-popular tipples and dopes. What is now needed is an amendment that will knock out the fraudulent sure-cure and cure-all. Any man who says that his salve or liniment will cure cancer is an unmitigated liar, for the simple reason that cancer is known to be an incurable disease. Some day, perhaps, it will be cured—maybe in the near future. But not by quack salves.

An amendment putting the sure-cure seller out of business would do no harm to those patent medicines that have genuine value. There are not a few such—remedies which, whatever the dangers attending their ignorant use, are at least efficacious when used intelligently. To that class belong the simpler laxatives, mouth washes, dentifrices, antiseptics, and so on. That these remedies may be misused is scarcely an argument against them. The law cannot undertake to protect the fool who is constantly dosing himself, ignorantly and unnecessarily. No matter what Congress says about it, he will continue to swallow elixirs and pills. But even this silly man should be given some assurance that he is getting what he pays for—that the beautiful pink liquid he buys for his stomachache is really not a furniture polish. [7 June 1911]

THE ANTI-VIVISECTIONISTS

The anti-vivisectionists of England, with characteristic mendacity, now endeavor to make it appear that the recent report of the Royal Commission on Vivisection gave support to their ridiculous and lying attack upon scientific medicine. The truth is, of course, that it did nothing of the sort. On the contrary, its general conclusion was wholly favorable to intelligent research, and it had this to say of anti-vivisectionist fictions:

> We desire to state that the harrowing descriptions and
> illustrations of operations inflicted on animals, which are freely
> circulated by post, advertisement, or otherwise, are in many cases
> calculated to mislead the public, so far as they suggest that the
> animals in question were not under an anæsthetic. To represent

that animals subjected to experiments in this country are wantonly tortured would, in our opinion, be absolutely false.

Going further, the commission agreed that experiments on animals were "morally justifiable and should not be prohibited by leglislation," and laid it down that "valuable knowledge has been acquired in regard to physiological processes and the causation of disease, and that useful methods for the prevention, cure and treatment of certain diseases have resulted from experimental investigations upon living animals." And yet the Hon. Stephen Coleridge, grand master of the English Anti-Vivisection Society, hails the report as "a striking and triumphant vindication of the struggle carried on by the society."

On what ground does the honorable gentleman base this absurd exultation? On the ground, it would appear, that the commission declared itself, at least by implication, against the wanton torture of animals. But is any such wanton torture carried on in the laboratories of England? Is it a fact, in brief, that animals are butchered in cold blood by ferocious pathologists, merely for the fun of it and without any benefit to man? Of course not. This charge has been made constantly by the anti-vivisectionists of England, just as it has been made constantly by the anti-vivisectionists of America, but the report of the commission, as might have been expected, showed that there is no truth in it whatever.

The trouble with the anti-vivisectionists is that their animus against all scientific medicine, regardless of the dependence upon expertmentation, is too, too evident. If they confined themselves to protesting against needless and over-cruel experiments every decent person, perhaps, would be with them, but they always go to the extreme of protesting against all experiments, however great and obvious their value. And, in order to justify that protest they must needs deny that value. That is to say, they must set up shop as destructive critics of the whole of modern medicine—as expert witnesses capable of controverting and flabbergasting such opposing experts as Ehrlich and Wright, Flexner and Welch.

Naturally enough, this preposterous effort does them far more damage than good. It is very difficult, in the present year of grace, to convince any wholly sane man that such things as the diphtheria, meningitis and tetanus antitoxins, the typhoid, smallpox and hydrophobia vaccines, the salvarsan of Dr. Ehrlich, and the revolutionary achievements of modern surgery are all useless and evil. He knows better. He himself, perhaps, has seen these things in operation, to his own relief or that or his friends, and if he hasn't, then he is at least content to take the word of those who have, and in particular, the word of those who are best fitted, by education and experience, to judge the matter. In brief, he believes, on the soundest conceivable grounds, that such a man as Dr. Welch knows vastly more about medicine than the average corn-fed osteopath or Christian Science healer-grafter, or patent medicine quack, and so he is willing to accept Dr. Welch's opinion.

Thus it happens that when the anti-vivisectionists undertake to prove that Dr. Welch is a fraud or an ignoramous they thereby lose the support of all persons of normal intelligence. But by the same token, they also draw to their banner all those persons whose intelligence is insufficient to distinguish between Dr. Welch's exact knowledge and a quack's empty balderdash. Therefore, you will find, if you look into the matter carefully, that the anti-vivisectionist movement, in this country as in England, tends to fall more and more into the hands of obvious foes of reason—that is to say, into the hands of persons who start out with the assumption that the liver is a mere delusion of the mind, or that massage will cure tuberculosis, or that Peruna is a certain specific for malaria.

With what result? With the result that the whole movement takes on the absurdity and borrows the chronic mendacity of such gladiators of nonsense. And with the secondary result that it becomes increasingly inadvisable, in the absence of overwhelming correlative proof, to accept any statement made by an anti-vivisectionist rabble-rouser. I do not say that all of these gentry are professional liars, for some of them, I believe, are merely credulous persons misled by those who are, but I do say that a campaign of incessant misrepresentation and slander, of indecent attack upon honest and useful men and women, of silly affirmations and ludicrous denials, now underlies the whole anti-vivisectionist propaganda.

It is well for the public to bear all this in mind. It is well for it to remember clearly, when sobs for boiled guinea pigs shake the air, that such sobs are too often evidence, not of any altruistic desire to save the guinea pigs, but of a purely selfish desire, on the part of some patron or toreador of quackery, to discomfit and discredit the men whose honorable labor stands between us and disease, and so work his own stupid satisfaction or personal profit. [29 March 1912]

ON CHRISTIAN SCIENCE

From a pleasant little note to the Editor of THE EVENING SUN, bearing the sign manual of the Hon. W. C. Williams, press agent of the local Christian Scientists:

> In one of his recent delightful outbursts he [the Hon. Mr. Mencken] stated very emphatically that Dr. Welch knew vastly more about medicine than the average Christian Science healer. I am surprised by this emphasis of Mr. Mencken, because it unmistakably implies that he believes Christian Scientists claim to know more about medicine than physicians. They do not make such an absurd claim * * * Christian Scientists do not use medicines. Then why should they care to know about them?

An almost classical example of Christian Science evasion, and hence worthy the attention of the judicious. I used the mord "medicine" in the broad sense of the art of combating disease; the Hon. Mr. Williams chooses to understand it in the narrow sense of a dose of castor oil—and there you are. Such silly juggling with words is to be encountered in practically all Christian Science writings. My meaning, I haven't the slightest doubt, was perfectly clear to the Hon. Mr. Williams, for I specifically mentioned surgery as a part of medicine, and surgery has nothing whatever to do with "medicines," and yet the honorable gentleman bases his whole answer upon the assumption that "medicine" and "medicines" are identical, and obviously regards that infantile trick as a proof of sagacity.

When a Christian Science healer-grafter essays to cure a case of cancer of the stomach by reading "Science and Health" to the patient he palpably practices medicine—first, by pretending to make a diagnosis, and, secondly, by prescribing a course of treatment. The fact that he does not prescribe "medicines"—*i. e.*, drugs or serums—is entirely immaterial. It is well known to everyone that, in the treatment of many diseases, drugs are of small value. Typhoid fever is an example and tuberculosis is another. An educated physician, in dealing with such a malady, sometimes finds it unnecessary to use any drugs at all. But he is practicing medicine nevertheless. And so is a psychotherapist who follows the same route.

It is my private belief that in the two chief departments of the art of medicine—diagnosis and treatment—the knowledge of Dr. Welch is infinitely greater than that of any Christian Science healer in Christendom, or, indeed, than that of all of them taken together. I may be wrong in holding to this belief, and I stand ready to abandon it whenever proof of my error is brought forward. But I do not reckon the idle word-juggling of the Hon. Mr. Williams as such proof, nor the preposterous and unsupported claims of mental healers. Going further, I hold that any person who does accept such evidence is a tedious and ridiculous ignoramus.

The Hon. Mr. Williams, in accordance with another familiar custom of Christian Scientist rhetoricians, endeavors to impale me upon a theological hook. That is to say, he seeks to make me deny, further on in his letter, that a direct appeal to Omnipotence will cure disease. I evade the issue by granting the fact. But if it be so, then why do Christian Scientist healers undertake an elaborate and recondite treatment, manageable only by the elect, and why do they make such depressingly material charges for something that must be free to all, and protest so bitterly when laws are passed forbidding then to do so?

Let the Hon. Mr. Williams come out from behind his theological breastworks. He knows very well that I can't reach him there. But if he cares to debate the question whether a Christian Science healer's diagnosis is likely to be as sound as Dr. Welch's, or the question whether or not Christian Science treatment (bought and paid for) will actually cure hydrophobia or jigger bites or caries of the teeth, then I shall be very glad to meet him on the mat.

Meanwhile I offer him my respectful compliments and grant freely that "the number of Christian Scientists is growing." Psychotherapy is now quite the rage in our fair republic, just as the scheme of the initiative and referendum is the rage. Both appeal powerfully to folk whose yearning to say something is unaccompanied by anything to say. Both are grounded firmly upon the theory that the man who knows nothing whatever about a given question is vastly more competent to answer it than the man who has sought to master it by hard study. [8 April 1912]

THE CASE FOR VACCINATION

Dr. A. L. Blessing, the calliope of medical freedom, in answer to my objection that his authorities against vaccination are either long dead or without professional standing:

> Unfortunately for his reasoning, by the same logical process
> the words of Christ, Shakespeare, Bacon and all the other great
> lawgivers and reformers are dead letters and of no value.

A typical example of anti-vaccinationist bosh. What possible comparison can there be between generalizations about human conduct and special knowledge about the facts of biology? The principles of ethics are the same today that they were in the time of Christ; the facts of immunization belong, in the main, to the medical progress of the last 30 years.

Nine-tenths of the objections that were brought against vaccination in the sixties and seventies are no longer valid today. At that time, as every intelligent man knows, it was still impossible to guard against the contamination of vaccines. On the one hand, they might contain impurities derived from the body of the human being or animal from which they were taken—for example, the germs of tuberculosis, tetanus or hydrophobia. And on the other hand, there was grave risk of polluting them in transmission or during inoculation, thus producing so-called blood poisoning.

But both dangers are now reduced to next to nothing. On the one hand it is possible to make sure that the laboratory calf is free from tuberculosis, tetanus and all other such infectious diseases, and on the other hand it is possible to perform the operation of inoculation under absolutely aseptic conditions. And not only is this possible, but it is actually done daily. The huge vaccination scars of 30 or 40 years ago— mute evidence of unclean surgery—are now encountered very seldom. An authentic case of tuberculosis following competent vaccination is almost as rare as an authentic case of delirium tremens. In brief, the business of getting vaccinated, provided the attending surgeon be decently equipped for his work, is now little more dangerous than the business of getting shaved.

For this benign advance the human race owes its thanks and respect to a long line of earnest and inspired men, and particularly to Joseph Lister and Emil Pasteur.[4] It was their patient experimentation, their long, tedious work in the laboratory, that made aseptic surgery possible. Not only must we thank them for the improvements made in vaccination against smallpox, but also for our growing control of other and even worse infectious diseases, and for the phenomenal advances in surgery in our time. As a direct result of their labors the death rate throughout civilization has been reduced fully 40 per cent. and the average span of human life has been lengthened more than five years.

But Lister and Pasteur get no grateful acknowledgments from medical freedomists. On the contrary, it is the chief effort of these grotesque bellowers of balderdash to deny and revile them. I do not say that Dr. Blessing himself is donkey enough to do it, but I do say that many fellow-members of his lodge are at it constantly, and that he encourages them to it by joining them in an ignorant and ridiculous war upon vaccination. He is, as he informs us, a graduate of the University of Maryland School of Medicine. Let him go back to that school and ask its professors what they think of his association with the Christian Scientists, anti-vivisectionists, osteopaths, chiropractors, perunists, vegetarians and other such mountebanks of medical freedom. Let him find a single university professor or student who is on the side of that absurd and lying bunch, and I shall very gladly kiss his hand.

If Dr. Blessing has any actual evidence against vaccination, his *alma mater* is the place to present it. There he will find men capable of judging it intelligently, and what is more, men willing to hear it patiently. If he has discovered sound objections to the operation, they will be given due consideration and he will go down into history as a respectable contributor to the progress of medicine. But he is not going to accomplish anything of value, either to himself or to the world, by allying himself with a camorra of bonesetters, masseurs, Eddyites, patent-medicine sellers, herb doctors and screaming old maids. He is not going to get any attention from intelligent folks so long as he adorns the League for Medical Freedom. [8 March 1913]

TONOTHERAPY AND OTHER REMEDIES

Medical freedom in all its myriad and lovely forms is given a lot of space in the current issue of the *Nautilus Magazine,* the New Thought organ. Mother Elizabeth Towne, editor of the *Nautilus,* is an ardent medical freedomist herself and has written a treatise "Just How to Wake the

Soler Plexus," which every New Thought knows by heart. But her present rave, it would appear, is not for this tickling of the plexus, but for tonotherapy, or musical therapeutics, the invention of Prof. Dr. Eva Augusta Vescelius, of Croton-on-Hudson, N. Y.

All one needs, to become a full-fledged practitioner of tonotherapy, is a phonograph and a set of records. The whole treatment, no matter what the disease, consists in wooing the patient's ears until he is well again. Thus a typical report from the Vescelius clinic:

> A case of chills and fever was cured by one application of
> Beethoven's "Moonlight" sonata, followed by "The Evening Star"
> and Pilgrim's chorus from "Tannhäuser" and "There Is a Land Mine
> Eye Hath Seen."[5] At the end of the last song the patient went to
> sleep. She awoke in perfect health, and has remained thus ever since.

A great discovery, but one that calls for further work by tonopathologists, for if music can cure, it can also kill, or, at any rate, wound. It is a well-known fact, for example, that the great majority of violoncellists suffer from cricks in the back, and that the constant playing of the oboe produces tonsilitis, sciatica and delusions of grandeur. Before the application of her remedy can be considered safe, Dr. Vescelius must investigate these contrary effects. Perhaps, of course, there is homeopathy mixed up with it—a familiar amalgam in the realm of medical freedom. Perhaps the strains of Schubert's "Serenade,"[6] which drive the average healthy man to the use of narcotics, may be a cure for the actual dope fiend. Such miracles are not unknown. The automatic piano, which rivals drink as a filler of our madhouses, is used in them to entertain the patients.

But tonotherapy is but one of the hundred or more great boons and inventions offered for medical freedom. Even more remarkable are the effects of the White Cross Electric Vibrator, which is sold by the Lindstrom-Smith Co., of 218 South Wabash street, Chicago. This wonderful appliance, according to the *Nautilus*,

> is the result of years of work and experiment. It is absolutely
> perfect. If you have your home wired for electricity, you can
> connect it up as easily as an electric lamp. If not, it will run
> perfectly on its own batteries. With this great machine you can
> get Nature's three greatest curative agents: Vibration, Galvanic

and Faradio Electricity. Give yourself vibrating chair treatments, Swedish massage in your own home.

The vibrator is useful in all conditions of ill health, but its specialties are wrinkles and baltitude. It makes a fine new thatch, soft and silky, upon the baldest head. And it knocks out wrinkles in a few rounds—and not only wrinkles, but "also other disfigurations."

It brings back the healthful glow of girlhood to pallid cheeks. Sagging muscles are strengthened and regain their beauty. Your complexion will be made as clear as a child's. If you have too much flesh, vibration will reduce it. If not enough, vibration will cause the hollows to be filled out.

I am sending for one of these magical vibrators and shall let you know its effects. My own beauty, once so blooming, has begun to wither and go stale. I have 2½ chins, a waist like a taxicab, and a pair of large zigzag wrinkles across my brow. My nose, growing pink in winter, stays pink all summer. I lose hair every time the wind blows. The White Cross Electric Vibrator would seem to be my rescuer foreordained.

And if it fails, medical freedom still has many remedies to offer. I pass over Christian Science, osteopathy, chiropractic, the Emmanuel Movement and bovotherapy as already familiar to all cognoscenti. More remarkable than any of them is the psycho-saline system of Prof. Walter De Voe, of 2057 East Sixty-ninth street, Cleveland, Ohio. You will find it described on page 85 of the *Nautilus*. Its basis is Prof. De Voe's discovery that "in healing the sick two conditions must be made," to wit:

1. The positive polarity of the body must be restored, so that every cell will be a positive centre of attraction for building elements, and will absorb them from food, etc.

2. The natural food elements must be provided in assimilable form.

But how to do it? Trust Professor De Voe! He is one of the whales of medical freedom—perhaps even its Ehrlich. This is how he goes about it:

1. I arouse the Organizing Power so that the entire body will become positive and attractive to vital elements in food, air, sunshine and earth radiance.

2. I provide refined food elements in the form of Nutrient Salts.

Just what these Nutrient Salts are Professor De Voe doesn't explain, but he has a large supply of them on hand and will sell them to any sufferer as a personal favor. He does not offer them by the pound, but by the month. A dollar for one month, or $5 for six months. "Send main symptoms when ordering."

Another medical freedomist who keeps one leg in the pharmacopœia, despite Mother Towne's declaration (page 20) that "drugs are going out of fashion," is Prof. Dr. Henderson, of Charleston, W. Va., who offers an "antiseptic mineral bath" that will "eliminate the body toxins" and cure "rheumatism, kidney disease, fevers, autotoxemia, joint troubles, catarrh, children's diseases * * * and uric acid conditions." Again, there is Prof. A. J. Straughan, of 820 Anheim street, Pittsburgh, Pa., with his system of astro-biochemistry, a compound of astrology and scientific feeding. Yet, again, there is Prof. G. H. Brinkler, of Washington. D. C., with his discovery that butter and cheese cause catarrh, and that radishes are stimulating.

But I go no further with these great boons of medical freedom. If you would enjoy them all, if you would escape from the foul clutches of the Medical Trust, then my advice is that you subscribe to the *Nautilus* and follow Mother Towne and her friends. They are pledged to achieve the goal of Dr. William H. Welch. They dream of the day when doctors will cease to poison and surgeons will cease to slaughter—when all our drugs will be thrown away as useless, and a delivered populace will put its whole trust in "Science and Health," bovotherapy, tonotherapy, the White Cross Electric Vibrator, osteopathy, Swedish massage, chiropractic, astro-biochemistry, the Subconscious, the Astral Self, Peruna, the Bhagavad Gita, the Aura, Deep Breathing, the Esoteric Atom, the solar plexus, the Emmanuel Movement and mechanotherapy. [24 April 1913]

THE TRIUMPH OF QUACKERY

Discoursing in the current *Atlantic Monthly* upon the vast success among us of such maudlin novelists as the Rev. Harold Bell Wright, the Hon. Owen Wister sweeps an illuminating ray or two through the general subject of quackery in the United States.[7] That quackery is of a special and incomparable brand, almost unknown in other parts of Christendom. We not only suffer it; we are even, in a sense, proud of it; it lies at the bottom of our dearest theories of the true, the good and the beautiful. In all combats between a quack and a man of genuine information and skill among us the quack has inordinate advantages and is sure to prevail. Not only in literature, but also in government, religion and morals he has only to emit his whoop to get the populace with him. The two Americans of today who can boast the largest and most enthusiastic followings are the Hon. Theodore Roosevelt and the Hon. William Jennings Bryan, both quacks in all departments of their protean activity.

The Hon. Mr. Wister finds the chief cause of this respect for quackery, this deification of the amateur, in the conditions confronting the pioneer American—conditions actually very easy, despite the legend of their hardship, and hence capable of being met and overcome by untrained and usually blundering men. Out of their overcoming the pioneer derived a high opinion of himself, and out of that high opinion of himself grew the doctrine that training and preparedness were after all of small consequence, and that the respect for them held in Europe was a mere illusion. Says Mr. Wister:

> The pioneer democrat had the backwoods and the Indian
> to fight. He won. * * * With an ax, and a gun and a vote and
> some patent medicine, he survived. * * * Suppose * * * he had
> had Napoleon, or Wellington, with some trained armies against
> him? Suppose some educated and civilized races had been his
> competitors? France, England, Germany, had *each other* to fight
> with, while the pioneer democrat was opposed by merely a virgin
> wilderness. New Orleans and Lundy's Lane do not outbalance
> our forlorn humiliation of 1812. Lack of education all hangs
> together—whether in soldiers, statesmen, doctors, or novelists.
> The pioneer democrat's easy success made him sure that quacks
> of whatever sort were just as good as anybody else. From this it
> was but a step to preferring them—and Europe was then too
> distant and too busy to disabuse him of this illusion.

This theory, perhaps, explains the genesis of American quackery, but it leaves unexplained the continued prosperity of quackery in these latter days. To find that explanation one must proceed by way of a doctrine enunciated by the late Wendell Phillips, the doctrine, to wit, that, "more than any other people, we Americans are afraid of one another." And why? Simply because no machinery can be provided, under a democracy such as ours, for the protection of genuine skill and information against ignorant and vicious attack, and the standing menace of that attack causes the man of sound knowledge to withdraw within himself, leaving the field to the quacks and their dupes.

One often sees the operation of this process in the field of medicine, where the difference between accurate knowledge and ignorant quackery is sharply defined. If it were possible to make a full use of this knowledge for the protection of the public health, the general death rate in the United States would probably decline at least 10 per cent. But, as everyone knows, it is not possible to make a full use of it, for the moment the educated physicians of the country propose to apply it in some new direction they are vigorously attacked by a host of quacks, and the best they can hope for after that is a more or less clumsy compromise. The result is that they come forward with new proposals as seldom as possible, and that a good deal of their sound and useful knowledge thus goes to waste.

The difficulty, of course, lies in the fact that, under a democracy, the ultimate adjudication of medical controversies, as of all other controversies, lies with the ignorant and unintelligent mob, and that this mob is animated by that chronic distrust of learning which always marks the lower orders of men. Under more civilized forms of government no such club is held over men who really know. Within the fields of their special knowledge they are not only heard with respect, but in addition they are given what amounts substantially to the power to legislate. This deprives the mob of all right to interfere with the solution of their special problems, and so there is no opportunity for quacks to enchant and mislead the mob with their brummagem sorceries. The net result is advantageous to all concerned. On the one hand, the mob enjoys the benefit of the experts' special knowledge, and, on the other hand, the experts are protected from rows and assaults which invade their self-respect.

So in all other fields. In this country, for example, the question as to the defense of the nation by sea to taken out of the hands of the men whose training fits them to deal with it and put into the hands of men who are notorious quacks, and whose whole fortunes depend upon their skill at political and other sorts of quackery—*e. g.*, the Hon. Josephus Daniels. At a time like the present, when the entire country is interested in the navy, the only men who really know anything about it are specifically forbidden, on pain of dismissal and professional ruin, so much as to discuss it. The quacks and mountebanks of Congress are free to discuss it to their hearts' content, and the quacks of the newspapers (of whom I have the honor to be one) are free to do likewise, but the admirals and captains of the fleet are muzzled, and if they ventured to disobey orders by publicly controverting the current sophistries and imbecilities, public opinion would be almost unanimously behind their punishment.

In brief, democracy works against all sound efficiency (as opposed to merely superficial dexterity) by filling the mob-man with the delusion that he is quite as good as any other man. From this false theory he deduces the quite natural corollary that any man who disputes it—*i. e.*, any man who presumes to superiority—is a charlatan and a rogue. The one leader that he acknowledges is the leader who ratifies and makes a virtue of the general ignorance and stupidity—*i. e.*, the rabble-rouser, the great democrat, the Bryan, the Roosevelt, the quack. He doesn't want advice; he merely wants approval. As the Hon. Mr. Wister says, "his notion of liberty is that everybody is free to agree with him." This is the fundamental belief of the mob-man, and this is also the fundamental principle of democracy. [5 June 1915]

XI

THE GREAT WAR

The German Emperor to the members of the Reichstag:

> The present situation did not arise from temporary conflicts
> of interest or diplomatic combinations, but is the result of ill
> will existing for years against the strength and prosperity of the
> German Empire.

Without any question, a fair and accurate statement of the case.
Ever since the Franco-Prussian War gave Germany her present solidar-
ity and started her upon her great career of prosperity and progress, she
has been viewed with baleful eye by France and England. For 44 long
years the French have menaced her security with their melodramatic
plans for *revanche*,[1] and all the while the English have come closer and
closer to an offensive and defensive alliance with her and their old foes.
Germany has stood in imminent peril ever since the Agadir incident
in 1911,[2] when the support of England gave France the courage for her
historic threat of war.

Nothing could better reveal the furious antagonism of both countries than their undisguised fear of Germany. That fear has frequently
taken grotesque and extravagant forms. Everyone knows how the
French have quaked and spluttered every time a German dirigible has

been sighted along the border, and everyone knows, too, what imbecile fictions about German ambitions and German plans have been printed in their newspapers. By the same token, everyone remembers the profound Germanophobia that afflicted England no more than three years ago, when the London papers devoted their chief news pages day after day to childish gabble about a "German invasion," and every strange light along the coast set the whole nation trembling, and even such sober men as Earl Roberts succumbed to the universal terror.

That terror was anything but creditable to the English people, but it would be difficult to show that the Germans tried to profit by it, or that they were in any way responsible for it. Their sole offense lay in attending strictly to their business, and in making it a go. They were pushing their trade into all parts of the world; they were trying to protect it against unfair attack by building up an effective navy; they were seeking legitimate outlets for their surplus population; they were beating the English at their own game. For these high crimes and misdemeanors they were denounced as pirates and worse. But behind that calling of names there was nothing more than respectable envy, and in that envy there was fear, and in that fear there was nothing to the honor and dignity of England.

England's belated entry into the present war may turn the tide against Germany, but it will certainly bring no glory to England. The world, as a world, sticks to old-fashioned notions of fair fighting. It has little admiration for the nation which waits to strike an enemy it fears until that enemy is beset by superior numbers, and battling for its life with its back to the wall. An attack at such a time may be effective; it may be prudent; it may be clever—but it is not cricket. What would the English say of it if Germany, seeing France beset by Austria and Italy, had waited until then to strike? In their own hearts, once this war is over, they will find such disquieting questionings. If they help to overwhelm Germany, the job will merely leave them with an open and irreconcilable foe, sure to pay them off soon or late. And if Germany, by any joke of fate, succeeds in holding them off, they will stand before the world in a highly ludicrous and embarrassing posture.

As for France, the situation is little more to her credit than to England's. For years she has been boring the world with her fantastic plans for punishing and annihilating Germany, but without ever passing

beyond the stage of loud boasting. She has fomented anti-German feeling in Alsace and Lorraine—and then left the protesting "prisoners of
war" to the mercies of the Germans. Beaten fairly and soundly in 1870,
she has spent 44 years talking about it. No known principle of good
sportsmanship has gone unbroken at her hand. And now at last, dragged
into it by the force of events, she stands fuming and flabbergasted before
her old foe, unable to take the offensive while the chance offers, unable
to protect the border States against the German invasion, deafening the
world with idle protests against German preparedness and enterprise,
waiting pathetically for England to join Russia in giving her aid.

Deutschland, Deutschland, gegen alles![3] [6 August 1914]

THE CAUSES OF THE WAR

The violently anti-German New York *World* on the causes of the war:

> The Austrian demands upon Servia were subversive of her
> nationality.

In exactly the same sense that our own demands upon Spain, after
the blowing up of the Maine, were subversive of *her* nationality. Search
all history, and you will have difficulty finding two situations more alike.
The Austrians had sound and abundant reasons for suspecting that the
assassination of the Archduke Franz Ferdinand had been planned by
Servians, with the connivance of the Belgrade Government, and so
they demanded representation on the Servian board of inquiry. We had
sound and abundant reasons for suspecting that the Maine had been
blown up by Spaniards, and so we demanded the right to make our
own inquiry. Two differences between the two cases now appear: (*a*) the
Austrians merely asked for representation, whereas we demanded that
the whole inquiry be in our hands, and (*b*) the Spaniards granted our
demand, whereas the Servians, backed by Russia, refused Austria's.

Nevertheless, we went to war with Spain. The Spaniards, as I say,
granted all our demands, and the inquiry conducted by Capt. W. T.
Sampson at Havana failed to fix responsibility upon any definite Span-
iard, or, indeed, upon the Spaniards at all, for many persons concluded
that the Maine had been blown up by Cubans to provoke the United
States to war. And yet we went to war. Would we have hesitated if all
Latin-America had stood behind Spain? Would we have hesitated if

even France and Italy had sent fleets to our coast? And did we denounce England when she stood ready to help us?

Let us, by all means, have a reasonable honesty and fairness in the discussion of this war. Let us not revile Austria for doing, in less measure, the very things that we ourselves did in 1898. The New York *World* is the principal organ of the Wilson Administration. It is an eager supporter of all the President's policies, including that voiced in his two proclamations of neutrality. And yet it practices neutrality by making violent attacks, day after day, upon the Germans and the Austrians, just as Dr. Wilson himself practices neutrality (or did, at least, for the first three weeks of the war) by cutting off all war news from Germany, and so giving a clear track to the outrageous charges of the French and the ridiculous lying and boasting of the Belgians.

Whatever fair and accurate war news we got in this country, up to a few days ago, we owed to the English. Dr. Wilson's "neutral" ban upon the German wireless had given the English cables a monopoly of the news. Over them came the manufactured news of the French and Belgians, but over them also came the honest announcements of the English themselves. Thus we had to go to one of the belligerents for a lesson in fairness. And thus that fairness put to shame our own Government's hollow and disingenuous pretense of neutrality. [26 August 1914]

THE CASE FOR GERMANY

We Americans, protected to the eastward and westward by the oceans and to the northward and southward by the fact that our neighbors are relatively weak and harmless, find it difficult to sympathize with the sacrifices that Germany has made to create her enormous war machine. It seems inconceivable to us that a free people should waste their money and energy upon any such enterprise, and so we jump to the conclusion that the Germans themselves must needs view it as we do, and that it has been forced upon them by their despotic Kaiser. To that view we are aided by the circumstance that nine-tenths of our news from Germany, even in times of peace, is derived from hostile sources. Practically everything that comes to us from the Continent comes through London. It is there that all of the great press associations have their headquarters and gather in their news. It is there that all of our great papers have their principal European correspondents. And naturally enough, our use of the same language makes us read the English papers, at first or second hand, vastly more than we read the German papers, and so leads us unconsciously into accepting the English point of view.

Hence the almost universal American feeling that the German war machine was created for the deliberate purpose of making trouble—that it represents, not any intelligible and righteous plan of self-defense, but merely the barbarous ambition and blood lust of one unconscionable man. But is this feeling justified by the facts? Is there, at bottom, any truth in the notion that the Kaiser is a professional bully, that he has yearned and plotted for a war, that the very existence of his huge army is a proof of his determination to make all Europe a howling wilderness? I think not. On the contrary, I see the German war machine as a means of defense only, as a necessary protection for a people beset by disingenuous and uncompromising enemies, as the one sure agent of ultimate peace in Europe. And to that view of it, I believe, more and more Americans will be inclined as the true history of the present war comes out.

Why is so much heard of the Kaiser's determination to make his army the best in the world, and so little of England's determination to rule and domineer upon the seas? If a chip has been carried upon a national shoulder, whose shoulder was it, England's or Germany's? Down to the time of the Franco-Prussian War the English were friendly to Germany. During that war they stood, albeit somewhat patronizingly, on the German side—that is, up to the fall of Paris. But the moment it became apparent that the disunited German principalities had been suddenly united into a strong and solid empire, the English made a rapid *volte-face*. Germany was now a great power, a rival to be reckoned with, even to be feared. And so the English began to be hostile to her, and out of that hostility there arose eventually two things—first, the creation of a huge English navy, and secondly, an open and ardent courtship of France. The old enemy was now useful against the new enemy. The *entente cordiale*[4] was born, and being born, it was assiduously nursed. Nothing could have been more undisguised than the English flattery of France during the last days of King Edward.

What was Germany to do? Her commerce was growing by leaps and bounds. Her ships were beginning to penetrate to every port of the world. Could she stand idly by while England prepared so openly to crush her when the time should come, and even discussed openly the nearness of its coming? Could she consent to leave her foreign commerce, the bulwark of her national prosperity, at the mercy of a rival so obviously jealous and belligerent? Could she put her head into the lion's mouth? And could she, on land, leave her frontiers undefended against England's new ally—that France which never ceased to cry for *revanche?* Or against Russia, that incongruous and terrible third member of the new firm?[5]

To ask the questions is to answer them. The one wise and prudent thing for Germany to do was to prepare to defend herself, not only against one power, but against all three together. To that end, under the present Kaiser, the military plans of Bismarck and Moltke were worked out to the last place of decimals. A vast army was organized, and to its training for war the best intelligence of the empire was devoted. And at the same time Germany began to build a navy. England was still far ahead, but bit by bit the Germans crept up. As it happened, war came at last before the navy was equal to a pitched battle, but not before it was able to protect Germany from invasion and annihilation. It is playing its part in this war—not a spectacular part, perhaps, but still a very valuable part. German commerce is destroyed, but the German coast is at least secure against England's enormous and once irresistible swarm of ships.

To picture the Germans as brigands and swashbucklers is to do a grave injustice to a people whose one genuine desire is for peace, a reasonable security, a chance to do their hard and useful work in the world. What have they ever done to provoke war? They kept hands off when England was paralyzed by the rising in South Africa.[6] They kept hands off when Russia was paralyzed by the disaster in Manchuria.[7] They submitted to the building of French forts along their Belgian frontier. They yielded to French aggressions in Africa. They permitted Italy to make war upon Turkey, their friend.[8] They made no protest against the astounding outbreak of Germanophobia in England four or five years ago. They showed no hatred of France, they listened without complaint to the eternal gabble about *revanche,* they did no crowing over their vanquished foe. Their one crime, during all the time that preparations were being made to crush and ruin them, was to attend strictly to business, beating the English in fair competition in all the open markets of the world. And their one crime today is that they fight gallantly and successfully against a combination of enemies which is so desperate and so eager that it stoops to any expedient to win, seducing Italy with promises of loot, inviting the Slavs to overrun Europe, turning loose the Japs in the East, even bringing up negro allies from Africa.

Did Germany strike the first blow? Did she, in the narrow, technical sense, start the war? Well, what of it? What sane man will deny that it was inevitable, soon or late—that it had to come, Kaiser or no Kaiser—that Germany was doomed to do battle for her very life? And what fair man will hold it an offense against the right to challenge glowering enemies boldly, to accept great odds without fear, to end an intolerable situation by forcing a stand-up fight? [27 August 1914]

A LAMENT FOR FRANCE

The poor French seem doomed to suffer all the worst horrors of this war. No matter which side wins in the end, the chief battles will be fought on French soil, and it appears highly probable that a number of French cities, including perhaps Paris, will share the fate of Louvain.[9] And meanwhile the whole of Normandy will be devastated by the clash of immense armies, and from end to end of the country industry and agriculture will be paralyzed. What is worse, France will probably lose more men in proportion of population than any other belligerent nation, not excepting Germany. The last line of reserves has been called out. The boys and the old men are going gallantly and pathetically to the front.

No man, whatever his sympathies, can contemplate this devastation and disaster without genuine distress. The French, alone among the contestants, stand free of any charge of bringing on the war. They yearned, true enough, for their long-delayed *revanche,* and in expansive moods they often talked of getting it, but not many intelligent Frenchmen, I believe, confused the desirable with the possible. Germany had grown too large and too strong to be conquered single-handed. The population across the Vosges had almost doubled since 1870. The population of France had stood still. The larger battalions were on the German side, and not only the larger battalions, but also the generalship. The thing that had proved impossible in 1870 was doubly impossible a generation afterward.

But then came the ingratiating English, with their open and even overwhelming offers of friendship. The French, at the start, were full of suspicion of these offers; they had not forgotten the "perfidious

Albion"[10] of the past; they distrusted the Greeks bearing gifts. But the wooing was conducted with such furious and un-English ardor that in the end the French were carried off their feet. There followed the famous *entente cordiale,* and on its heels the Triple Entente. England, laying plans against Germany, needed the help of the France that she had threatened in 1870. And when, the time being ripe, she raised her moral banners and sounded the advance, it was upon her new ally that the chief burdens of the conflict fell. The French were outnumbered and saw their frontiers overrun. England sent enough men—and no more— to hold back one wing of the German horde 24 hours. Over the ground that she essayed to guard the Germans have delivered their boldest and most devastating blow at France.

Nothing could be plainer or more inspiring than the courage and enthusiasm of the French soldiers. They are throwing themselves into the fight with heroic vigor, and taking their ghastly punishment without whimpering. But all the chances of war are against them. At least in trained men, they are outnumbered by their foes; the help of England is delayed and cut off; worst of all, they suffer again from that stupid and childish leadership which brought them to disaster in 1870. On every field, from the first days in Alsace to the retreat from the Meuse, their leaders have been outgeneraled and made ridiculous by the diabolical General von Stab.[11] Consider, for example, General Joffre's "rescue" of the "imprisoned" provinces—and his sonorous proclamation to their people. What a humiliation to read it now!

The trouble with the French Army, today as in 1870, is politics. It is under the control, not of military experts, but of self-seeking and empty-headed politicians. Promotion does not go by merit, but by pull and favor. There is, in peace as in war, an endless series of scandals. Jobbery enters into the purchase of supplies; incompetents are put in command; good men are persecuted and kept down; the whole estab- lishment is crippled by that corruption which is universal in French officialdom. And in time of war the inevitable collapse is concealed by the diligent spreading of false news of victories. I have shown in this place how it was done in 1870; everyone knows how it has been done in the present war. In 1870 the French people finally arose against their deceivers and drove them out. No doubt they will do the same thing again, once they learn and comprehend the truth.

But all that will not take anything from the burden of their misfortune. They are doomed to pay two-thirds of the price of the English attack upon Germany, and the most they can hope to gain is the recovery of Alsace-Lorraine, a province that Germany will be sure to wrest from them again at the first opportunity. And even here the chances are against them, for if the war ends with Germany in possession of any part of Belgium, the English will undoubtedly trade it for Alsace-Lorraine. Germany and England will be the survivors. Austria is already crushed; Belgium is German soil; Russia will be crumpled up and hurled back. And in the west Germany will have the land and England will have the sea, and France will have to take whatever the two together choose to give her. [3 September 1914]

WHAT IS THIS WAR ABOUT?

Rising to a question of personal privilege, I beg to assure those gentlemen of the Letter Column who mistake my defense of the slandered and hard-pressed Germans for a laudable (or heinous) manifestation of patriotism that I am not a German and am not bound to Germany by sentimental ties. I was born in Baltimore of Baltimore-born parents; I have no relatives, near or remote, in Germany, nor even any friends (save one Englishman!); very few of my personal associates in this town are native Germans; I read the German language very imperfectly, and do not speak it or write it at all; I never saw Germany until I was 28 years old; I have been there since but twice;[12] I am of English and Irish blood as well as German.

What is more, the most massive influences of my life have all been unmistakably English. I know Kinglake's "Crimea" and Steevens' "With Kitchener to Khartoum"[13] a great deal better than I know any history of the American Revolution or Civil War; I make a living writing the language of Thackeray and Huxley, and devote a good deal of time to studying it; I believe thoroughly in that imperialism for which England has always stood; I read English newspapers and magazines constantly, and have done so for 15 years; I regard the net English contribution to civilization as enormously greater than the German contribution; I am on good terms with many Englishmen, always get along well with them, and don't know a single one that I dislike.

All this by way of necessary explanation. But the Englishman upon whom the glory and greatness of England rests in not the Englishman who slanders and blubbers over Germany in this war. The England of Drake and Nelson, of Shakespeare and Marlowe, of Darwin and Huxley, of Clive and Rhodes is not the England of Churchill and Lloyd-George, of Asquith and McKenna, of mongrel allies and bawling suffragettes, of "lime-housing" and "mafficking,"[14] of press-censors and platitudinarians, of puerile moralizing and silly pettifogging. The England that the world yet admires and respects was a country ruled by proud and forthright men. The England that today poses as the uplifter of Europe is a country ruled by cheap demagogues and professional pharisees. The slimy "morality" of the unleashed rabble has conquered the clean and masculine ideals of the old ruling caste. A great nation has succumbed to mobocracy, and to the intellectual dishonesty that goes with it.

What is the war really about? Why are the nations fighting one another? In so far as Germany and England are concerned, the cause is as plain as a pike-staff. Germany, of late years, has suddenly become England's rival as the boss of Europe, and with Europe, of the world. German trade has begun to prevail over English trade; German influence has begun to undermine English influence; even upon the sea, the new might and consequence of Germany have begun to challenge England's old lordship. The natural result is that the English have grown angry and alarmed, and the second result is that they yearn to crush and dispose of Germany before it is too late—*i.e.*, before the Germans actually become their superiors in power, and so beyond their reach.

Such a yearning needs no defense. It is natural, it is virtuous, it is laudable. National jealousies make for the security, the prosperity and the greatness of the more virile nations, and hence for the progress of civilization. But did England, filled with this yearning, openly admit it, and then proceed in a frank and courageous manner to obtain its satisfaction in a fair fight? England did not. On the contrary, she artfully dissembled, her mouth full of pieties, until Germany was beset by enemies in front and behind; and then she suddenly threw her gigantic strength into the unequal contest. And did she, even then, announce her cause, state her motive, tell the truth? She did not. She went into battle with a false cry upon her lips, seeking to make her rage against a rival appear as a frenzy for righteousness, shedding crocodile tears over Germany's sins, wearing the tin halo and flopping chemise of a militant moralist.

I do not like militant moralists, whether they be nations or individuals. I distrust the man who is concerned about his neighbor's sins, and who calls in the police (or the Turcos, or the Sikhs, or the Russians) to put them down. I have never known such a man who was honest with himself, nor is there any record of such a one in all history. They were a nuisance in the days of Christ, and His most bitter denunciations were leveled against them. They are still a nuisance today, though they impudently call themselves Christians, and even seek to excommunicate all persons who object to their excesses. That their shallow sophistries appeal to the mob, that they are especially numerous and powerful under a mobocracy, is but one more proof that mobocracy is the foe of civilization, and not only of civilization, but also of the truth.

For the manly, stand-up, ruthless, truth-telling, clean-minded England of another day I have the highest respect and reverence. It was an England of sound ideals and great men. But for the smug, moralizing, disingenuous England of Churchill and Lloyd-George, of hollow pieties and saccharine protestations, of Japanese alliances and the nonconformist conscience—for this new and oleaginous England, by Gladstone out of Pecksniff, I have no respect whatever. Its victory over Germany in this war would be a victory for all the ideas and ideals that I most ardently detest and upon which, in my remote mud-puddle, I wage a battle with all the strength that I can muster, and to which I pledge my unceasing enmity until that day when the ultimate embalmer casts his sinister eye upon my fallen beauty.

When I think of this new, this saponaceous, this superbrummagem England, so smug and slick without and so full of corruption and excess within, I am beset by emotions of the utmost unpleasantness. I snort; I swear; I leak large globulous tears. It in my hope and belief that this sick and bogus England will be given a good licking by the Deutsch, to the end that truth and health may prevail upon the earth. If the Mailed Fist cracks it, I shall rejoice unashamed. The Mailed Fist is dedicated to the eternal facts of life, to the thing behind the mere word, to the truth that is above all petty quibbling over theoretical rights and wrongs. I am for the Mailed Fist, gents, until the last galoot's ashore.[15] [29 September 1914]

THE FATE OF BELGIUM

The Hon. Vivian C. Leftwich, Acting Belgian Consul at Baltimore, on the ethical and theological implications of the war:

> Happily for Belgium and the world, a power exists which
> is still above Germany, her idea of justice and her culture. It is
> called the justice of God. It is to this judgment that the Belgian
> nation appeals.

Nevertheless, even allowing this to be a fair statement of the case, it cannot be argued that there is much hope in the situation. Finland made the same appeal; so did Poland; so did the Boers. What good did it bring them? The history of England shows almost endless conquests of little peoples with right and justice on their side and full confidence in their ultimate triumph.

Let me not appear here to be mocking the Hon. Mr. Leftwich's apparent faith. But the facts of life have a bitterness that cannot be concealed. They show clearly that, in the reactions of nation upon nation, no intelligible process of justice can be discovered. The strong usually prevail over the weak; the sinful often violate and enslave the virtuous; the cunning and ruthless have an advantage over the simple and tender-hearted. Justice was on the side of Ireland for more then a hundred years, and yet Ireland had to get home rule at last by a political deal of the most undisguised sort. It was her wire-pullers and manipulators that freed her, not her patriots and heroes.

In the case of Belgium the justice or injustice of her cause need not detain us: the question will always remain academic and sentimental, and hence unworthy of serious discussion. Her fate depends, not upon her deserts, but upon the measure of aid that England extends to her. If the English, abandoning their old maid's campaign of scandal against the Germans, resolve at last to take to the field, and if the huge but clumsy army that they then muster proves stronger than Germany's smaller but far more efficient force, then the Germans will be driven out of Belgium, and what remains of the country will revert to the Belgians—no doubt with an English "army of occupation," *à la* Egypt, in Brussels. But if the English, as seems more probable, continue to confine their help principally to moral exhortations and encouraging cheers, then Belgium will disappear from the family of nations as surely as Finland has disappeared, and not all the justice under heaven will avail to save her.

Hard lines, true enough, but life itself is very hard. I am not one, I hope, to gloat over the Belgians in their hour of overwhelming disaster (perhaps the worst disaster that ever overtook a civilized people in the whole history of the world), nor do I argue that there is justice in it. But neither do I adopt the sentimental view they are ravished innocents and that their sufferings prove the Germans to be unconscionable savages. The Germans, facing a situation of the utmost danger, had their choice of two bitter alternatives. On the one hand they could attack France head on and so expose themselves to a death blow through Belgium, whose unfriendliness to them (or, at any rate, whose inability to protect them) was apparent to everyone. And on the other hand they could sacrifice Belgium to save themselves. They chose the latter alternative, and it is my contention that any other intelligent people would have done the same. They were not prepared to dally over moral issues; they were fighting for their very lives.

The Belgians, by the same token, were also confronted by harsh alternatives. On the one hand they could stand aside and let the war of the titans go on, and on the other hand they could strike a gallant blow for what they conceived to be their honor. (On this question of their honor I merely ask two questions. 1. In view of their secret arrangement with England, did they actually act here in good faith? 2. Of what actual value is the honor of a nation which exists merely by a diplomatic fiction and the sufferance of its neighbors?) The Belgians chose the latter of these alternatives, and came swiftly to grief. If they expected to stop the Germans unaided, they were very stupid. If they looked for help from England or France, they were again very stupid. And if they put glory above security, the empty sound of words above a valuable reality, they were yet again very stupid.

The essential point here is that the Belgians had a free choice, and that they chose deliberately. If, now, that exercise of their free choice has brought them to disaster, surely they cannot allege that their troubles were inflicted upon them by a wholly external agency—that is, by no fault or error of their own. The simple truth is, as I have said, that fate presented them with two alternatives, both very harsh, and that they fatuously embraced the worse. That these alternatives were presented to them was not the fault of Germany, for Germany herself was in the same predicament, and even the most bilious anti-German must allow that to the Germans themselves at least, their own safety was of far more importance than the theoretical honor of the Belgians. The original cause of the collapse of the Belgians is then to be sought behind the Germans—to wit, in the obscure and incomprehensible original causes of the war. But they had a chance, if not to escape all damage, at any rate to make that damage relatively small, and they foolishly adopted a contrary course. In so far as human volition may be blamed at all for their present appalling plight, that blame lies chiefly upon their own folly.

In brief, there is no merit in the argument that the devastation of Belgium is a monument to the sheer ferocity of the Germans. The Germans did there what any other intelligent and determined people, facing the same staggering odds and hazards, would have done—what the English, in point of fact, have often done—what the Japs have since done, and with vastly less excuse, in China.[16] Moreover, nothing is going to be accomplished by abusing them for it. If they are ever rooted out of Belgium, it will not be by angry words nor even by any disembodied spirit of justice, but by superior force. The German people, encompassed by a horde of merciless and unscrupulous enemies, have had to put their trust in blood and iron.[17] And only more blood and more iron will ever overcome them. [10 December 1914]

THE PLIGHT OF THE GERMAN-AMERICAN

The estimable "Wanderer" in the long-suffering Letter Column:

> The Hon. Mr. Mencken * * * says that because our sympathies favored Prussia in 1870, they should have favored them [her?] now. But he knows quite well that the Imperial Government of Napoleon III had nothing in it to make it beloved in this country. The French Imperial Government in 1870 was the same swaggering, bullying militarist despotism that rules at Potsdam today * * *

A noble example of the sonorous piffle that passes for logic among bogus "neutrals." In the first place, I have never employed the argument that the hon. gentleman mentions, and he must be well aware of it. In the second place, he must also know very well that the preponderance of American sympathy was *not* with the Prussians in 1870, but with the "swaggering, bullying militarist despotism" that he describes. The Know-Nothing spirit was still rampant in 1870, though the party itself had gone to pieces during the Civil War. The Germans and the Irish were the chief victims of that madness, and it took the form of a widespread Prussophobia during the Franco-Prussian War. Besides, the majority of Americans expected the French to crush the Germans, just as, until lately, they expected the Allies to achieve the same moral feat.

At the beginning of the present war the German-Americans did not ask their fellow-citizens of English origin and sympathy to begin whooping for Germany. On the contrary, they had every reason to believe that the opinion of the majority would be in favor of the Allies, and they were prepared to face that hostile opinion with as much calm and dignity as they had shown in 1870–71. But when, the German cable being cut, the country was flooded with a mass of imbecile, English-made lies about the conduct of the German Army, and a constant succession of reports of ignominious German routs, and an endless series of libels upon the German Emperor and the German people by screaming English press agents—when this hysterical Germanophobia broke out and the American newspapers helped it along with ignorant and idiotic misrepresentations of German ideals and German aims, then the German-Americans arose as one man to defend the honor of their race.

They didn't ask for sympathy; they didn't ask for any violation of American neutrality in favor of Germany; they merely asked for a reasonable justice, a square deal. And considering the studied and atrocious falseness of the libels they had to face, they made that demand with notable self-restraint. But at once they encountered the astounding theory that the mere making of it was an offense against the United States—that it was treason for an American citizen to ask for fair play from his countrymen! To that theory they refused to subscribe, and they persist in their refusal today. So long as the English defamers of Germany are heard, the German-Americans will demand that they too be heard, and no threats and revilings, however supported, are going to make them recede from that position. Threats, indeed, are poor weapons to use against men of German blood.

Regarding the resolutions passed at various public meetings of German-Americans, Irishmen and other German sympathizers, protesting against the ghoulish sale of arms to England, France and Russia, I have hitherto discoursed at length, and so I shall not go into the merits of the matter again. But there is one thing that the Germanophobes constantly overlook, and that is that the attitude of the United States to the war, considering the nature of our population, cannot be wholly remote and disinterested. The Germans who have become American citizens are just as much citizens as the men of any other race, and they have just as much right as the Irish or the English to protest against dishonorable attacks upon their brothers in blood across the sea. Suppose England were engaged in a war upon Ireland, and the United States, taking advantage of Ireland's lack of a navy, were supplying England with arms and ammunition. What would the Irish in the United States think of it and say of it? They would think and say, I believe, just what the German-Americans now think and say, and the proof of it lies in the fact that the majority of them are ardently supporting the German-Americans today.

Let those Americans who are genuine friends of neutrality and peace bear a couple of facts in mind. One is that the Americans of German origin or sympathy have had a lot to bear in this war, not only in the form of abominable libels but also in the form of even more abominable preaching. Another is that nothing is going to be accomplished by denouncing them as traitors and scoundrels for demanding a greater measure of fair play. They know their rights and they are going to insist upon getting their rights, and no emission of balderdash, however pious, however ill-natured, however menacing, will be sufficient to terrorize them into silence. They know very well what good citizenship means, and they have proved it on many a day. But they do not think that good citizenship involves a tame submission to ignorant, dishonest and poltroonish attacks upon the courage, the decency and the honor of their race. [25 February 1915]

BRITISH LINERS AND GERMAN SUBMARINES

The sinking of the British liners *Aguila* and *Falaba*[18] by the German submarine *U-28*, with the loss of a number of passengers, is giving the "neutral" newspapers of the United States another admirable opportunity to shed crocodile tears over German "barbarism," and no doubt the "deserving Democrats" of the State Department are already preparing a pious note of protest to Berlin. But a diligent study of the facts shows that the loss of passengers was due quite as much to the two English skippers as to the German commander, and that the latter made every reasonable effort to give them time to take to the boats.

It is the invariable rule of the sea that a merchant ship, when hailed by a man-of-war, whether in time of war or in time of peace, must heave to at once and await orders. But when the commander of the *U-28* (which was on the surface, and *not* submerged) hailed the *Aguila,* the captain of the latter crowded on all steam and so tried to escape. The submarine thereupon "fired across the bows of the steamer," but "she speeded up to 14 knots." Then came a solid shot and she was brought to a halt. Meanwhile, she had been calling for help by wireless. The Germans, knowing that British warships were near, had no time to wait. They sank the ship at once. Three passengers more lost, but it is significant that the captain and 19 members of the crew were saved.

As every reader of the London war news is well aware, very few lives have been lost in the German war upon the British merchant marine. The German submarine commanders always give the crews of the overhauled ships plenty of time to take to their boats, and whenever it is necessary and possible they tow those boats to safe waters. But when the captain of a ship carrying passengers calls to warships and tries to escape by flight, he plainly offers resistance to the submarine that has captured him, and so the responsibility for any loss of life that may ensue rests upon his own shoulders. It is his duty to obey the rules of the sea for merchant ships and not to attempt a vain engagement against a submarine carrying both torpedoes and guns.

The case of the *Falaba* was exactly like that of the *Aguila.* When the *U-28* signaled her captain to heave to, "he ignored the order and promptly started at full speed ahead." The liner was a relatively fast craft, and it took half an hour for the submarine to overtake her. Again there were wireless calls to British warcraft, and again the commander of the submarine was forced to make quick work of the ship, once he had overtaken her. Not a passenger would have been injured if the captain had halted when he was hailed, instead of making a vain and hazardous effort to escape.

So long as the masters of British passenger ships continue to take such chances, they must assume full responsibility for the safety of their passengers. And any passenger who books upon a British ship, knowing that it will attempt escape if overhauled by a submarine, takes his life into his own hands. If the Germans permitted merchant ships to go unharmed on the ground that they had passengers aboard, the moral English would see to it that there were passengers aboard every ship leaving their ports. Let those who have to travel by sea take passage under other flags. The Union Jack is now far more a menace than a protection, and it will become more and more a menace as the war goes on. No matter what the objection of bogus "neutrals," the Germans will pay the ignoble English off in their own coin and to the last penny.

Two or three weeks ago, it will be recalled, the London press bureau was sending out eloquent accounts of the "destruction" of various German submarines, and of the total failure of Admiral von Tirpitz's campaign against the British merchant marine. But the submarines are still hard at it, and the British destroyer fleet seems wholly unable to halt them. Day after day more ships are sunk, and day after day they are larger and more important ships. This steady attrition will inevitably produce the effects that the Germans aim at. The British are by means plentifully supplied with ships. They have had to commandeer thousands for their far-flung transport services, and more thousands will have to be sent to the Mediterranean if they are ever to make any progress against Turkey. The result will be a growing shortage of bottoms in the merchant service, and growing distress in the United Kingdom. The English have sought to starve out Germany; unless all signs fail, they will presently taste some of that bitter medicine themselves. [2 April 1915]

THE *LUSITANIA*

It is natural, of course, that the sinking of the *Lusitania*[19] should startle and horrify the world, for it brings home to all of us, and more vividly than a dozen sanguinary battles, the ruthless tragedy and cruelty of war; and it is equally natural, perhaps, that the foes of Germany in this country should seek to make the most of the excuse it offers for American intervention. These persons have been very diligently engaged, since the first weeks of the war, in efforts to embroil us on the side of England, and they have been gallantly aided in that benign endeavor by the London press bureau, by a horde of publicity-seeking politicians and other such gentry, and by a number of American newspapers, including the senile but still charming *Sunpaper*. More than once it has appeared strongly probable that they would get their wish—and maybe the time has come at last. Dr. Wilson will be strong, indeed, if, in the face of a national running amuck, he stands firmly for a strict and prudent attention to our own business.

Meanwhile, two salient facts stick out, and it may be well to direct notice to them before the band begins to play. One is the fact that the *Lusitania* was an armed vessel of the English naval reserve, engaged in transporting munitions of war to the enemies of Germany. The other is the fact that the persons who took passage upon her were specifically warned that she would be sunk at sight. These persons assumed a known and positive risk when they set sail; they were exactly in the position of persons who refused to leave a beleagured town upon notice of bombardment. The notion that their presence upon the ship should have protected it from the normal hazards of war is empty and idiotic. The Germans gave fair and open warning that they disputed that theory. They gave fair and open warning that they would sink the *Lusitania*. They have done exactly what they said they would do, and they will undoubtedly continue in that course until England is brought to her knees, regardless of the moral protests of their enemies.

Much will be made, I daresay, of the fact that the *Lusitania* was not hailed before the two torpedoes were launched at her, and of the alleged violation of international law in that proceeding. More bosh. It is a first principle of international law that a merchant ship shall stop at once on the hail of a vessel of war: it is a notorious and undisputed fact that English merchant ships have been instructed to attempt flight at full speed, and that all of them actually hailed have essayed to carry out those instructions. The Germans have no submarine capable of making more than half of the *Lusitania's* 26 knots. If they had hailed her, she would have crowded on steam, taking all the ensuing risks, including that to her American passengers. The *Falaba*, a slower boat, did that same thing—and came to grief thereby. The *Lusitania* would have probably got away. The Germans therefore torpedoed her first and hailed her afterward. If international law was violated by that act, then the blame was upon the English.

It would be much better for us if, instead of wasting time ranting against the Germans, we recognized and took to heart the true lesson of this staggering incident of the war. The lesson is this: that we cannot expect to put 'our eggs' in the English basket without running a grave risk of having them smashed. If we send our ships to England bearing contraband of war, and they sail through the war zone with English patrol boats guarding them, we must not be offended if the Germans attack and sink them. A ship so laden and guarded is to all intents and purposes a vessel of war, and must take all the risks of a vessel of war. And if our people put to sea in ships of the English naval reserve, after plain and specific warnings that those ships will be sunk at sight, we can have no reasonable ground for complaint when the warnings are made good. The theory that England is free to hide behind our flag and our people, and that any challenge of that privilege is an offense against our neutral rights, is not one that the Germans are going to accept. They are engaged in a war to the death with England, and they cannot be expected to increase the already heavy odds against them by standing aside politely every time an unfriendly "neutral" appears on the field. As the Philadelphia *Record* said of the *Gulflight* case:[20]

> Being contraband, the lading of the *Gulflight* was amenable
> to belligerent seizure and confiscation. A neutral flag does not
> protect contraband of war. On the contrary, a neutral vessel
> engaged in contraband trade *is herself impressed with a hostile
> character* and forfeitable to the captor, and the persons employed
> in such trade *take all the risks of belligerents.*

The Germans, you may be sure, will not stop with the *Lusitania*. They will not stop until the iron ring is squeezed so tightly around John Bull's neck that he gasps for breath and begs for mercy. This is no ordinary war, waged according to the books. The English started out by announcing, not merely that they would defeat Germany, but that they would devastate and destroy Germany; they are engaged even today in a deliberate effort to starve out and murder *all* Germans, without regard to age or sex. The German reply to that threat is to have at England with exactly the same stick. The only difference between the two enterprises, despite all the howling of the English, is that that of the Germans begins to succeed. They have proved that they have nothing to fear from the English on land; they are beginning to prove that they have nothing to fear from the English on the sea. That the English themselves are beginning to realize their true situation is shown by their endless screaming about Germany's "atrocities," and their frantic efforts to hide behind neutral countries and to drag them into the war on their side.

These efforts, particularly in the cases of Italy and the United States, begin to take on a pathetic grotesquerie. Every time a neutral ship is sunk in the North Sea the English press bureau floods the American newspapers with "moral" buncombe about the deviltries of the Germans. The truth is, of course, that the English have committed vastly more offenses against our commerce than the Germans have, and with vastly less excuse. They have held up our ships without rime or reason; they have misused and made a mock of our flag; they have seized our cargoes, both eastbound and westbound; they have even (as in the *Brynhilda* case, reported by Captain Duffy)[21] pressed our ships into service for purposes of actual war.

But whatever the relative weight of our grievances against the two combatants, it must be plain that the Germans intend to proceed with the war in their own way, and that that way contemplates a systematic and relentless effort to isolate England. The English challenge has been boldly accepted. The bully among the nations has at last met an antagonist who knows how to strike boldly and terribly. Fighting Germans is an infinitely more arduous business than slaughtering Boer farmers or unarmed savages. The English are slow of comprehension, but this much, at least, they begin to realize, and the realization turns them cold with fear. They see before them a resolute and warlike—perhaps even a ferocious—people, armed, eager and unafraid. The future before them is black with disaster. [8 May 1915]

THE UNITED STATES AND GERMANY

The text of Dr. Wilson's note to the German Government[22] makes it plain that Germany and the United States have come to an irreconcilable difference of opinion, and that the only way to avoid an open rupture will be for either the one Government or the other to withdraw from its position. In the present state of public opinion in the United States it is inconceivable that this Government will ever make any such withdrawal, or, for that matter, even consent to any extended discussion of its demands. And the Germans, on their side, will probably stand just as steadfast, for they are sincerely convinced that if they yield it will put intolerable burdens upon them in the conduct of the war and perhaps turn the tide of battle, which is now in favor of them, against them. We thus come to an impasse. The American note, though not actually a declaration of war, is obviously an unmistakable notice that a declaration of war is belind it.

In this situation, of course, it is useless to attempt any discussion of the merits of the American demands. The time for that discussion was before they were definitely framed. Now that they are in plain English and the country is irrevocably committed to their enforcement, the only thing to do is to bow to the accomplished fact. But meanwhile, before affairs proceed to the next and apparently inevitable stage, it may be well to remember that the Germans, too, think that they are right, despite the American verdict that they are wrong, and that the thing they struggled for against great odds is just as sacred in their sight, and just as worthy of their supreme sacrifices, and just as much an inherent and inalienable right, as the thing that the United States threatens to go to war for. We may dispute the righteousness and justice of their cause, but we cannot dispute their earnest belief in it, nor decry the resolution with which they fight for it.

Perhaps a good many Americans may yet think it worth while, before the band begins to play, to put the United States in Germany's place, and so strive for some comprehension of the German point of view, as the Germans themselves have sought to understand (and even, to some extent, to sympathize with) the French and Russian points of view. Suppose that the United States, instead of having ample room for expansion within its own borders, were imprisoned in a small and crowded area by a ring of hostile neighbors, and suppose the most hostile and most powerful of these neighbors, stirring the others to war, were to announce openly that it proposed to overthrow the American Government, invade and conquer American territory, exile the President of the United States to St. Helena,[23] destroy the American Navy, break up American trade in all parts of the world, restore the divisions of 1860–65, and reduce the whole American people, men, women and children, to ruin and starvation. And suppose Germany, 3,000 miles away and unconcerned in the war, were to give aid to this enterprise by manufacturing arms and ammunition for these hostile neighbors, and by giving the transportation of such arms and ammunition, either directly or indirectly, the protection of her flag.

In the face of such a combined attack, would we stop at any method of counter-attack which promised to spread terror and consternation among our overwhelming hordes of enemies, and so reduce the heavy odds against us? Would we, in such a situation, accept rules of war which put fresh burdens upon us, and which we regarded as deliberately designed to nullify our enterprise and our prowess? Would we, even supposing us to admit the intrinsic soundness of such rules, put our duty to obey them above the incomparably higher duty to save our country from destruction and desolation? And if Germany, in particular, sought to lay down the doctrine that the presence of any of her citizens among enemies engaged in enterprises hostile to us should protect those enterprises against our attack, would we accept that doctrine or dispute it? And if Germany sought to enforce it by threats, would we submit to those threats tamely or resist them to the limit of our power?

This, in brief, is the case for Germany, here stated for the last time. The American people, through their high officers of state, have decided that it is a bad case, and from that decision there is no appeal. [14 May 1915]

The reply of the German Government to the American note of May 15[24] affords the jingo newspapers a capital opportunity to bawl names and make faces at the Germans, and one may be sure that they will take full advantage of it. Led by the estimable New York *Herald,* some of them are already hard at it, and during the next week or two they may be trusted to flood the country with all sorts of wild tales of German plots and German-American treasons, and a multitude of brave demands for immediate and merciless war. The true patriotism of these virtuous gazettes may be very accurately gauged by the patriotism of the gentleman who owns and edits the chief of them. This gentleman, the Hon. James Gordon Bennett, of the *Herald,* loves the United States with such deep and unselfish devotion that he has lived in France for 40 years, and his passion for the higher virtue is so vast that he was lately fined $30,000, a record penalty, for printing obscene "personal" advertisements in his moral paper.

That the American people will permit themselves to be inflamed and led astray by the tub-thumping of such dubious persons is very improbable. Despite the gallant whooping which followed the sinking of the *Lusitania,* nothing approaching a genuine demand for war arose in this country. The people generally disapproved that act of war and felt deeply the loss of American lives, but the great majority of them were still able to see clearly the provocation offered to the Germans, and to separate the true facts from the fustian emitted by the London press bureau and diligently spread broadcast in this country. The German reply makes that provocation even plainer. It is by no means an affront to the American Government, as the press-agents of quaking England would have us believe, but a straightforward presentation of the German point of view and of what the Germans honestly believe to be serious grievances.

Americans are not so blind to fair play that they cannot see the odds against which Germany so gallantly and effectively fights, nor are they inclined to increase those odds in favor of England. If neutrality means anything at all, it means refraining from acts which put upon one party to a conflict a hopeless and intolerable handicap. The arms traffic, perhaps, may be defended, legally if not morally, but surely no American who calls himself a fair man is going to defend the doctrine that the presence of our citizens on munitions-bearing ships of the English naval reserve shall protect those ships against attack with the only means at Germany's present command. To lay down such a doctrine is, to all intents and purposes, to make war upon Germany, and it would be more honest and more courageous, if that is our true intent, to follow Italy with an open declaration and so put an end to hypocritical equivocations.

Without the help of the United States England faces an almost absolute certainty of defeat and destruction in this war. Her navy has failed to protect her coasts against the enterprise and daring of the Germans; her army has been repeatedly routed and made a mock of on land, even by the Turks; the great majority of her citizens refuse to fight for her, or even to work for her, in her hour of sore need. Worse, her efforts to raise new allies in all parts of the world, by promise of loot, by threats of revenge later on and by downright bribery, have brought her nothing but fresh difficulties and disasters. Her one remaining hope is to enlist the United States on her side, and to this endeavor she brings every resource of her unrivaled casuistry and dishonesty. The deliberate exposure of the *Lusitania* and the so-called Bryce report[25] were but two incidents of a frantic campaign to get American ships into the North Sea and American soldiers into Flanders.

Surely the American people are not going to be seduced into a costly and unjust war upon a friendly people bound to us by ties of blood, long amity and common interest, by such oblique maneuvers of a country which despises us, and has twice tried to destroy us, and played dirty tricks upon us during our days of civil war. We have got on with the Germans for 139 years; they have been our firm friends when we were doing the fighting and they were standing by; all they ask of us today is honest fairness and good-will, and a reasonable allowance for the difficulties besetting them. They have a heavy job on their hands; they meet it and put it through with magnificent courage. Are we to see that they get a square deal? Or are we to blackmail and bully them while their backs are to the wall? [31 May 1915]

The obvious determination of the Administration to brush aside all negotiations with Germany and so enter the war upon the side of England has at least this salient merit: that it is vastly more straightforward, and hence vastly more creditable to an honorable nation, than our former pretense of neutrality. Against the hollowness of that pretense I have composed and printed pieces since the first month of the war, and more than once I have been denounced therefor by various anonymous Englishmen and ardent English sympathizers. But I doubt that any American of reasonable fairness, whatever his opposition to the Germans, would venture to argue for the genuineness of our neutrality today. The United States, in point of historical fact, has been against Germany from the start, not only in sympathy but also in act, and a frank acknowledgment of it will clear the air and put an end to hypocrisies that have excited quite as much scorn in England as in Germany. We cannot be neutral in such a war and still aid and protect one contestant at the expense of the other. And if we are not neutral, then let us by all means be honest enough to say so in the open.

The approaching entrance of the United States into the war will put a heavy burden of regret upon all Americans who believe that this country has been grossly unjust to Germany, and, in particular, upon all of those Americans of German blood whose conviction is emotionally supported, perhaps wholly, perhaps only in part, by the most sacred and intimate of human ties. These persons cannot expect that any allowance will be made for their terrible agony of mind. They have already faced the doctrine that it is criminal for them to take the side of Germany against England; they must yet face the doctrine that it is treason for them to deplore the commitment of the United States to England's broken and abominable cause. No allowance will be made for the cruel difficulty of their position. They will be fair game for the superpatriots; they will have to expect every sort of attack and injustice that popular passion knows; they will be lucky, indeed, if the thing stops at mere slanders and denunciations. It will take all of their traditional steadiness to withstand that bombardment without losing their heads.

This steadiness, I am convinced, will be forthcoming. There are bitter days ahead for all men of German blood in the United States, and they will be more than human if the whooping against them does not destroy some of their old faith in American fairness and good will, but they will put up philosophically with what they cannot help, trusting to the ultimate emergence of a saner and truer point of view. In all the American hysteria against the Germans there is evidence of an uneasy conscience. If we were not so diligently betraying their old friendship, one would hear far fewer moral homilies upon their immorality. Soon or late the American people will came to their senses, and see clearly how they have been misled by false issues and cunning sophists. They will not be proud of their course in this war, once they see it calmly in retrospect. Even now, deep down in their hearts, a great many of them know that their country is wrong. [2 June 1915]

THE UNITED STATES AND MILITARISM

The pronunciamento of the Maryland League for National Defense is so full of sound logic and plain speaking that it is somewhat surprising to find it closing with a couple of paragraphs of conventional rumble-bumble about the differences between the militarism which is militarism and the militarism which is not militarism. As a matter of fact, no such difference exists. If a country prepares for war in time of peace, that country straightway becomes militaristic, and it is idle to assess its virtue according to its motives, for once it has attained to military strength those motives may very easily change and the army of defense may become an army of conquest. Our own navy was set up by MM. Cleveland and Windom for the purpose of defending our long coasts, but once its potency became apparent a desire to make further use of it possessed the American people, and the result was a series of flamboyant doings in Latin-America, culminating in the Spanish-American War. Had there been no white squadron,[26] there would have been no battle of Manila Bay, and had there been no battle of Manila Bay we would not be moving toward a war with Japan today.

It is upon just this theory, indeed, that the Germans are now denounced as international trouble-makers, and that the Germans themselves denounce the English. Every sane man must be well aware that the rise of militarism in Germany was not due to any desire for conquest, but to a desire to protect the young and weak empire against the aggressions of miltaristic neighbors, particularly France. The Germans of a century ago were not militarists; so late as 1840, indeed, the majority of them opposed militarism. But they were forced into it by national necessities, and with characteristic conscientiousness they converted the necessary into the efficient. The result was undoubtedly a great growth of the military spirit: they were proud of their strength and impatient of any flouting of it. So with the English Navy. It began as a means of necessary defense against France, Holland and Spain. Its final fruit was "Britannia Rules the Waves"—*i. e.*, the feeling that its mere power gave England certain rights upon the high seas that all other nations were bound to respect. Today the English fleet fights to cripple the German Army and the Germans fight to tame the English Navy. Militarism eats navalism.

Thus it is useless to talk of adopting a militarism which shall not be militarism. Either we must depend upon improvisation for our defense, and so run the risk of destruction, or we must go the whole hog. And going the whole hog will inevitably expose us to the temptation of exerting our military power, not alone when our actual safety at home is endangered, but also and more especially when offense is offered to what we conceive to be our interests and honor abroad. That the Swiss brand of militarism offers less menace to the peace of Europe than the

German brand, the Russian brand or the French brand is not due to any inherent virtue in it, or to any other difference in quality, but simply and solely to the fact that the Swiss are a small people. No other nation in Europe fears their aggressions. Moreover, no other nation covets their national territory, and they have no colonies and no sea-borne commerce to intrigue the lustful eye. Thus the Swiss, roosting upon their mountain peaks and engaged in their innocuous hotel keeping, offer neither menace nor temptation to their neighbors.

But if the United States begins to arm it will be unable to maintain any such benign isolation, for on the one hand its arming will constitute a vastly greater menace to other nations, if only because of its mere hugeness, and on the other hand, its people will be unable to restrict themselves to such modest ambitions as those which animate the Swiss. Given an adequate navy—*i. e.,* one able to protect us against a first-rate power—and we'll soon be using it for snouting and big-stick flourishing in far waters. Given an army strong enough to protect New York, and we'll soon have an army strong enough to cast longing glances toward Mexico, Yokohama and perhaps even Montreal. Moreover, an armed nation, save it be very small, cannot remain a thing in vacuo. On the contrary, it inevitably finds itself either for or against the other armed nations—that is, it sees them either as possible friends or as possible foes. And so seeing them, it must needs be drawn into their rows. Even today, badly armed as it is, the United States is plunging with dizzy speed into an alliance with England.

Here, of course, I do not argue against militarism. As a matter of fact, I am thoroughly in favor of militarism, whether it be German or American. All I seek to do is to show that we cannot be militarists one day and pacificists the next day, We must choose our course carefully, and then stick to it resolutely, taking the bitter of it with the sweet. If the role that destiny has laid upon us is that of an international moralist, if it is our duty to teach the more backward nations of the earth the principles of the higher ethic, then we must be prepared to enforce our teachings. Moral suasion and good example will get us nowhere. Even President Wilson, who seemed inclined to think, a few months ago, that they might, has now gone over very frankly to the doctrine of force, and is seeking to impose his ideas upon other nations, not by persuading them, but by threatening them.

The international moralist must learn from the experience of the domestic moralist. The latter does not try to bring sinners to his superior standards of virtue by mere argument, nor does he rely on the spirit of emulation in them. He knows, in fact, that most sinners are not only not eager to be as good as he is, but that many of them are so far gone in carnality that they are even disposed to deny that he is better than they are. So he passes over all psychic appeals and has at them with a club, or urges the police—*i. e.,* his army—to club them for him. This plan would go to pieces if the moralist were not a militarist—that is, if he allowed any sentimental regard for the sinners' antagonistic desires, and in particular their desire for peace, to interfere with his own desire to save them from their sins. The international moralist must make the same choice. Militarism may be a theoretical evil, but without embracing it he must see the utter failure of his plan to bring the whole world up to grace. [29 July 1915]

A FINAL WORD ON BOGUS NEUTRALITY

Nothing could better reveal the poverty of the case for bogus neutrality—that is, for a covert and dishonest alliance with England in this war—than the oblique and idiotic devices employed by the *Sunpaper* and other such stupid gazettes to defend it. These devices seldom make any approach to intelligible argument, or show any sign of an honest desire to get at the truth; they consist almost entirely of violent and indecent defamations of the pro-Germans, whether German or American, and of silly efforts to terrorize them into silence and submission. On the one hand these pro-Germans are accused of participation in sinister conspiracies of which they actually know nothing, and which, in most cases, do not even exist (as the *Sunpaper* is well aware); and on the other hand they are denounced as "disloyalists" because, forsooth, they favor Germany instead of England, both being at peace with the United States, and claim the same right to state and advocate their views that the pro-English, including the *Sunpaper,* exercise so copiously and so deafeningly.

Time and again, in defending the arms traffic, the *Sunpaper* has had to abandon its childish legal quibbles about the obligations of neutrality and fall back upon the doctrine that for some mysterious reason, we should help the Allies all we can. And yet, whenever anyone has presumed to argue that the arms traffic should be stopped. It has screeched, in high falsetto, that he has sought to help Germany, and that this should be a sufficient argument against him. What feeble nonsense is this! Why should it be more patriotic to favor England than to favor Germany? By what rule of law or reason is an American compelled to take the side of our old enemy against our old friend? And why should a German, because he happens to be in the United States, be denounced for answering the call of his blood and an Englishmen be flattered and praised?

The theory that the United States is bound to continue the arms traffic, and to lift it to gigantic proportions under Government patronage, is so false and so dishonest that it scarcely deserves an answer. The utmost that can be said for this traffic is that we have a right, under international law, to engage in it. But by the same token we have a right to abandon it if we see fit, and during the Spanish-American War we asked the Germans to do this, the shoe being upon the other foot, and they promptly agreed. But now we not only reject a similar request when it comes from Austria, but we also make plans to engage in the business upon a scale hitherto unknown in the world. That is to say, we not only sell our customary merchandise; we convert our country into a huge arsenal for the Allies, and so make a deliberate effort to give them an advantage over their opponents. And all this on the plea that it is our duty, under international law, that we should be unfair to friendly nations if we refrained! Could hypocrisy take more extravagant forms? Is it possible to imagine a more empty and obscene quibbling?

The United States, remember, is not a participant in this war; it stands before the world, not only as a professed neutral, but also as the special advocate of humanity. It sends up pecksniffian prayers to God that the slaughter in Europe shall cease; it attempts to browbeat Germany, rejecting all her efforts at legal justification for her acts of war, on the ground that its concern is for humanity, that it abhors bloodshed. And yet this bumptious and self-righteous champion of humanity, when a chance offers to turn a profit out of the killing going on, at once takes refuge behind transparent legal quibbles, and the defenders of its policy—*e. g.*, the *Sunpaper*—seek to scare off all who call attention to the inconsistency by accusing them falsely of all sorts of mythical crimes.

This last effort, I need not say, is going to fail, and the sooner the *Sunpaper* and other such tarletan bravos understand it, the better it will be for their cause. The people of the United States, in the long run, are not going to be fooled by the daily gabble about German "conspiracies" that never get any further than their announcement, nor by the endeavor to prove that self-respecting and reputable American women are concerned with bomb-throwers and murderers, nor by the endless lies from England about German "atrocities" and English "victories," nor by the insane theory, so diligently propagated, that the Germans aspire to conquer the United States, and that after they have finished with England they will turn to these shores. Whatever their faults, the Germans are not lunatics: they know very well that they couldn't conquer the United States, even if they would; what is more, they haven't the slightest desire, and never had, to seize any of our territory, or to violate our rights, or to interfere with our Government. Did they interfere with the French Government when they had the chance? They found a monarchy and left a republic. Have they ever sought to overthrow their own republics, Hamburg, Bremen and Lubeck, three city-states that are just as free today, despite all we hear of Kaiserism, as Maryland, Delaware and Virginia? Nay, this bugaboo of despotism will not serve the pro-English. It is empty and absurd, and the *Sunpaper,* employing it deliberately to arouse prejudice, in well aware of its absurdity.

But, as I say, such deliberate efforts to injure the Germans by lying about them and to alarm the pro-Germans by raising the cry of treason against them will get the English apologists nowhere. As for the pro-Germans, they simply refuse to be scared. They have stuck to the truth, as they see it and understand it, through a year of unexampled reviling, and they will stick to it until the last galoot's ashore. Those persons who hope to intimidate them by accusing them of disloyalty, or by gabbling ridiculously about imaginary plots, or by charging that they plan to set up a despotism in the United States, or by donkeyish braying about the duty of upholding the President—such persons had better give it up. Honest and self-respecting men are not going to pay any heed to the cackling of a horde of puny mountebanks, too feeble in mind to present their case intelligently and too steeped in sanctimonious drivel to present it honestly. [13 August 1915]

NOTES

INTRODUCTION

1. "A Genealogical Chart of the Uplift," in *A Book of Burlesques* (1916), was taken from the Free Lance column of 12 March 1914. Carl Bode's compilation *The Young Mencken* (New York: Dial Press, 1973) included eight columns. A few other columns have been reprinted in other volumes.

2. *Thirty-Five Years of Newspaper Work: A Memoir by H. L. Mencken,* ed. Fred Hobson, Vincent Fitzpatrick, and Bradford Jacobs (Baltimore: Johns Hopkins University Press, 1994), 26–27.

3. Ibid., 30.

4. Ibid., 32. Later on (42) Mencken notes, "I invented all sorts of opprobrious nicknames for himself and his friends." One such nickname was Mahoni Amicus, cited in the first selection in this book. *Mahoni* is a coined Latin genitive (possessive) case of "Mahon" (i.e., Sonny J. Mahon [see n. 7 below]), while *amicus* is Latin for "friend." Hence the term means "friend of Mahon."

5. The Monthly Feuilleton, *Smart Set* 69, no. 4 (December 1922): 140; rpt. in *H. L. Mencken on American Literature,* ed. S. T. Joshi (Athens: Ohio University Press, 2002), 9.

6. Ibid.

7. *The Philosophy of Friedrich Nietzsche* (Boston: John W. Luce, 1908; rev. ed. 1913), 110. Mencken's adherence to the notion of the superman allowed him to make game of the powerful Baltimore political boss Sonny J. Mahon, referred to consistently in the Free Lance columns as the super-Mahon.

8. For a selection of these arguments, see *In Her Place: A Documentary History of Prejudice against Women,* ed. S. T. Joshi (Amherst, NY: Prometheus Books, 2006).

9. "The Report of the Vice Commission," *Baltimore Evening Sun,* 28 December 1915, 6; 30 December 1915, 6; 1 January 1916, 6.

10. "What Is to Be Done about Divorce?," *New York World Magazine,* 26 January 1930, rpt. in *H. L. Mencken on Religion,* ed. S. T. Joshi (Amherst, NY: Prometheus Books, 2002), 281.

11. For a liberal selection of these columns, see *H. L. Mencken on American Literature* (n. 5 above).

12. *Thirty-Five Years,* 33.

13. Fred Hobson, *Mencken: A Life* (New York: Random House, 1994), 132.

14. *Thirty-Five Years,* 59.

15. Hobson, 160.

16. See *My Life as Author and Editor,* ed. Jonathan Yardley (New York: Knopf, 1992), 299–300.

17. *Thirty-Five Years,* 33.

I. ON BEING A FREE LANCE

1. The Lord's Day Alliance was a religious organization founded in 1888 as the American Sabbath Union in Washington, DC, by delegates from Baptist, Methodist, Reformed Church, and United Presbyterian churches, and was devoted to lobbying for the passage of Sunday-rest laws. It was responsible for pressuring a number of state legislatures to ban many activities (including baseball, golf, and the delivery of the mail) on Sunday.

2. In this sense, *punk* is a slang term referring to various matter that will smolder when lighted, used to set off fireworks.

3. Loudon Park Cemetery is a large cemetery in the southwestern part of Baltimore. One of Mencken's earliest publications was some advertising copy included in *Loudon Park Cemetery Company 1853–1902* (Baltimore: Williams & Wilkins, 1902).

4. The New York Society for the Suppression of Vice was founded in 1873 by Anthony Comstock for the purpose of censoring matter perceived to be obscene or indecent. Analogous organizations were subsequently established in many other states. The Anti-Saloon League, founded in 1895, was a lobbying organization that spearheaded the passage of the Eighteenth Amendment.

5. The statement is found not in any of Paul's epistles but in John 8:32: "And the truth shall make you free."

6. Peruna was a patent medicine devised by Dr. Samuel B. Hartman in 1879; by 1900 it was one of the most popular medicines in the country. Mencken frequently used the word to refer to a bogus remedy or panacea.

7. Osseocaputs: Mencken's neo-Latin coinage, meaning "boneheads."

8. A yellowback was a cheap and often lurid novel published in yellow paperback covers, chiefly in England during the later nineteenth century.

II. THE CENTRAL QUESTIONS OF EXISTENCE

1. A hangover, or a headache caused by a hangover.

2. The term *mugwump* was first applied to Republicans who refused to support the candidacy of James G. Blaine in the presidential election of 1884; it later came to be used, both favorably and pejoratively, to characterize anyone who refused to follow a party line or demonstrated independence of mind.

3. Pediculidæ is the Latin scientific name for the family of lice that attacks human beings.

4. Mencken evidently refers to President Woodrow Wilson's desire to keep the United States out of World War I and his efforts to bring about a reconciliation between Germany and the Allied Powers.

5. Local option is a policy of allowing individual communities to determine whether to ban the sale or consumption of alcoholic beverages. It was generally supported by prohibitionists as a means of incrementally enforcing statewide prohibition.

6. Back River Neck is a peninsula to the east of the city of Baltimore. In Mencken's day it was a popular resort area for the working classes of Baltimore.

7. Siemanns: Mencken's error for Werner von Siemens (see Glossary of Names).

8. Mencken probably intended to write "other" here.

III. THE FOLLIES OF AMERICAN GOVERNMENT AND SOCIETY

1. A collective noun derived from Solon (640?–561? BCE), Greek statesman who reputedly reformed the Athenian constitution.

2. In 1901, pressured by the Woman's Christian Temperance Union and other antiliquor groups, Congress outlawed army canteens (shops where food and other provisions were sold to soldiers), on the ground that their selling of liquor was causing widespread drunkenness. The unintended consequence of the action was that drunkenness became more widespread, as soldiers sought out liquor from other and less reputable sources.

3. Thomas F. Farnan, chief of police in Baltimore, customarily given the honorific title of Marshal.

4. Wiskinski: a favorite slang word of Mencken's, defined by him as "signifying a functionary told off to collect campaign assessments from officeholders" (*The American Language: Supplement I* [New York: Alfred A. Knopf, 1945], 296).

5. A bravo is an assassin, frequently one who has been hired by someone else to kill. A thimble-rigger is a con artist who is an adept of the game of thimble-rig, in which a pea or pellet is placed under one of three thimble-like cups and shifted around as spectators place bets to determine under which cup the pea rests. Mencken uses both terms metaphorically for corrupt politicians.

6. *Ferae naturae:* Latin for "wild beasts."

7. The Florestan Club was a dinner club organized in 1910. Mencken was a charter member.

8. The Hon. Dashing Harry: Mencken's jocular reference to Baltimore mayor J. Harry Preston (see Glossary of Names).

9. From "History" (*Edinburgh Review,* May 1828) by British historian and essayist Thomas Babington Macaulay (1800–1859).

10. The Industrial Workers of the World, founded in 1905, was a radical labor organization whose purpose was the overthrowing of capitalism. It engaged in direct confrontation with employers and public officials, often inciting violence. Membership by 1917 may have reached as many as 100,000, but with the onset of World War I the Justice Department, granted enhanced powers to crack down on perceived sedition, arrested most of the IWW's leaders, causing its rapid decline.

11. The *Menace* (1911–19; succeeded by the *Torch,* 1920–22, then by *Menace: Successor to the Torch,* 1922–25) was a virulently anti-Catholic periodical whose circulation reached 1.5 million in 1915.

12. Between 1895 and 1910, seven Southern states passed so-called grandfather clauses, amending their constitutions so that those who had the right to vote on 1 January 1867 were exempt from literacy tests, property qualifications, and other voting restrictions. The effect of these grandfather clauses was to allow poor, illiterate whites to vote but to bar African Americans. The US Supreme Court declared the clauses unconstitutional in 1915.

IV. THE BOZART

1. *The Follies of 1910* was the annual revue of the Ziegfeld Follies, with its customary display of scantily clad dancing girls. It presumably played at Ford's Theatre at 318 West Lafayette Street in Baltimore, operated by John T. Ford and his descendants.

2. *The Girl from Rector's* (1909) is a romantic comedy in four acts by Paul M. Potter (from the French of Pierre Veber). Its dialogue was considered risqué for the period. M. J. Lehmayer was the manager of the Academy of Music.

3. Henrik Ibsen's *Ghosts* (1881) was staged privately in London in 1891, as the examiner of plays, E. F. S. Pigott, refused to license it. No public performance occurred in London until 1914. Gilbert and Sullivan's *The Mikado* (1885) was banned for a time in England out of concern that it might offend the Japanese.

4. Black Friday occurred on 24 September 1869, when a financial panic was caused on Wall Street by the attempts of Jay Gould and James Fisk to corner the gold market.

5. Central characters in Joseph Conrad's "Falk" (1902) and William Makepeace Thackeray's *Barry Lyndon* (1844, 1852).

6. Dreiser continued the Trilogy of Desire with *The Titan* (1914), reviewed by Mencken, and *The Stoic* (1947).

7. Mencken refers to Charles Gallaudet Turnbull's *Anthony Comstock, Fighter* (1913).

8. Henry R. Jones was the president of the Children's Aid Society of Brooklyn.

V. MEN, WOMEN, AND THE VOTE

1. Mencken refers to the German phrase *Kirche, Küche, und Kinder* (church, kitchen, children).

2. The Lyric Theatre, at 140 West Mount Royal Avenue in Baltimore, opened in 1894 and featured opera and orchestral performances as well as drama, boxing matches, and political meetings.

3. Phospine is an archaic term for phosphuretted hydrogen gas, which can be used to incapacitate a person in the manner of chloroform.

4. Homer describes the Amazons coming to the aid of the Trojans sporadically in the *Iliad* (e.g., 2.814, 3.189, 6.186). The theme was elaborated in Arctinus's *Aethiopis*. For the Amazons in Attica, see Plutarch, *Theseus* 26.

5. The Duke of Wellington (1769–1852), victor at Waterloo, is said to have remarked: "The battle of Waterloo was won on the playing fields of Eton."

6. Edmond Beall (1848–1920) was an Illinois state senator.

7. Mencken's jocular phonetic spelling of what he took to be the pronunciation of *café* in the American language. See *The American Language,* 4th ed. (New York: Knopf, 1936), 177, 347.

8. See Section III, n. 4.

9. Zechia Judd was a physician in Baltimore. Bishop Wegg, Clark d'Arlington, Alice Hackett, and Jane Snookum are writers of letters to the *Evening Sun.* Snookum is probably fictitious.

10. Cheyne-Stokes breathing is a term used for a type of irregular breathing associated with coma or cerebral injury. The term was derived from the names of two physicians, John Cheyne (1777–1836) and William Stokes (1804–1878), who first identified it.

VI. THE BANE OF RELIGION

1. An organization of clergymen (identified in the following selection as the Wilson Clergy Contribution Fund) who sought to secure the election of the Democrat Woodrow Wilson in the presidential campaign of 1912, when he ran against the Republican incumbent William Howard Taft and Theodore Roosevelt, running on the Bull Moose ticket.

2. The Peabody Institute at East Vernon Place opened in 1868, housing a conservatory of music, a library, and an art gallery.

3. An allusion to Horace's celebrated phrase *Eheu fugaces . . . labuntur anni* ("Alas, the fleeting years slip by") (*Odes* 2.14.1–2).

4. Mencken took to referring to the Anti-Saloon League as the Anti-Saloon Leg because of the publication in the 24 January 1914 issue of its

organ, the *American Issue,* of an ad for hosiery that showed a woman's extended leg.

5. Blattidae is the Latin scientific name for a family of cockroaches.

6. "Spot" Mitchell ran an amusement park in eastern Baltimore County.

7. "But woe unto you, scribes and Pharisees, hypocrites! for ye shut up the kingdom of heaven against men: for ye neither go in yourselves, neither suffer ye them that are entering to go in. . . ."

VII. THE VICE CRUSADE 1: GENERAL NOTES

1. George D. Porter, director of public safety in Philadelphia at the time.

2. Havelock Ellis, *The Task of Social Hygiene* (Boston: Houghton Mifflin, 1912), 287.

3. Mencken alludes to the hysteria, in the early decades of the twentieth century, over the possibility that white slave traders were abducting thousands of young white women and forcing them to become prostitutes. The hysteria led to the passage in 1910 of the widely ridiculed Mann Act, which forbade the transportation of women across state lines "for immoral purposes."

4. "Thou shalt not commit adultery" (Exodus 20:14).

5. Exodus 20:16.

VIII. THE VICE CRUSADE 2: PROHIBITION AND OTHER PANACEAS

1. A *blind tiger* (also *blind pig*) is a slang term for a place used for the illicit sale of liquor.

2. Towel Building is a reference to the Baltimore American Building. Mencken referred to the *Baltimore American* newspaper as the *Hot Towel* because its publisher, General Felix Angus, had reputedly come to the United States from France as a barber. The Anti-Saloon League had an office on the eleventh floor of the building.

3. "Let him that stole steal no more: but let him labor, working with his hands the thing which is good, that he may have to give to him that needeth."

4. Tartuffe is a religious hypocrite in Molière's play of that title (1664).

5. Charles L. Mattfeldt was a member of the board of county commissioners of Baltimore County.

6. A *nautch* was an East Indian style of dancing performed by dancing girls.

7. Emory Grove was a Methodist camp-meeting ground about twenty miles northwest of Baltimore.

8. The editorial, appearing in the Editorial Comment section of *American Medicine* 19, no. 10 (October 1913): 634, was presumably written by the two editors of the magazine, H. Edwin Lewis, MD, and Charles E. Woodruff, MD. The italics in the passage are Mencken's. The phrase "demnition bow-wows," found in Dickens's *Nicholas Nickleby,* is generally equivalent to "going to the dogs."

9. Clarence V. T. Richeson was a clergyman found guilty of murdering a woman in a Boston YCWA in 1911. He was executed on 20 May 1912. Hawley Harvey Crippen (1861–1910) was an American-born physician who settled in London in 1900. He was convicted of the murder of his wife and hanged on 23 November 1910. Johann Hoch was a Chicago janitor who was a bigamist and convicted of murdering one of his wives in 1905; he may have committed as many as eleven other murders.

10. Derived from *black hand* (*mano negra*), or a purported member of an Italian criminal mob.

11. Derived from one of Mencken's favorite terms, *camorra,* another term for a gang of Italian mobsters.

12. Chickens: i.e., *chicks,* attractive young women.

13. Especially cornetists who played at Salvation Army meetings.

14. Dips: i.e., pickpockets (see *The American Language,* 4th rev. ed. [New York: Alfred A. Knopf, 1936], 576).

15. *Ganov* is a Yiddish term for a thief.

16. A moll-buzzer is defined by Mencken as "a pickpocket who specializes in robbing women" (*The American Language: Supplement II* [New York: Alfred A. Knopf, 1948], 670n3).

17. A road agent is a highway robber.

18. *Schnorrer* is a Yiddish term for a beggar.

19. A yeggman is a small-time criminal.

IX. THE VICE CRUSADE 3: PROSTITUTION

1. The chandala are the lowest ("untouchable") caste in Indian society.

2. For Tartuffe, see VIII, n. 4. Sganarelle appears in several Molière plays, but Mencken is probably referring to the character in *L'Ecole des maris* (1661; The School for Husbands), a man who brutally keeps his ward confined at home.

X. SUNDRY FORMS OF QUACKERY

1. The Emmanuel Movement was a medico-religious movement advocated by Episcopal clergyman Elwood Worcester (1862–1940) beginning in 1904, when he was rector of the Emmanuel Church in Boston. Worcester believed that disease could be more efficaciously treated by a fusion of conventional medicine with religious and psychological insight.

2. "Spring Song" is the unauthorized name for no. 30 of *Lieder ohne Wörte* (songs without words), Opus 62, no. 6, a piano solo by Felix Mendelssohn.

3. In 1911 the Supreme Court ruled that a key provision of the Pure Food and Drugs Act of 1906, which decreed that statements on medicine labels should not be "false or misleading in any particular," applied only to the actual ingredients listed on the label. Justice Oliver Wendell Holmes Jr., in his majority opinion, maintained that Congress did not intend to enter into a therapeutic

controversy over the actual curative claims of the medicines in question. The decision revealed a weakness in the 1906 law, leading Congress to pass the Sherley Amendment in 1912, which explicitly declared that labels containing "false or misleading" statements regarding curative properties of medicine were illegal.

4. Mencken's error for Louis Pasteur.

5. Piano Sonata no. 14 in C-sharp minor ("Moonlight"), Opus 27, no. 2, by Ludwig van Beethoven. "The Evening Star," a bass solo ("O du, mein lieber Abendstern"), is in act 3, scene 2 of Richard Wagner's opera *Tannhäuser* (1845). There are two Pilgrims' choruses in *Tannhäuser,* the first in act 1, scene 3 and the second in act 3, scene 1; probably the latter is meant. "There Is a Land Mine Eye Hath Seen" is a hymn (1843) by Gurdon Robbins (set to music by Daniel B. Towner, 1897).

6. Franz Schubert's "Serenade," a song for voice and piano, is no. 4 of his *Schwanengesang* (Swan song), D. 957.

7. Owen Wister, "Quack-Novels and Democracy," *Atlantic Monthly* 115 (June 1915): 721–34.

XI. THE GREAT WAR

1. The term *revanche* (revenge) refers to the French desire to reclaim the provinces of Alsace and Lorraine, which Germany had annexed following its victory in the Franco-Prussian War (1870–71).

2. The French, in their attempt to occupy Morocco, sent a military mission to Fez in early 1911. In response, Germany occupied the port of Agadir. England demanded that Germany lift the occupation, and after several tense months Germany accepted a French compromise in October. Throughout the summer and early fall, it was widely expected that the three countries would go to war.

3. "Germany, Germany, against all," an adaptation of the German national anthem, "Deutschland, Deutschland, über alles" (Germany, Germany, over all).

4. The Entente Cordiale of 1904 resolved all previous colonial disputes between France and England, but it did not commit the two countries to mutual defense in the event of war.

5. Mencken refers to the Anglo-Russian Agreement of 1907, with terms similar to those of the Entente Cordiale.

6. I.e., the Boer War (1899–1902).

7. Russia occupied Manchuria at the conclusion of the Boxer rebellion in 1900, but was ousted by the Japanese in the Russo-Japanese War of 1904–5.

8. Italy and Turkey engaged in a war in 1911–12, leading to Turkey's ceding the port of Tripolitania to Italy.

9. Louvain, in Brabant province in central Belgium, fell to the Germans on 19 August 1914 and, in an incident that shocked the world, the university library was destroyed on 25 August, resulting in the destruction or damage of

hundreds of thousands of books. In addition, historic churches were damaged by fire and the citizens were subject to summary execution.

10. The phrase "perfidious Albion," referring to England, was reputedly uttered by Napoleon in 1803, but it had already become widely used during the French Revolution.

11. General von Stab is a personification of the German term *Generalstab* (general staff, including a military staff or headquarters), alluding to the German army.

12. Mencken first visited Germany in 1908. He visited it again in 1912 and 1914, the latter trip leading to the writing of *Europe after 8:15* (1914; with George Jean Nathan and Willard Huntington Wright), in which Mencken wrote the preface, the section on Munich, and parts of the section on London.

13. Alexander William Kinglake (1809–1891), *The Invasion of the Crimea* (1863–87; 8 vols.), an immense history of the Crimean War (1853–56), in which England, France, and Turkey were arrayed against Russia. G. W. Steevens (1869–1900), *With Kitchener to Khartum* (1898), a journalist's account of the British invasion of the Sudan in 1897–98, led by Lord Kitchener (1850–1916).

14. *Limehousing* is a slang term referring to fiery political speeches, derived from speeches of this sort made by David Lloyd George in 1909 in the impoverished London district of Limehouse. *Mafficking* refers to uproarious and jingoistic celebrations by crowds, derived from such celebrations when a British garrison, under siege by the Boers at the South African town of Mafeking, was relieved on 17 May 1900.

15. See Mencken's article "The Mailed Fist and Its Prophet," *Atlantic Monthly* 114 (November 1914): 598–607, a discussion of Nietzsche and his influence on the "new Germany."

16. Japan entered World War I on the side of the Allies, using the conflict as an opportunity to occupy the German leasehold at Kiaochow Bay in China.

17. Mencken refers to the phrase "blood and iron" (*Blut und Eisen*), popularized by German chancellor Otto von Bismarck in a speech in 1862 ("The great questions of the time will not be resolved by speeches and majority decisions . . . but by blood and iron").

18. The British liner *Falaba* and the British steamer *Aguila* were sunk by a German submarine on 28 and 29 March 1915, respectively. Of the *Falaba*'s crew of 90 and 130 passengers, 80 were killed and an additional 8 who had been rescued subsequently died from exposure. The *Aguila* had a crew of 42 and 3 passengers; 23 crewmen and all the passengers were killed. In both cases, the respective captains attempted to flee once the German U-boat had been sighted.

19. The British liner *Lusitania* was sunk by a German submarine on 7 May 1915, killing 1,200 people, including 128 Americans. The incident led to a momentary groundswell of public enthusiasm for entering the war on the side of the Allies, but President Wilson maintained a position of neutrality, declaring famously: "There is such a thing as a man being too proud to fight."

20. The American oil tanker *Gulflight* was torpedoed on 2 May 1915; the captain and two sailors were killed.

21. According to a German dispatch, a Captain Duffy, commanding the American sailing vessel *Brynhilda,* claimed on 5 May 1915 that, while delivering a cargo of cotton from New York to Bremen, he had been stopped by a British cruiser, whereupon the commander of the cruiser attempted to force Duffy to convey a large quantity of ammunition along with armed marines to the war zone. Duffy protested, and the *Brynhilda* proceeded to Bremen without the ammunition or marines.

22. On 13 May 1915, President Wilson sent a note to his ambassador to Germany, James W. Gerard, expressing indignation at the loss of American lives and vessels in Germany's campaign of submarine warfare and demanding the cessation of this kind of warfare. The German government would, he stated, be held in "strict accountability" for any further attacks that resulted in the loss of American lives or shipping. Wilson's note was delivered to the German government on May 15.

23. St. Helena, an island in the South Atlantic, was where Napoleon was exiled from 1815 until his death in 1821.

24. On 29 May 1915, Germany replied to President Wilson's note, stating that it had sunk the *Lusitania* in "justified self-defense" because the vessel had been armed. Although apologizing for any destruction of unarmed neutral vessels, Germany refused to suspend its campaign of submarine warfare. The unconciliatory tone of the reply was found by the Wilson administration to be surprising and disappointing.

25. The Bryce Report, a document prepared by a British committee led by James Bryce, Viscount Bryce (1838–1922), England's ambassador to the United States (1907–13), outlined German atrocities in Belgium. It was issued on 7 May 1915, the very day the *Lusitania* was sunk, and seriously damaged support for Germany in the United States; but several of its claims were subsequently found to be false.

26. The White Squadron was the term used for the first four steel vessels produced by the US Navy in 1883: the cruisers *Atlanta, Boston,* and *Chicago,* and the dispatch boat *Dolphin.*

GLOSSARY OF NAMES

ABBREVIATIONS

AM   *American Mercury*

BES   *Baltimore Evening Sun*

CST   *Chicago Sunday Tribune*

P1–6   *Prejudices: First–Sixth Series* (New York: Alfred A. Knopf, 1919–27)

SS   *Smart Set*

All names are of Americans, save where indicated.

Addams, Jane (1860–1935), social reformer who established Hull House in Chicago, one of the first social settlements in the United States. She won the Nobel Peace Prize in 1931.

Aldrich, Nelson Wilmarth (1841–1915), US representative (1879–81) and senator (1881–1911) from Rhode Island and one of the most powerful Republican politicians of his day. He was a strong advocate of protectionism and big business.

Anderson, William H. (1874–1959), prohibitionist long associated with the Anti-Saloon League in Illinois, New York, and Maryland, and a member of the executive and legislative committee of the Anti-Saloon League of America (1912–24).

Asquith, Herbert Henry (1852–1928), British statesman who was prime minister of England (1908–16) during the early stages of World War I.

Bennett, Arnold (1867–1931), British novelist and critic best known for *The Old Wives' Tale* (1908). Mencken regarded him as one of the leading novelists of his day and consistently reviewed his books as they appeared, including *What the Public Wants* (1909), *Hilda Lessways* (1911), *Paris Nights* (1913; reviewed in *SS*, February 1914), *The Lion's Share* (1916), *The Pretty Lady* (1918), and *The Roll-Call* (1918).

Bennett, James Gordon, Jr. (1841–1918), son of James Gordon Bennett (1795–1872), who had founded the *New York Herald* in 1835. Bennett Jr. assumed proprietary control of the paper in 1867, on his father's retirement, and made it one of the most popular newspapers in the nation. In 1877 he was forced to move to Paris because of a personal scandal, remaining there for forty years but still retaining editorial control of the *Herald*.

Bismarck, Otto von (1815–1898), prime minister of Prussia (1862–73, 1873–90) and founder and chancellor of the German Empire (1871–90). Under his regime Germany formed numerous alliances in Europe and markedly strengthened its army.

Blease, Coleman L. (1868–1942), governor (1910–16) and US senator (D) from South Carolina (1924–30) who defended lynching and denounced African Americans.

Boggs, Thomas G., secretary of the Merchants and Manufacturers Association of Baltimore (which Mencken parodied as the Honorary Pallbearers) and editor of the *Merchants and Manufacturers Journal* (1904–14; parodied by Mencken as the *Baltimoreische Blaetter*).

Bonaparte, Charles J. (1851–1921), great-nephew of Napoleon, secretary of the navy (1905–6) and attorney general (1906–9) in the Theodore Roosevelt administration. Early in his career Mencken had written an effusive article on him, "Charles J. Bonaparte: A Useful Citizen" (*Frank Leslie's Popular Monthly*, December 1903), but later he looked askance at his moral crusading.

Bourne, Jonathan, Jr. (1855–1940), US senator (R) from Oregon (1907–13).

Bryan, William Jennings (1860–1925), leading Democratic politician of the later ninetenth and early twentieth centuries. He was the Democratic candidate for president in 1896, 1900, and 1908, and secretary of state under Woodrow Wilson (1912–15). His role in the prosecution of the Scopes trial of 1925 is infamous, made the more so by Mencken's pungent and cynical coverage of it.

Bryan, William Shepard, Jr. (1859–1914), a Baltimore lawyer who served as counsel for the Board of Supervisors of Elections (1890–92) and was subsequently city solicitor (1892–95) and attorney general of Maryland (1903–7). He never married.

Burgess, John W. (1844–1931), professor of political science at Columbia University (1876–1912) and author of numerous treatises on politics and constitutional law.

Carnegie, Andrew (1835–1919), financier who gradually gained nearly total control of the US steel industry until he sold the Carnegie Steel Company to J. P. Morgan in 1907. He later became a noted philanthropist.

Churchill, Winston (1874–1965), British statesman. He was First Lord of the Admiralty (1911–15), but his failure to capture Gallipoli in May 1915 brought down the Asquith government and led to his resignation. Prime Minister David Lloyd George made Churchill minister of munitions in July 1917. He later served as secretary of war, chancellor of the exchequer, and prime minister (1940–45, 1951–53).

Cleveland, Grover (1837–1908), twenty-second and twenty-fourth president of the United States (1885–89, 1893–97), and a political figure whom Mencken always respected. During his two administrations he presided over a significant reorganization of the Navy Department, an action that was instrumental in the United States' victory in the Spanish-American War.

Clive, Robert (1725–1774), British soldier and statesman who led British forces in suppressing native revolts in India (1751–57). He later became governor of Bengal (1765–72).

Coleridge, Stephen William (1854–1936), British lawyer and antivivisectionist. He was a member of the Victoria Street Society for the Protection of Animals and became its executive director in 1898, when it was renamed the National Anti-Vivisection Society.

Comstock, Anthony (1844–1915), founder of the New York Society for the Suppression of Vice in 1873. Attaining tremendous power and influence, Comstock and his allies carried on numerous campaigns to prevent the distribution of "obscene" books and other matter. He was one of Mencken's *bêtes noires*. See his review of Charles Gallaudet Turnbull's *Anthony Comstock, Fighter* (1913; *SS*, April 1914), the lengthy chapter on "Puritanism as a Literary Force" in *A Book of Prefaces* (1917), and the essay "Comstockery" (*P5*).

Conrad, Joseph (1857–1924), Polish-born British novelist. Mencken regarded him as perhaps the leading writer of his time and became his most vigorous American advocate. He wrote extensively on Conrad in *A Book of Prefaces* (1917) as well as in many reviews of his novels and tales. Among Mencken's favorite works were the stories "Youth" (1898), "Heart of Darkness" (1899), and "The End of the Tether" (1902), in *Youth and Two Other Stories* (1902); "Typhoon" (1902) and "Falk," in *Typhoon and Other Stories* (1903); and the novels *Almayer's Folly* (1895), *An Outcast of the Islands* (1896), *The Nigger of the*

"Narcissus" (1897), *Lord Jim* (1900), *Nostromo* (1904), *The Secret Agent* (1907), and *Under Western Eyes* (1911).

Cornell, John J. (1826–1909), a Quaker minister in Baltimore. His *Autobiography* was published in 1906.

Daniels, Josephus (1862–1948), secretary of the navy under Woodrow Wilson (1913–21). He earned Mencken's wrath by prohibiting the use of alcohol on navy vessels in 1914 and by an extensive build-up of the navy in accordance with the Naval Appropriation Act of 1916, which Mencken believed was part of the US government's covert support of the Allies against Germany in World War I.

Dodge, William E., Jr. (1832–1903), New York businessman and philanthropist who served as president of the American branch of the Evangelical Alliance and of the National Temperance Society, and was vice president of the American Sunday School Union.

Dowie, John Alexander (1847–1907), Scottish-born theologian who founded the Christian Catholic Apostolic Church in Zion. He was a predecessor of Billy Sunday in his use of emotive preaching, faith healing, and abstention from tobacco and alcohol.

Dreiser, Theodore (1871–1945), pioneering novelist; Mencken became his chief advocate. Dreiser's first novel was the controversial *Sister Carrie* (1900), a grim naturalistic work about a working-class woman. Mencken wrote substantial reviews of many of Dreiser's subsequent books, including *Jennie Gerhardt* (1911; *SS,* November 1911), *The Financier* (1912; *New York Times Review of Books,* 10 November 1912), *The Titan* (1914; *Town Topics,* 18 June 1914, and *SS,* August 1914), *The "Genius"* (1915; *SS,* December 1915), *A Hoosier Holiday* (1916; *SS,* October 1916), and *An American Tragedy* (1925; *AM,* March 1926). He wrote a substantial chapter on Dreiser in *A Book of Prefaces* (1917). For their tortured personal relationship see *Dreiser-Mencken Letters* (Philadelphia: University of Pennsylvania Press, 1977; 2 vols.) as well as Mencken's *My Life as Author and Editor* (New York: Knopf, 1993).

Eddy, Mary Baker (1857–1910), founder of Christian Science and author of the Christian Science Bible, *Science and Health* (1875). See Mencken's essay "On Christian Science" (*BES,* 23 October 1916).

Ehrlich, Paul (1854–1915), German medical scientist renowned for pioneering work in immunology and chemotherapy. Chief among his discoveries was the first effective treatment for syphilis. He won the Nobel Prize for Physiology or Medicine in 1908.

Ellis, Havelock (1859–1930), British critic and sexologist who wrote a pioneering account of sexual behavior, *Studies in the Psychology of Sex* (1897–1928;

7 vols.). The first volume, *Sexual Inversion* (1897), was seized by the British censors and banned. The work was never banned in the United States, but many booksellers sold it circumspectly. He also wrote *The Task of Social Hygiene* (1912). Mencken reviewed Ellis's *Impressions and Comments: Second Series* (1921; *Literary Review, New York Evening Post,* 24 September 1921) and wrote several brief articles on him.

Erickson, Matilda (1880–1957; later Matilda [Erickson] Andross), author of *Temperance Torchlights* (1910), *Alone with God: Fitting for Service* (1917), *Story of the Advent Message* (1926), and other works on Christianity and Seventh-Day Adventism.

Fiske, Charles (1868–1941), rector of St. Michael and All Angels (Episcopal) Church in Baltimore (1910–15) and later a bishop.

Flexner, Simon (1863–1946), pathologist and bacteriologist who taught at Johns Hopkins (1895–99) and the University of Pennsylvania (1899–1903) and helped found the Rockefeller Institute for Medical Research (now Rockefeller University) in 1903. His chief work was in the treatment of dysentery.

Frank, Leo M. (1884–1915), Jewish American manager of a pencil factory in Atlanta who was accused of murdering a thirteen-year-old Irish American worker at the factory, Mary Phagan. Although overwhelming evidence pointed to his innocence, Frank was convicted and was lynched in jail while awaiting execution.

Freud, Sigmund (1856–1939), Viennese founder of psychoanalysis. Mencken wrote a review-article of several works by Freud and his colleagues: "Rattling the Subconscious" (*SS,* September 1918).

Gaynor, William J. (1849–1913), jurist who, as a member of the appellate division of the New York State Supreme Court (1905–9), vigorously supported individual rights against misuse of power by the government, especially the police. He pursued further campaigns of reform as mayor of New York City (1909–13).

Goldsborough, Phillips Lee (1865–1946), governor (R) of Maryland (1912–16), US senator from Maryland (1929–35), and member of the board of directors of the Federal Deposit Insurance Corporation (1935f.).

Grannan, Eugene E., longtime police magistrate in Baltimore and one of the Commissioners for Opening Streets. Mencken devotes much space to him in the chapter "Recollections of Notable Cops" in *Newspaper Days* (1941).

Grgurevich, John J., special agent in charge of the enforcement of the Mann Act (see section VIII, n. 3) in Baltimore.

Haeckel, Ernst (1834–1919), German zoologist and enthusiastic proponent of Darwin's theory of evolution, today best known for a widely influential popular treatise on biology and physics, *Die Weltrathsel* (1899; Eng. trans. as *The Riddle of the Universe*, 1900).

Harris, Carlton D. (1864–1928), Methodist minister who was pastor at several churches in Baltimore, including Calvary Church (1894–98), Emmanuel Church (1905–7), Central Church (1907–11), and Alpheus W. Wilson Memorial Church (1921–27). He was editor of the *Baltimore Southern Methodist* (1911–22, 1927–28).

Harrison, Carter Henry, Jr. (1860–1953), mayor of Chicago (1897–1905, 1911–15) who resisted the recommendations of the Chicago Vice Commission and other reform groups to wipe out prostitution in the city. Instead, he chose to segregate prostitution within certain districts, a policy Mencken supported.

Hemberger, Theodor (1870–1956), German-born violinist and composer and a member of the Saturday Night Club, a social and musical group in Baltimore of which Mencken was a member.

Hoar, George Frisbie (1826–1904), US representative (1869–77) and senator (1877–1904) from Massachusetts. He argued vehemently against the election of senators by popular vote.

Hook, Jacob W., tax collector of Baltimore during the mayoralty of James Harry Preston.

Hooker, Donald R. (1876–1946), professor of physiology at Johns Hopkins University (1906–20) and longtime managing editor of the *American Journal of Physiology*.

Howe, Frederic C. (1867–1940), lawyer and director of the People's Institute, New York (1911–14), and commissioner of immigration at the Port of New York (1914–19). Among his books are *The City: The Hope of Democracy* (1905) and *The High Cost of Living* (1917).

Howells, William Dean (1837–1920), novelist, editor, and critic who was perhaps the most highly regarded American writer of the later nineteenth century, chiefly on the strength of *The Rise of Silas Lapham* (1885) and other novels of social realism. Mencken, however, considered him only a second-rater. By the time Mencken began reviewing, Howells's best days were over, and Mencken's reviews of *New Leaf Mills* (1913; *SS*, June 1913) and *The Leatherwood God* (1916; *SS*, January 1917) are condescending at best.

Huxley, Thomas Henry (1825–1895), pioneering British naturalist and enthusiastic supporter of Darwin whose "plain English" and fearless challenging of religious orthodoxy were much appreciated by Mencken. See "Huxley" (*CST*, 2 August 1925).

Ibsen, Henrik (1828–1906), Norwegian dramatist. See Mencken's extensive introductions to new translations of *A Doll's House* (1909), *Little Eyolf* (1909), and *The Master Builder, Pillars of Society,* and *Hedda Gabler* (1918).

Janney, O. Edward (1856–1930), Baltimore physician, minister of the Society of Friends (Quakers), and chairman of the Friends' General Conference (1900–1920). He was the author of *The White Slave Traffic in America* (1911).

Jesup, Morris K. (1830–1908), a wealthy banker who became a leading philanthropist, giving large amounts of money to a variety of organizations, notably the American Museum of Natural History.

Joffre, Joseph Jacques Césaire (1852–1931), French general who was appointed chief of the General Staff in 1911. In the early stages of World War I, he launched a counterattack against the German invasion of Belgium and France, stopping the Germans on the Marne; but later efforts to confront the Germans in Artois and the Somme foundered, and he was relieved of his command in December 1915, although nominally he was promoted to marshal of France.

Johnson, Jack (1878–1946), the first African American heavyweight champion of the world; he held the title from 1908 to 1915. Johnson provoked anger among whites by his lavish and flamboyant lifestyle, which frequently involved his driving around the country with a variety of white girlfriends. In 1913 he was convicted of violating the Mann Act. He fled the United States, returning only in 1920 and serving a year in prison.

Jones, Sam (1847–1906), itinerant Methodist evangelist.

Kean, Jefferson Randolph (1860–1950), army officer who served in various medical capacities from the Spanish-American War through World War I. From 1906 to 1909 he was adviser to the department of sanitation for the Provisional Government of Cuba; from 1909 to 1913 he was in charge of the sanitary division of the surgeon general's office.

Kelly, Howard A. (1858–1943), gynecologist and surgeon who taught at Johns Hopkins Hospital (1889–1919) and Johns Hopkins Medical School (1893–1919). Aside from many works on medicine, he wrote *A Scientific Man and the Bible* (1925; reviewed by Mencken in *AM,* February 1926), in which he made clear his devotion to a literal reading of the Bible. Kelly also spoke out on moral and social subjects, advocating the abolition of prostitution and siding with Anthony Comstock and other vice crusaders.

Kenney, Annie (1879–1953), British trade unionist and militant suffragist. She assisted Christabel Pankhurst in advocating woman suffrage for the Women's Social and Political Union. She was arrested and imprisoned on several occasions.

Kenyon, William Squire (1869–1933), US senator (R) from Iowa (1911–22) and judge on the US Circuit Court of Appeals (1922–33). A Progressive, Kenyon was a friend of labor and a strong critic of unethical business practices.

Kluck, Alexander von (1846–1934), German general who took part in the Franco-Prussian War (1870–71), became a major general in 1899, and was appointed general of infantry in 1906. As commander of the First Army, he defeated the British and French in several early battles of World War I. He retired in 1916.

La Follette, Robert (1855–1925), governor (1901–5) and US senator from Wisconsin (1906–25), and vigorous proponent of Progressive causes such as the direct primary and fairness in taxation. He ran for president in 1924, obtaining more votes than any third-party candidate up to that time.

Lankester, Sir Edwin Ray (1847–1929), British zoologist whose research in parasitology was instrumental in the diagnosis and treatment of malaria. He also made contributions in anatomy, embryology, and anthropology.

Lee, Bernard J., warden of the Baltimore city jail.

Levering, Eugene (1845–1928), Baltimore banker and a member of the firm of E. Levering & Co., importers of sugar and coffee. He was president of the National Bank of Commerce in Baltimore (1878–1921) and, when it merged with Merchants National Bank, became chairman of the board.

Lister, Joseph (1827–1912), British surgeon largely responsible for the development of antiseptic surgery. Developing the theories of Louis Pasteur, he came to realize that infections in wounds were caused by microorganisms, and he pioneered the use of carbolic acid to sterilize instruments and ligatures.

Lloyd George, David (1863–1945), British statesmen. He was chancellor of the exchequer (1908–15) and prime minister (1916–22); in the latter capacity he vigorously led the Allies against Germany in World War I.

Lodge, Henry Cabot (1850–1924), US senator (R) from Massachusetts (1893–1924), supporter of Theodore Roosevelt, and ardent foe of Woodrow Wilson. He led the opposition to the United States' joining the League of Nations in 1920.

Logan, John, captain of the Baltimore branch of the Volunteers of America, a Christian human services organization founded in 1896 and devoted to assisting alcoholics, drug abusers, and the disabled.

Mahon, John J. ("Sonny") (1852–1928), longtime Democratic political boss in Baltimore.

Marx, Karl (1818–1883), German political theorist and author of *Das Kapital* (1867–95) and (with Friedrich Engels) *The Communist Manifesto* (1848), which laid the groundwork for socialism and communism. See Mencken's essay "Das Kapital" (*BES*, 20 and 27 March 1922; in *P3*). Mencken also published a debate with a socialist, *Men versus the Man: A Correspondence between Rives La Monte, Socialist, and H. L. Mencken, Individualist* (1910).

McKenna, Reginald (1863–1943), British politician who was appointed First Lord of the Admiralty in 1908, serving until 1911, when Prime Minister Asquith replaced him with Winston Churchill. McKenna then became secretary of the Home Office (1911–15) and chancellor of the exchequer (1915–18). He was later chairman of the Midland Bank.

McNulty, Thomas F. (1859–1932), sheriff of Baltimore (1913–23) who gained celebrity by singing songs in support of a wide array of Democratic candidates.

Moltke, Helmuth von (1800–1891), chief of the Prussian and German General Staffs (1858–88) and a leader in Germany's defeat of France in the Franco-Prussian War (1870–71).

Morgan, John Pierpont (1837–1913), banker and financier who invested heavily in railroads and helped form the U.S. Steel Corporation. He was also a noted philanthropist, contributing substantially to the Metropolitan Museum of Art and the American Museum of Natural History.

Müller, Johannes Peter (1801–1858), German physiologist and anatomist who did pioneering work on human sense organs and in comparative anatomy.

Münsterburg, Hugo (1863–1916), German-born psychologist and director of the then newly established psychological laboratory at Harvard. He wrote several studies of American culture: *American Traits* (1901), *The Americans* (1904), *American Problems* (1910), and *American Patriotism* (1913). He elicited controversy by publishing a book, *The Peace and America* (1915), defending Germany's invasion of Belgium.

Munyon, James M. (1848–1918), a hugely popular and successful manufacturer of homeopathic patent medicines. Although not an actual physician, he always referred to himself as "Dr. Munyon." His pet phrase, circulated widely through advertisements, was "There is hope."

Murphy, Charles F. (1858–1924), a powerful political boss in the Tammany Hall organization in New York City.

Murray, Kenneth G., Methodist clergyman in Baltimore who was pastor at a church on West Fayette Street, near the city's red-light district. He was later caught by the police in a homosexual liaison and forced to leave town.

Nearing, Scott (1883–1983), socialist and prolific author on politics and society. In 1915 he was dismissed as professor of economics at the University of Pennsylvania for speaking out against child labor. Although he subsequently served for two years (1915–17) as professor of social sciences at the University of Toledo, he then found it impossible to secure another teaching position. In 1932 he and his wife Helen retired to a farm in Vermont. Mencken later reviewed his *Where Is Civilization Going?* (1927; *AM,* January 1929).

Nietzsche, Friedrich (1844–1900), revolutionary German philosopher whose anticlericalism and theories of the superman significantly influenced Mencken. See Mencken's *The Philosophy of Friedrich Nietzsche* (1908), his slim selection, *The Gist of Nietzsche* (1910), and his translation of *The Antichrist* (1920). Mencken wrote frequently of Nietzsche in *SS* (see the issues of November 1909, March 1910, March 1912, August 1913, and August 1915). See also "Nietzsche" (*CST,* 23 August 1925).

Osler, Sir William (1849–1919), Canadian-born physician and professor of medicine who taught at Johns Hopkins Medical School (1888–1904), then emigrated to England, becoming the Regius Professor of Medicine at Oxford. His textbook, *The Principles and Practice of Medicine* (1892), long remained standard.

Pankhurst, Emmeline (1858–1928), British social and political reformer who, with her daughters, Christabel (1880–1958) and Sylvia (1882–1960), led the movement for woman suffrage in the United Kingdom, often resorting to acts of civil disobedience that led to her repeated imprisonment. Sylvia was the author of *The Suffragette: The History of the Women's Militant Suffrage Movement, 1905–1910* (1911).

Pasteur, Louis (1822–1895), French chemist who developed the germ theory of fermentation and also did pioneering work in the identification of microorganisms that cause disease and the decay of organic matter.

Pentz, Samuel E., chief agent of the Maryland Society for the Suppression of Vice. He was forced to resign when he was caught in a compromising situation with an underage girl.

Phillips, Wendell (1811–1884), prominent abolitionist and social reformer.

Pinkham, Lydia (1819–1883), proponent of patent medicines who created, in the 1870s, a "Vegetable Compound" from ground herbs and alcohol, claiming that it could cure any "feminine complaint." It continued to be sold well into the 1920s.

Preston, James Harry (1860–1938), mayor of Baltimore (1911–19) and a member of many political and social organizations in Baltimore.

GLOSSARY OF NAMES

Rainsford, William Stephen (1850–1933), Protestant Episcopal clergyman born in Dublin. He came to the United States in 1870 and was minister at St. George's in New York City (1882–1904). During this time he caused a scandal by recommending the reform, not the abolition, of the saloon and of dance halls.

Rhodes, Cecil (1853–1902), British imperialist who amassed a huge fortune in gold and diamonds in South Africa. He became prime minister of the Cape in 1890 and established the region that he named after himself, Rhodesia.

Roberts, Frederick Sleigh, first Earl (1832–1914), British army officer who served for more than fifty years in the British military. From 1900 to 1904 he was commander-in-chief of the British army. In 1905 he became president of the National Service League, which argued for compulsory military training.

Romanes, George John (1848–1894), naturalist who was born in Canada but lived most of his life in England. He studied natural science at Cambridge and at University College, London, where he became acquainted with Charles Darwin. Family wealth allowed him to devote all his energies to research. Romanes did pioneering work in invertebrate biology as well as in the physiology and psychology of animals (including human beings), embodied in such works as *Animal Intelligence* (1882), *Mental Evolution in Animals* (1883), and *Mental Evolution in Man* (1888). Much of his work was, however, criticized as lacking in scientific rigor and was quickly superseded by more objective studies. He became a leading advocate of the theory of evolution and wrote the three-volume treatise, *Darwin, and After Darwin* (1892–97).

Roosevelt, Theodore (1858–1919), vice president under William McKinley; he became twenty-sixth president of the United States (1901–9) when McKinley was assassinated. Mencken heaped scorn upon his bluff persona and was particularly hostile to Roosevelt's vehement calls for the United States to enter World War I on the side of the Allies. See Mencken's "Roosevelt: An Autopsy" (*P2*).

Root, Elihu (1845–1937), secretary of war under William McKinley and Theodore Roosevelt (1899–1904), secretary of state (1905–9), and US senator (R) from New York (1909–15). He won the Nobel Peace Prize in 1912 and was president of the Carnegie Endowment for International Peace (1910–25). His treatise *Experiments in Government and the Essentials of the Constitution* (1913) is a series of lectures on the adaptation of laws and government to modern conditions.

Rubenstein, Charles Aaron (1870–?), rabbi at the Har Sinai synagogue in Baltimore and author of *History of Har Sinai Congregation* (1918).

Russell, Lillian (1861–1922), star of the American musical stage who was featured in many Broadway musicals from 1879 to 1912. She was renowned for her soprano voice and her good looks but gained notoriety for her volatile temperament and several tempestuous marriages.

Russell, William T. (1863–1927), Roman Catholic priest and secretary to James, Cardinal Gibbons in Baltimore (1894–1908); subsequently rector of St. Patrick's church in Washington, DC (1908–17).

Sampson, William Thomas (1840–1902), naval officer and chairman of the board of inquiry investigating the sinking of the *Maine* in Havana harbor in 1898.

Sanborn, Herbert C. (1873–1967), member of the faculty at Vanderbilt University (1911–42) and author of works on education, language, philosophy, and politics.

Sanger, Margaret (1879–1966), birth control pioneer (she coined the term birth control in 1914) who frequently endured prison terms in her quest to legalize the sale and distribution of contraceptive devices and to permit the dissemination of information on family planning. She was indicted in 1914 under the Comstock Act for publishing "obscene" information about birth control. She fled the United States in October 1914 before her trial. Returning the next year, she found public opinion now on her side, and the prosecutor dropped all charges.

Siemens, Werner von (1816–1892), German electrical engineer who, with his brother, Karl Wilhelm (later Sir William) Siemens (1823–1883), played an instrumental role in the development of the telegraph industry.

Sloane, William M. (1868–1928), secretary to the historian George Bancroft in Berlin (1873–75) and professor of history at Princeton (1876–96) and Columbia (1896f.). He wrote such treatises as *The French War and the Revolution, 1756–1783* (1893) and *The Balkans: A Laboratory of History* (1914).

Stone, William J. (1848–1918), governor (1893–97) and US senator (D) from Missouri (1903–18) and chairman of the Senate Committee on Foreign Relations.

Sunday, Billy (1862–1935), itinerant evangelist who became immensely popular in the first two decades of the twentieth century by his histrionic outdoor sermons. Mencken discussed his witnessing of one of Sunday's lecture tours in *BES* (17 February, 14 and 27 March, 2 May 1916); see also "Savonarolas A-Sweat" (*SS*, July 1916), a review of a biography of Sunday.

Tirpitz, Alfred von (1849–1930), German officer. He was state secretary of the Navy Office (1897–1916) and was named the first grand admiral of Germany in 1911. He was instrumental in building up German naval power before World War I, but the navy's lack of preparedness at the outbreak of the war and his shortcomings as a strategist led to his removal in March 1916.

Towne, Elizabeth (1865–1961), author and editor who founded the New Thought journal *Nautilus* in 1898. She was director of the New Thought Alliance (1918–30) and its honorary president (1924–32), and was a charter member of the New England Federation of New Thought Centers. Among her books are *You and Your Forces* (1905) and *How to Use New Thought in Home Life* (1915).

Veeder, Van Vechten (1867–1942), lawyer who became a judge of the US District Court of the Eastern District of New York (1911–17). He resigned to serve in a private law practice. He later became an authority on maritime law, becoming a member of the International Maritime Commission (1930–36) and president of the Maritime Law Association of the United States.

Venable, Richard M. (1839–1910), professor of law at the University of Marland (1870–1905) and member of the Baltimore City Council (1899–1903).

Vescelius, Eva Augusta (d. 1917), pioneer of music therapy and author of *Music and Health* (1918).

Welch, William Henry (1850–1934), pathologist at Johns Hopkins University (1883–1918) and president of the Maryland Board of Health (1898–1922). He was a leader in the development of pathology and bacteriology.

Wharton, Edith (1862–1937), American novelist of New York society whose many novels—including *The House of Mirth* (1905) and *The Age of Innocence* (1920; reviewed in *SS*, February 1921)—have given her high rank among American writers of her time. Mencken, however, had praise only for the grim New England tale *Ethan Frome* (1911; reviewed in *SS*, December 1911), and had little regard for her other work.

Whitlock, Brand (1869–1934), mayor of Toledo, Ohio (1905–13), and US minister to Belgium. Mencken frequently recommended Whitlock's essay, *On the Enforcement of Law in Cities* (1910), which outraged doctrinaire reformers in its urging of moderation in the pursuit of moral infractions.

Wilde, Oscar (1854–1900), British novelist, poet, and playwright whose name fell under a cloud for a generation following his conviction for homosexuality in 1895.

Windom, William (1827–1891), US representative (R) from Minnesota (1859–69), US senator from Minnesota (1871–81, 1881–83), and secretary of the treasury under James A. Garfield (1881) and Benjamin Harrison (1889–91).

Wister, Owen (1860–1938), novelist and essayist best known for the Western novel *The Virginian* (1902) but also a prolific writer on political and social issues. Developing a strong antipathy to President Woodrow Wilson, he opposed US entry into World War I and wrote a harsh sonnet on Wilson that aroused widespread criticism.

Wood, Henry (1849–1925), professor of English and German at Johns Hopkins University (1881–1920) and author of numerous treatises on German literature, many of them written in German.

Wright, Sir Almroth Edward (1861–1947), British bacteriologist who introduced antityphoid inoculation and was a pioneer in vaccination. Hostile to woman suffrage, he wrote *The Unexpurgated Case against Woman Suffrage* (1913), favorably discussed by Mencken in *In Defense of Women* (1918).

Wright, Harold Bell (1872–1944), clergyman and novelist who wrote a succession of novels that made him one of the most popular writers of the first three decades of the twentieth century. Mencken had little good to say of his work; he formally reviewed only *The Calling of Dan Matthews* (1909; *SS*, November 1909), saying of it: "The author's style wanders far from the canons of good English, but his story shows no little earnestness and plausibility. It is, in brief, not half so bad as the publisher's encomiums lead you to expect."

INDEX